Owning William Shakespeare

MATERIAL TEXTS

Series Editors
Roger Chartier   Leah Price
Joseph Farrell   Peter Stallybrass
Anthony Grafton   Michael F. Suarez, S.J.

A complete list of books in the series
is available from the publisher.

Owning William Shakespeare

The King's Men
and Their Intellectual Property

JAMES J. MARINO

PENN

UNIVERSITY OF PENNSYLVANIA PRESS

PHILADELPHIA

Copyright © 2011 University of Pennsylvania Press

All rights reserved. Except for brief quotations used for purposes of review or scholarly citation, none of this book may be reproduced in any form by any means without written permission from the publisher.

Published by
University of Pennsylvania Press
Philadelphia, Pennsylvania 19104-4112
www.upenn.edu/pennpress

Printed in the United States of America on acid-free paper

10 9 8 7 6 5 4 3 2 1

Library of Congress Cataloging-in-Publication Data
Marino, James J.
　Owning William Shakespeare : The King's Men and their intellectual property / James J. Marino.
　　p. cm. — (Material texts)
　Includes bibliographical references and index.
　ISBN 978-0-8122-4296-6 (hardcover : alk. paper)
　　1. Shakespeare, William, 1564–1616—Stage history—To 1625. 2. Shakespeare, William, 1564–1616—Criticism, Textual. 3. Shakespeare, William, 1564–1616—Authorship. 4. Intellectual property—England—History—16th century. 5. Intellectual property—England—History—17th century. 6. Transmission of texts—England—History—16th century. 7. Transmission of texts—England—History—17th century. 8. King's Men (Theater company) 9. Chamberlain's Men (Theater company) 10. Repertory theater—England—London—History—16th century. 11. Repertory theater—England—London—History—17th century. 12. Theatrical companies—England—London—History—16th century. 13. Theatrical companies—England—London—History—17th century. I. Title.
PR3095.M37 2011
792.9'5'09420931—dc21

2010028881

CONTENTS

Introduction — 1

Chapter 1. Secondhand Repertory: The Fall and Rise of Master W. Shakespeare — 19

Chapter 2. Sixty Years of *Shrews* — 48

Chapter 3. *Hamlet,* Part by Part — 75

Chapter 4. William Shakespeare's *Sir John Oldcastle* and the Globe's William Shakespeare — 107

Chapter 5. Restorations and Glorious Revolutions — 143

Notes — 161

Works Cited — 179

Index — 195

Acknowledgments — 203

INTRODUCTION

> I stand here for him.
> —*Henry V,* 2.4

Editors and Owners

The tradition of editing Shakespeare is as old as English copyright law, and they enter history together. Until the eighteenth century, printing rights were governed by the rules of London's guild of booksellers, printers, and binders, the Worshipful Company of Stationers, and members of the company considered their "copy," their right to republish books that they or their predecessors had published, both exclusive and perpetual. In 1709, as Parliament debated legislation that would set a finite term for exclusive copyrights and vest them in authors rather than in publishers, the bookseller Jacob Tonson devised a strategy to help maintain his perpetual control over the rights to Shakespeare's plays. Tonson republished the collected plays, identified for the first time as the poet's *Works*, including the first biography of Shakespeare and for the first time publicly citing an editor, Nicholas Rowe, who took responsibility for setting the text.[1] As the copyright term of each subsequent edited *Works* neared expiration, Tonson and his successors would publish new editions, with new editors.[2] After print copyright had become a question of black-letter law rooted in the concept of an author's personal rights, rather than a collection of industrial rules and customs focused on the rights of Stationers, the publishing industry sought a new category of owner whose legal rights the Stationers could exercise in order to retain control of books whose writers were long dead. The passage of the first English copyright law, the 1710 *Act for the Encouragement of Learning*, sometimes called the "Statute of Queen Anne," meant that a publisher such as Tonson could not own Shakespeare's plays forever, at least not in theory. But surely Rowe owned Rowe's edition of Shakespeare, and after him, Alexander Pope owned Pope's edition of Shakespeare and Lewis Theobald owned Theobald's, and each of these editors' authorial rights had in the due course of publication been assigned or franchised to their publisher, Jacob Tonson.

The Tonson publishing family's strategy of serial editions was only one part of the English publishing magnates' long campaign to maintain perpetual copyright despite the letter of the law; the landmark *Donaldson v. Becket* decision did not break the great London publishers' hold on their traditional properties until 1774.[3] But in a larger sense, Tonson's innovation of 1709, claiming Shakespeare through a commissioned editor's copyright, remains fundamental to the practice of publishing Shakespeare's texts and therefore to the practices of reading them, studying them, preparing acting versions of them, and teaching them in classrooms. Editing is an essential component of the twenty-first-century intellectual property regimen, because editing creates intellectual property. In order to exert a proprietary claim upon a work whose basic copyright protection has expired, which now generally means any work created before 1923, publishers need an editor.[4] While Shakespeare's works have themselves long since entered the public domain, the intellectual labor of setting a text creates a new and unique intellectual property that the editor legally owns and may therefore license or sell to a publishing firm. Shakespeare is public property. *The Arden Shakespeare*, *The Oxford Shakespeare*, *The Riverside Shakespeare*, *The New Cambridge Shakespeare* and all of their many marketplace competitors are private property. That no two editions of *Hamlet* are precisely alike may be a reflection of the play's textual difficulty, but it is also an economic necessity. An edition of *Hamlet* whose text was identical to another's would be unpublishable. Shakespeare's texts must be made new, again and again, in order to remain in print.

This basic fact of business has been a gift to learning in many ways and has required publishers to underwrite textual scholarship. As Andrew Murphy puts it, the series of eighteenth-century Tonson editions midwived "the Birth of the Editor," and "the evolution of editing as a discipline with its own clear theoretical underpinnings."[5] Each editor's need to distinguish his work from his forerunners' led to explicit disagreements with earlier editors, formal statements of methodology, and vigorous critical debates between rival scholars. The third of Tonson's editors, Theobald, had a very public feud with Pope, the second, beginning soon after Pope's edition was published; the tradition of controversy began early. By the time the Tonson cartel lost its exclusive hold, there was already a rich body of bibliographical scholarship for new editors to reckon with. Neither did increased marketplace competition weaken the proprietary imperative to reedit the text.

While editing Shakespeare is now almost exclusively the province of academics, the practice is not native to academia and long preceded the institution of English departments. Shakespeare was not edited by university professors until the 1860s, and so-called amateurs continued to advance and improve editorial scholarship well into the twentieth century. (Even common use of the term "amateur" to describe such editors is perverse, since "amateurism" is imagined here as *not* having a specific full-time occupation in another field.) Editing Shakespeare is far older than teaching Shakespeare, and older than any other form of Shakespeare scholarship except biography, which also began with Rowe's edition. Scholarly editing, like literary biography, is a previously independent enterprise which was eventually subsumed into a larger set of academic pursuits; editing is in the English department but not of it. And while editing makes natural and invaluable contributions to the academy's intellectual mission, it remains fundamentally oriented toward the imperatives of its original institution, the publishing house, rather than to those of the university.

Editing's defining involvement with the press does not make it more commercial than the scholarly activities that evolved inside universities, or less serious, or more concerned with financial reward. Neither is there a substantial intellectual difference between editing Shakespeare for nonprofit publishers and editing for a commercial press. Editors do not compromise their scholarly principles for business reasons, most also practice other forms of literary criticism and scholarship, and all are engaged with the continuing research in their fields.

They themselves, being academics, are governed by the academy's rules and customs. But the activity of editing remains conditioned by the needs of the press and focused on producing the very specific kind of intellectual product that publishers require. Editors who are also literature professors may successfully and even brilliantly serve more than one master, but the duty to establish a text is never omitted. It is the basic job description. Implicit in that duty is the obligation to provide a text which can legally be published and enjoy protection under the laws of copyright, an original edition sufficiently distinct from all those that have gone before it.

The surviving texts of Shakespeare's plays, richly endowed in variants and mess, provide editors with almost inexhaustible resources for new iterations of the text. But editors must rhetorically circumscribe their freedom to use those resources. The cultural value invested in literary authorship, and especially in William Shakespeare's authorship, and the rhetorical stance Shakespeare's editors have adopted toward him have precluded any uninflected appeal to the editor's personal tastes since the original textualist feud between Pope and Theobald. The Tonsons engaged the first Shakespeare editors not for their erudition but for their own literary reputations and talents. Rowe was a successful dramatist, associated with the acting company at Lincoln's Inn's Fields and with the leading Shakespearean actor of the day, Thomas Betterton. (Indeed, it was Betterton who collected most of the material for Rowe's biographical sketch of Shakespeare.)[6] Rowe cheerfully admits at the outset of his edition that reconstruction of Shakespeare's authorial draft is impossible, as "the Author's Original Manuscripts . . . are lost, or at least are gone beyond any Inquiry I could make."[7] Rowe proposes instead "to compare the several Editions," choosing the best reading from his collation of early printed copies, and to "render" thorny passages in the text "Intelligible." Indeed, the title page of the 1709 *Works* advertises the collection as "*Revis'd and Corrected*" by Rowe, which leaves ambiguous the question of whether the seventeenth-century printings or Shakespeare himself was being "revis'd"; such an ambiguity would have seemed scandalous to later generations, who have come to view outright revision of Shakespeare as a kind of secular sacrilege.

The next editor of the *Works*, Alexander Pope, corrected and revised Shakespeare in earnest. Pope, the dominant poetic talent of his day, understood his project as an editor to be the improvement and modernization of the plays: updating vocabulary, making the iambic pentameter stricter, degrading passages he disliked to the margin, and generally imposing his own polished eighteenth-century aesthetic. Indeed, Pope is perfectly open about what he considers Shakespeare's "Faults" and "defects" (even though he allows Shakespeare's "Beauties" and "Excellencies" to outweigh them).[8] It was Pope's free hand that drew the first attack on him by Theobald. The year after Pope's edition was published, Theobald's *Shakespeare Restored* criticized him for unnecessary meddling with Shakespeare's text. Although Theobald worried that "private property"—Tonson's proprietary claim—would prevent him from publishing his own properly "restored" edition of Shakespeare, the Tonson house eventually gave him the next commission.[9] Theobald's actual editing practice was not terribly distinct from Pope's when compared to later approaches, but his victory over Pope is one of the most influential in the history of Shakespearean bibliography.[10]

What Theobald won was a debate over the proper objective of editing, and his basic position, however modified in the details, has held the field for almost three centuries. Theobald views the project of editing Shakespeare as historical and restorationist, just as the title *Shakespeare Restored* implies. The text is to be corrected, but not revised, and it is the text, not the author, that falls under the editor's correction. The editorial project is to return the text to something approaching an original state, although different schools of editing have subsequently theorized that "original" text in many different ways. The text is not to be modernized in any substantive way (although the question of what constitutes a substantive change requires its own theoretical debate). The editor should emend the text only where it seems somehow corrupt or defective, rather than where it happens to displease the editor. The task calls upon the editor's philological and antiquarian knowledge, rather than upon personal literary taste. The editor shall not substitute his or her own literary judgment for Shakespeare's. None of these axioms is at all simple in application; each opens a set of thorny philosophical questions. But it is a testimony to the thoroughness and magnitude of Theobald's triumph that today they all seem largely uncontroversial, and the approach Pope adopted unthinkable.

What Pope's edition offered to readers was a living text, a Shakespeare that changed with the English language and the literary fashion. The underlying logic of his method presumes that the edition would eventually be supplanted, not by a more historically correct text such as Theobald's, but by a later, further-modernized version of Shakespeare. Pope's approach might seem strange to those educated within the discourse that Theobald initiated, but it is "wholly reasonable within his historical context," as Marcus Walsh argues,[11] and perfectly logical and coherent within its own chosen terms. Moreover, Pope's editorial approach was entirely in line with what eighteenth-century actors did in the theaters, where Shakespeare's plays were routinely modernized and adapted. Theobald himself was such a theatrical adapter; his edition, and his attack on Pope, implicitly propose that Shakespeare's plays should be freely altered for performance but remain nominally stable and static in print, making concessions to ease listeners' understanding but demanding effort from the understanding reader. Theobald's approach defines Shakespeare's text as a historical artifact, increasingly remote from each generation of readers, edited like the works of Virgil or Horace.[12] And while Theobald's preservationist model has a powerful appeal, the choice between Pope's strategy and Theobald's was not strictly necessary. Editions of both species might have hypothetically coexisted, just as printed editions following Theobald's general program would coexist with radically adapted stage versions. But the choice between models was made, decisively, in the eighteenth century.

Pope's editorial policy, in retrospect, represents the road not taken. Shakespeare would never again be handed over to a generation's leading poet for an aesthetic makeover. There would not be a Wordsworth's Shakespeare, or a Tennyson's Shakespeare, or a T. S. Eliot edition of Shakespeare, although Eliot was a sometime scholar of early modern drama. The next important literary figure to edit Shakespeare, Samuel Johnson, cast his project in Theobald's restorationist terms (even as Johnson's former pupil, David Garrick, adapted Shakespeare as he pleased on stage, cheerfully discarding the fifth act of *Hamlet* for an "improved" finale).[13] To hire an editor for her or his own poetic talents now seems at best beside the point, or even dangerously wrongheaded; Shakespeare is not to be trifled with. Personal literary authority is not seen as a qualification for editing Shakespeare, in the way the Tonsons saw Rowe's and Pope's literary authority as qualifying them, because Shakespeare's poetic authority no longer admits any rival. An edition is meant to be Shakespeare and nothing else.

Editors, therefore, renounce their own prerogative over the text and present their task as a duty rendered to Shakespeare. This is the foundation of Theobald's success; no one would argue that he was a better judge of verse than Alexander Pope. But he could claim greater fidelity to his original and frame the debate as a contest between Pope and Shakespeare. Such framing allows Theobald to protest his "Esteem for Mr. Pope" and his "high . . . Opinion of his Genius and Excellencies," performing the very respect for poetic authority that he implicitly accuses Pope of omitting. "Tho' I confess a veneration, almost rising to Idolatry, for the Writings of this inimitable Poet," Theobald writes of Pope, "I would be very loth even to do *him* Justice at the Expence of *that other* Gentleman's Character."[14] Theobald is not offering the most brilliant possible text but the most authentic possible text, and he underwrites his edition with Shakespeare's authority rather than his own. Authenticity, or at least professed authenticity, remains indispensable for publishers of Shakespeare. A text that does not present itself as Shakespeare's cannot compete seriously in a marketplace filled with texts that do so present themselves. Although the existence of every edition is founded upon the editor's legal authorship, editors since Theobald have needed to disavow their own authority. The publisher acts as the curate of the editor's authorial rights; the editor volunteers to serve as the curate of the author's intentions.

Every published edition of Shakespeare must therefore satisfy two fundamentally opposite demands. It must be demonstrably new, and demonstrably the editor's own, but persuasively authentic and archaic, imagined as entirely Shakespeare's. The basic tension between fidelity and novelty places every editor in a double bind but requires no bad faith because the official goal of editing is ultimately impossible. The three hundred years since Rowe's edited *Works* have greatly increased the accuracy and reach of editorial inquiry, but the condition of the author's original manuscripts still remains beyond it. Absolute success can only be pursued asymptotically, edition after edition, with each editor arriving at an individual approximation. The establishment of an incontrovertibly "correct" text would be a catastrophe for the enterprise of publishing Shakespeare. The texts of his plays could no longer be converted into marketable private properties. Achieving the editorial profession's intellectual end would be the end of editing as a profession.

Players as Possessors

In a rhetoric of editing that casts Shakespeare as the sole authority and the editor as the prime arbiter and champion of Shakespeare's intentions, the question of Shakespeare's theatrical collaborators, his partners in the playhouse, will always be an uneasy one. Pope justifies cutting and marginalizing large sections of text by claiming that both the 1623 Folio and the quarto texts were corrupted by their theatrical provenance. He deduces this provenance, reasonably enough, from the participation of Shakespeare's partners, John Heminges and Henry Condell, in the Folio's publication, and from their implicit claim to have provided the manuscripts for the printer. But Pope disputes Heminges's and Condell's claim to have provided the "True Originall Copies," imagining the copy-text manuscripts as "those which had lain ever since the Author's days in the playhouse, and had from time to time been cut, or added to, arbitrarily."[15]

With this claim, Pope begins a long critical discourse which construes actors as a source of interference and textual corruption. Any revisions made in the theater are conceived of as arbitrary; plays are imagined lying in the playhouse, passive and vulnerable, rather than living there. Pope is careful to emphasize the gap between the end of Shakespeare's writing career and the publication of the Folio, and he expresses it in terms that invite careless readers to conflate that gap with the distance between "the Author's days" and their own. (The "ever since" refers to the decade or so between Shakespeare's retirement and 1623, or else to the seven years between his death and the printing of the Folio, but equivocally evokes the whole century between the Folio and Pope's audience.) And while Pope foregrounds his objection to theatrical revisions made after Shakespeare's "days," he also objects to those made during Shakespeare's own theatrical career and gives no more authority to quartos published during the writer's lifetime than to folios published after it: "this edition [the Folio], as well as the Quarto's [*sic*] was printed (at least partly) from no better copies than the *Prompter's Book*, or *Piece-meal Parts* written out for the use of the actors."[16]

Even the texts used for original performances are being derided here; presented with the King's Men's "prompt-book" for *Hamlet*, or the acting part written out for the actor playing the Ghost, Pope would lament that he had "no better copies." This was not merely abstract principle but practice. Pope had especially strong objections to *Loves Labors Lost*, for example, and tampered with it more thoroughly than any other play,[17] although its earliest surviving quarto dates from the heyday of Shakespeare's own documented career as an actor; if that text reflects strictly theatrical corruption, then William Shakespeare must have conspired to corrupt it. But even Shakespeare's own status as an actor marks him as unreliable to Pope, who opines "that most of our Author's faults are less to be ascribed to his wrong judgment as a Poet, than to his right judgment as a Player."[18] For Pope, a play's literary integrity is compromised by the very act of preparing it for the stage.

While few later editors would articulate such an extreme and explicit antitheatrical animus, theatrical production has long been considered as source of tampering, and many editors have focused on identifying playhouse additions, actor's interpolations, and other theatrical changes to the text. At worst, as Steven Urkowitz puts it, "The process of 'theatrical adaptation' or 'theatrical cutting' is universally described as a destructive assault, carried out by persons whose interests are alien to the author's artistic concerns."[19] Such descriptions are less universal now than they were when Urkowitz wrote that sentence, but Urkowitz's is an all-too-accurate characterization of routine editorial practice throughout most of the twentieth century, and "theatrical adaptation" remains a widely accepted explanation for variant texts and especially for inferior ones. Theatrical practice has persistently been treated as a rival for authority, rather than as a legitimate source of authenticity. Any authority ceded to the players is imagined as diminishing Shakespeare's, and their role as interpretive agents threatens to muddle the editors' claims to be the author's primary representative. Even critics such as Urkowitz and Leah Marcus, who have embraced theatrical revision as a beneficial process, focus strongly and often exclusively on Shakespeare himself as the reviser; he remains the only widely acceptable agent for explaining textual development or evolution. The rest of Shakespeare's fellows are only sources of potential contamination or, at best, his cooperative proxies. Various bibliographers have argued that Shakespeare's acting partners sometimes worked to block publication of his plays—or argued that the actors promoted such publication—in concordance with Shakespeare's personal wishes. Actors can be assigned agency only if they serve as someone else's agents.

Pope's implicit conflation of Elizabethan and Jacobean playhouse texts with eighteenth-century theatrical adaptations plays an important part in demoting actors' authority, because it equates Shakespeare's fellow players, who exerted a fiercely proprietary influence on the text, with eighteenth-century actors who pressed no such claims to ownership or unique authority. Before the Civil War, playing companies had maintained physical custody of their plays, but these manuscripts were lost to Restoration actors, who depended upon printed copies of old plays for their performance scripts. After 1660 the theater no longer enjoyed any primary textual authority but clearly used secondary and derivative texts; a playing script was, for Pope, a doctored version of a printed book. Moreover, no actor or group of actors could still claim to be the exclusive owner of a Shakespeare play, as they had before the English Civil War. The closure of the theaters between 1642 and 1660 had meant an end to proprietary claims upon the plays an acting company had originated, because the original companies did not survive until the Restoration.

Although the restored regime instituted a new arrangement of exclusive theatrical properties, assigning specific plays to specific companies, that system broke down in 1695. Thereafter, while performances of Shakespeare were officially confined to a few "legitimate" government-licensed theaters, all of those theaters were free to stage whichever pre-Restoration plays they liked, and none had any special claims. Indeed, each of the licensed theaters could offer its own version of a Shakespeare or Jonson play, in competition with the versions offered on other London stages, something that had not been officially permitted by the Masters of the Revels before 1642 or by the royal patentees who controlled the London companies after 1660. But Pope imagined that Elizabethan playing companies operated as eighteenth-century companies did, with plays available to more than one troupe and proper to none. He suggests that variant quartos of the same play derive from competing acting versions; his survey of early printed quartos sometimes reveals "two or more editions by different printers, each of which has whole heaps of trash different from the other: which I should fancy was occasion'd, by their being taken from different copies, belonging to different Playhouses."[20]

Although Pope does not appeal to the company names printed upon the title pages of early dramatic quartos and octavos, those company names would have been misleading for him; the basic scholarship about those companies' histories and identities had not yet been done. Pope could not know that the Lord Chamberlain's Servants, the King's Servants, and Lord Hunsdon's Servants were all names for a single company at various times in its history. Neither could he know that Lord Strange's Servants, the Earl of Pembroke's Servants, or Queen Elizabeth's Servants were names for playing companies whose London heydays preceded the formation of the Lord Chamberlain's Men, and whose plays passed, by one means or another, into the Chamberlain's Men's repertory. Pope seems to have read those company names as signs of concurrent rather than consecutive possession and to have imagined each repertory company adapting an authorial original in its own way. But the model of theatrical repertory upon which Pope's surmise rests, a model in which no acting company owns a play, was not even thirty years old when Pope did the surmising.

Players' quartos, taken from recent stage productions, continued to be published in the eighteenth century, with theatrical ascriptions that superficially resembled those on Elizabethan and Jacobean quartos. But because eighteenth-century actors were offering their own versions of old plays that rival companies were free to perform, eighteenth-century playhouse quartos explicitly present themselves as adaptations, rather than originals, distinguishing the "authorial" or "Shakespearean" text, which lay in the public domain, from the individual company's own distinct and marketable alterations. Title-page formulas describing plays "as acted" or "as played" by a specific company took meanings diametrically opposed to the implications such phrases had carried before the Civil War. To publish "A midsummer night's dream. A comedy. As it is acted at the Theatres-Royal in Drury-Lane and Covent-Garden. By Shakespeare"[21] is to propose a distinction between the play "as it is acted" at a specific place and time and the play itself. To publish "A Midsommer nights dreame. Written by William Shakespeare. As it hath beene sundry times publickely acted, by the Right honourable, the Lord Chamberlaine his seruants"[22] is to propose the printed text's authenticity, because what the Lord Chamberlain's Servants act publicly is the play, and also to propose the Lord Chamberlain's Servants' authority as the guarantors of the play's authenticity. Since the Restoration, actors have been tenants of early English plays, bound to leave them unchanged by their tenancy; players before the Civil War were those plays' owners and masters.

Even the proliferating variants within early printed playbooks, long construed as signs of corruption and derivation, are more properly understood as an expression of the players' authority. Early editions of Shakespeare's plays do not define their relationship to some other foundational version of the text, as eighteenth-century players' editions must, because the early editions present themselves as the foundational text itself, and the players' ownership of the text gave them authority both to change it and to define it. When subsequent editions of an Elizabethan or Jacobean playbook offer multiple versions of a dramatic text, the players should not be imagined as adapting an underlying base text which maintains its own separate, integral identity. Rather, they should be imagined (as they seem to have imagined themselves) as changing the foundational text. What post-Restoration actors do with *Hamlet* remains imaginatively distinct from *Hamlet* itself. What pre–Civil War players did was *Hamlet*, by virtue of the fact they did it. They were never unfaithful to their texts. The texts were theirs. The most fundamental expression of authority is the power to authorize the text: to define its nature and to identify it the as correct approved version. To approve subsequent changes does not diminish one's discursive authority but reasserts it. Indeed, the production of Shakespeare's authority in print continues to work by this very method and has since Tonson and Rowe, at least. The editorial tradition maintains Shakespeare's authority and the publishers' proprietary claims, by issuing a succession of changing texts each of which is the newly "authoritative" version. The Tonson cartel could publish a hypothetically endless series of new versions of Shakespeare's *Works*, each of which was "Shakespeare," precisely because they owned those *Works*, and the exercise of their prerogative to reshape and reissue the plays underscored the Tonsons' possession.

Early modern playbooks do not diverge from the authorized text as much as they reflect authorized changes. The *Essays* of Bacon or Montaigne did not diminish in authority as the essayists revised successive editions, nor did John Milton sacrifice any of his authority by making *Paradise Lost* twelve books rather than ten. Neither are the later editions adaptations of the earlier ones; they replace and supplant the earlier published works. Such public revisions underscored the singular and indispensable authority of the writer, the prerogative to say what the work is and what it is not. When multiple versions of a single play were published over a period of years under the discursive authority of Shakespeare's playing company, it was likewise a performance and public confirmation of their rights over the text. In this, playing companies behaved very much as nondramatic authors in the period did; it is mainly the more recent scholarly constructions of theatrical and literary revision that differ.

While the project of reconstructing Shakespeare's original texts belongs firmly inside the institution of print, those texts were originally created within the institution of the early modern playhouse and formed by that institution. I would not dispute Pope's basic intuition about the theatrical nature of the Folio's copy, but only his derogatory judgment of such copy's value. The quest to rid Shakespeare of theatrical interference is fundamentally quixotic. The theatrical elements of drama are not distortions. They are the nature of drama. Isolating and eliminating the contributions to Shakespeare's plays by other agents in the playhouse is neither empirically feasible nor genuinely worthwhile. Shakespeare's partners and collaborators in the acting company to which he belonged, the group known originally as the Lord Chamberlain's Servants and later as the King's Servants, were not his agents in the sense that modern editors position themselves as his agents, nor servants variously faithful or unfaithful to his artistic intentions. They were his fellows: fellow owners of the plays he created with them and for them, and fellow authors of those plays. The Chamberlain's Men owned those plays, exclusively, as subsequent actors have not, and they exerted substantial authority over them. The plays are shaped by their artistic and commercial goals, goals shared by their partner William Shakespeare. When the company changed the texts of the plays, they were not adapting them. They were continuing the process of creating them. A King's Men's play changed by the King's Men should not be imagined to be a derivative work. It is better thought of as an original work, shaped by its authors. The project of reconstructing "Shakespeare" by stripping away the King's Men's contributions seeks to recreate a work that none of its makers ever sought to create.

Before and after the New Bibliography

Nor should the original work be imagined as the singular, unchanged object that editing seeks and fails to establish in print. No single state of an early modern play's text is the play itself; the play was a changing and evolving artwork. The extant evidence about the Elizabethan and Jacobean theater indicates that revision was a routine practice. The theatrical landlord and financier Philip Henslowe frequently records payment for "additions" to older plays, including such landmark works as *Dr. Faustus* and *The Spanish Tragedy*.[23] These documented additions and revisions can be seen in the printed texts of those plays, with the first published versions of the plays eventually being supplanted by longer versions. No internal documents such as Henslowe's so-called *Diary* survive from the Chamberlain's Men, but many of Shakespeare's plays have publication histories resembling those of the revised Henslowe plays, histories in which an initially published text is superseded by a longer and often more sophisticated version of the same text. It seems reasonable to suspect, if not to conclude absolutely, that the changing texts of *Hamlet* and *King Lear* were influenced by something like the processes that altered the similarly evolving texts of *The Spanish Tragedy* and *Faustus*. And indeed, this is precisely what the mainstream of nineteenth-century bibliographers, following Edmond Malone, took as presumptively likely. Early printed texts which differed from later printed versions of the same plays were typically taken to be either early drafts of, or sources for, the later, fuller, and more accomplished versions.

Yet beginning in the early twentieth century the main school of Shakespeare bibliography labored to cast suspicion on such straightforward chronology and to construct a scholarly paradigm within which the notion of such straightforward revisions seemed nonsensical. From the viewpoint of the so-called New Bibliographers, the idea that a longer, later-published text was a revision of a shorter, earlier, and often inferior text seemed at odds with common sense. The New Bibliographical chronology, damaged and undermined as it has been by more recent scholars, still remains the privileged starting place for discussions of dating Shakespeare's plays. It is important, therefore, to examine how that paradigmatic sense of scholarly presumption and expectation, that communal narrative, was created.

As Paul Werstine and E. J. Honigmann have both argued, the movement now called the New Bibliography did not have an internally cohesive program, nor were its major figures in agreement about many of the key premises that now define the New Bibliographic approach. Werstine isolates four basic positions around which the orthodoxy formed, although none of the leading figures assented to all four ideas: A. W. Pollard's division of the Shakespeare plays printed before 1623 into legitimate "good" and garbled "bad" quartos; W. W. Greg's argument that some quartos were created by rogue "reporters" using a technique that Greg called "memorial reconstruction"; R. B. McKerrow's confident speculative description (abetted by Greg) of Shakespeare's "foul papers," or authorial drafts, and their features; and the tendentious identification of "Hand D" in the manuscript play *Sir Thomas More* as Shakespeare's personal handwriting, made by Pollard in conjunction with John Dover Wilson and others.[24] While, as Werstine objects, these divergent hypotheses "cannot be forged into a coherent body of knowledge,"[25] and while both Werstine and Honigmann are right to caution against imposing any illusory consistency upon these very different bibliographers, the New Bibliography still needs to be understood as a movement with undeniable consequences for the history of Shakespeare studies. Even now, after each of the positions Werstine enumerates has been sharply critiqued by later textual scholars, the New Bibliography continues to shape the ways that editing and textual scholarship are done. The very lack of coherence Werstine cites may help to explain the resilience of New Bibliographical approaches. Because the movement never had any central indispensable doctrine, it could survive the refutation of any specific claim, and has. The New Bibliography was not a unitary philosophy but a movement of scholars with overlapping concerns; movements, unlike philosophies, cannot be refuted.

If the New Bibliography was never quite a theory, it was very much a set of practices. The New Bibliographers shared a deep interest in the material nature of the early modern book and in reconstructing the processes by which those books were made. Greg, Pollard, McKerrow, Dover Wilson and their later followers have contributed a huge and detailed store of scholarly knowledge about early modern printing, manuscript culture, and theatrical practices. Textual scholarship is now vastly more rigorous and better informed than it was in the nineteenth century, and every subsequent bibliographer is in the New Bibliographers' debt. The tools they have left for their successors are indispensable. The project to which they applied these tools, an intellectual project which unified them more than any specific shared precept, was the reconstruction of the copy text underlying the printed play, and ultimately of the author's original holograph, by studying the material traces left upon the playbook during its production. What theoretical coherence the movement had came from the New Bibliographers' profound and often reflexive investment in William Shakespeare's authority, an investment so deep and so universal as to go largely unexamined.

The internal fissions and inconsistencies in each individual New Bibliographer's methods rise from the inescapable tensions between their project and their techniques. Their splendid empirical tools were applied to an impossible and distinctly nonempiricist task, the "reconstruction" of an ideal and hypothetical text whose existence cannot be established. The New Bibliography applied rigorously materialist means to strictly idealist ends. Empiricism is merely a jealous god; William Shakespeare is a beloved one. Scholars follow one from duty, and the other from desire. But when empiricism is set as the means to an end whose own feasibility cannot be demonstrated, it ceases to be empiricism.

The leading New Bibliographers sometimes subordinated material evidence to their editorial goals. They were interested in theatrical practice, or in early modern collaboration and revision, primarily to the extent that they could be used to reconstruct a singular, individual, and authorial text. This effort frequently led them to overlook or misconstrue evidence with which they were extremely familiar, for example by ignoring the presence of allegedly "authorial" and nontheatrical features within clearly theatrical manuscripts; many of the internal contradictions of their work have been illuminated by a newer generation of textual scholars to whom this work is indebted, including Paul Werstine, David Bevington, Eric Rasmussen, Steven Urkowitz, Leah Marcus, Jeffrey Masten, Peter Stallybrass, Margreta de Grazia, Randall McLeod, and others. The New Bibliographical project also led to many ingenious, counterintuitive narratives which remain influential even after the weakness of their foundational premises has been exposed.[26] The "bad quarto" and memorial reconstruction hypotheses have led, for example, to a paradigmatic chronology which imagines the copy texts for many first quartos as later than the texts underlying later printings, including printings decades later. This New Bibliographical chronology remains the default starting position for many discussions of dating. The canonical text is presumed to precede any texts printed before it; arguments that variant editions of a play were created in the same order in which they were published are typically met with demands for positive evidence, reversing the usual burden of proof.

Pollard, Greg, and their disciples also shored up the "bad quarto" and memorial reconstruction hypotheses with appeals to property rights that they were learned enough to understand were anachronistic. If the late good texts were really anterior to the early bad ones, rather than being later revisions, then the bibliographers needed a plausible explanation for the inferiority of the allegedly derivative early text. Some of the blame was laid on theatrical adaptation, it being presumed that working actors would damage a text for performance reasons; early quartos resulting from theatrical adaptation remains a standard narrative available to Shakespeare editors. But the rest of the blame was laid on illicit agents whom Pollard colorfully labeled "pirates": rogue actors and unscrupulous printers who mangled playtexts in the act of stealing them. While this narrative has little to do with the actual ways Stationers and players divided their properties, and while its specific details have been repeatedly shown to be inaccurate, it continues to obscure critical understanding of how theatrical property actually functioned in the early modern period.

Elements of New Bibliographical practice persist in contemporary editing of Shakespeare, partly because some editors still share Greg's and McKerrow's impossible goals and focus on re-creating a purely authorial text, but more broadly because the New Bibliographers' techniques, while insufficient to their ultimate ends, remain very effective tools for generating editions of Shakespeare. The New Bibliographers, for all their appeals to "scientific" methodology, were at heart applied rather than pure scientists. Their techniques are not designed to discover truths but to establish texts. The resulting product may not be the longed-for authorial copy, but it will be a publishable edition. Many of the New Bibliographers' practices continue to thrive because they are so productive, in such concrete ways. They produce scholarly editions, they produce answers to questions, they produce conclusions. They are more effective in application than a purer textual skepticism might be; editing has far less space for indeterminacy than literary criticism does. And they offer editors a set of methods for discriminating between theatrical and authorial material within a playbook, even if the foundations of those methods have been challenged.

Even the 1986 *Oxford Shakespeare*, hailed upon publication as a radical advance in Shakespearean editing, relies heavily on New Bibliographical concepts, such as memorial reconstruction and authorial foul papers, designed for the recuperation of authorial manuscripts and freighted with author-centric presumptions. Indeed, the Oxford editors explicitly defend an updated version of the New Bibliographers' project and express their interest in reconstructing the "lost manuscripts of Shakespeare's plays." Their stated method is "to restore certain features of a lost material object (that manuscript) by correcting certain apparent deficiencies in a second material object (this printed text) which purports to be a copy of the first."[27] But the manuscript they seek to restore, or to restore elements of, was not necessarily a single manuscript, written at a single time, nor is it axiomatic that Shakespeare's plays resulted from acts of integral composition. Their lost material object remains hypothetical, because it cannot be determined that all of the features that the Oxford editors seek to restore ever coexisted within the same manuscript.

The New Bibliography, at least in Pollard's account and in Greg's, counted certain kinds of textual variation as signs of corruption or piracy. A text that changed radically was a text that had been garbled in the act of theft: a memorial reconstruction, a surreptitious printing, a "bad" quarto. But many such textual variants should be considered as signs of continued and appropriate possession, of the theatrical owners continuing to shape a living and evolving text. I would not propose that every variant can be explained by this hypothesis. Every early modern playbook contains a certain number of errors which cannot be ascribed to any intention; such inevitable informational noise is no more a sign of legitimacy than it is of illegitimacy. But many traditional bibliographical puzzles can be resolved or obviated when considered outside the New Bibliographer's paradigm, and most importantly when Shakespeare's originary authorship is not taken as an axiomatic principle.

I propose to examine a number of plays that lie firmly within the Shakespeare canon as we now understand it but once lay much less securely in the Lord Chamberlain's Men's control: plays that the company may not have originally owned, and that might not have always or immediately been conceived of as William Shakespeare's. Those plays constituted most of the company's original repertory upon its formation. The process of attributing these plays to Shakespeare accompanies the progressive variation of their texts; the very textual changes which later scholars have imagined as belying authorial control are correlated with the intensification and consolidation of Shakespeare's discursive authority. They become publicly Shakespeare's as their published texts increasingly resemble the canonical versions. And their attribution to Shakespeare accompanies their attribution to the Lord Chamberlain's Men. The variants in those texts are not signs that they have changed hands illicitly, unless one considers Shakespeare and his fellows the thieves. The evolution of the dramatic text can also be read as a sign of the legitimate owner's continuing control, and even as a public performance of that control. The King's Men revised their plays in many ways, for many reasons; among those reasons was the need to assert and defend their claims to those plays.

My first chapter begins in 1594, with the formation of the playing company to which Shakespeare belonged, and the general question of the plays, formerly the possession of other groups, with which they began their long collective career. All of those plays which have survived were eventually attributed to William Shakespeare; in 1594, none of them had been.

The second and third chapters examine signs of revision and evolution in two of the plays from that original 1594 repertory. The second chapter deals with the texts of *The Taming of the Shrew* and the problems of the "foul papers" hypothesis. The third deals with *Hamlet*, with the specific revision techniques available to early modern players, and with the discontents of the memorial reconstruction narrative. The fourth chapter deals with the King's Men's efforts to control the print rights to the plays from their original 1594 repertory, as illuminated by the puzzling case of *Sir John Oldcastle* and by the rhetorical construction of Shakespeare in the First Folio. The final chapter considers the life of Shakespeare's plays in the Restoration, after they had left the custody of the King's Men for the first time, and examines the way Shakespeare's plays ceased to be the property of any playing company, concluding with Thomas Betterton's theatrical triumph over the idea of exclusive theatrical rights to Shakespeare. It is during the Restoration and the aftermath of Betterton's dramatic rebellion that publishers rather than actors became the unrivaled proprietors of Shakespeare. Betterton's victory was both a victory and a loss for Shakespearean actors. It was the moment when Shakespeare's plays became public domain for performers, but also the moment when those plays ceased belonging to performers as they once had: the moment when Shakespeare retired from the stage into the study, when his plays were forced to sit still and keep a librarian's quiet. The pages that follow are my best tribute to those plays' original protean energy and their clamorous nature.

CHAPTER I

Secondhand Repertory: The Fall and Rise of Master W. Shakespeare

> He was an actor. He was other people.
> —Michael Martone, "Everybody Watching
> and the Time Passing Like That"

Beginning with Errors

William Shakespeare's name appears for the first time in any theatrical record on March 15, 1595. Shakespeare scholarship typically asserts that this record is in error.

Shakespeare's name had previously appeared on his poem *Venus and Adonis* in 1593 and on *The Rape of Lucrece* in 1594, and a pamphlet in 1592 had glanced at a player who had taken to "bombast[ing] out a blanke verse" and considered himself "the onely Shake-scene in a countrey."[1] That pamphlet links the versifying "upstart Crow" to a line from the play known either as *The True Tragedy of Richard, Duke of York* or as *The Third Part of Henry the Sixt*, jeering at a "*Tygers hart wrapt in a Players hyde,*" but no version of that play would be attributed to Shakespeare explicitly for another quarter-century, and the allusion in the compounded "Shake-scene" only becomes unambiguously convincing after one is already convinced that William Shakespeare was a player, a dramatist, and the author of *The Third Part of Henry VI*. That "Shake-scene" is the identifying word, rather than "Iohannes" or even "Crow," is only clear once it has become clear. Had William Shakespeare left London in 1594 and been mentioned in no further records, there would be no conclusive way to link the upstart player attacked in the pamphlet to the fashionable erotic and narrative poet. Shakespeare was not mentioned as writer of a plays until 1598. Until 1595, there is nothing to confirm that Shakespeare was involved in the theater at all.

On March 15 of that year, a warrant for £20 from the Chamber accounts is made out "To Willm Kempe Willm Shakespeare & Richarde Burbage seruantes to the Lord Cham^bleyne . . . for twoe seuerall comedies or Enterludes shewed by them before her Matie in x^pmas tyme laste paste . . ."[2] specifically on St. Stephen's Day (December 26) and Innocents' Day (December 28). Shakespeare appears for the first time accompanying the partners and associates with whom he would spend the rest of his career, and who would define that career even after his retirement and death: the Lord Chamberlain's Servants. Shakespeare was apparently already a prominent member, joined in delegation with the company's leading man, Burbage, and their star clown, Kemp. (The chief performers only appear as payees this one time, after the company's first Christmas at court.) Since the document in March deals with performances from the previous December, scholars have taken it to confirm his company membership by the time of those Christmas performances; since the Chamberlain's Men originally formed sometime during the first half of 1594, theater history has generally presumed Shakespeare's presence at the company's founding. This warrant is thereby used in the way Elizabethan theatrical documents are often, indeed as they are typically used: to reconstruct a narrative about an earlier, undocumented period in Shakespeare's career. Shakespeare is being given priority, in every sense of that word. The evidence is valued to the extent that it can be used to create a coherent biographical narrative about William Shakespeare, even if scholars must preserve that narrative coherence by emending the evidence and labeling it as mistaken.

Although the warrant explicitly refers to "Innocentes daye," meaning December 28, 1594, this detail is pronounced erroneous by standard histories and reference works because it conflicts with another document, a record that mentions neither Shakespeare nor the Chamberlain's Servants by name. The *Gesta Grayorum*, an account of student entertainments at Gray's Inn, reports that "a Comedy of Errors (like to *Plautus* his *Menechmus*) was played by the Players" to conclude the celebrations "upon *Innocents-Day* at Night" in 1594.[3] The "Players" themselves are not identified. But since *The Comedy of Errors* is alluded to by plot and title, the players have been presumed to be the Chamberlain's Men. Two performances on Innocents' Day by the same company has struck many theater historians as impossible; to resolve the difficulty, the wording of the court warrant is often disregarded and the date it gives replaced with a speculative date, in order to keep Shakespeare, his company, and his plays imaginatively inseparable.[4] If someone gave *The Comedy of Errors* on the night of December 28, the implied logic goes, then it must have been Shakespeare and his partners, even if they were somewhere else.

Moreover, the plays are imagined as inseparable from their author from the outset, taking what was Shakespeare's as forever and uninterruptedly his. That the Chamberlain's Men were only months old, that Shakespeare's previous company membership is practically impossible to establish, and that the date of *The Comedy of Errors*'s composition is unknown makes no difference to the scholarly debate over who might have performed the comedy in December, 1594. Almost no such scholarly debate exists.[5] Shakespeare's possession, and by extension that of the Lord Chamberlain's Men, is taken as self-evidently secure, secure enough to adjust the date on an apparently contradictory piece of evidence, and questions of date and provenance work backward from the security of this principle. Even if the conclusion itself is plausible, the methodology is unsettling. A serious case can be made that the Chamberlain's Men performed *The Comedy of Errors* on the night in question, but no one has bothered to make it. The conclusion is not defended or advanced but treated as an initial premise. The explicit documentary record of Shakespeare's life in the theater begins with a record that Shakespeareans refuse to accept at face value, and this refusal is presented as common sense.

This evidentiary sunspot may seem a small matter compared to the larger questions of Shakespeare's canon and Shakespeare's biography. And it may seem superficially logical to consider a single anomaly within the context of a broad, established pattern of theatrical ownership. But in the case of the Chamberlain's Men's initial repertory, virtually all of the evidence is anomalous, and the pattern is a scholarly construction. The general rules do not hold true in any of the specific cases. The presumption of the company's claim to *The Comedy of Errors* might be strengthened by its demonstrated claim to a number of other Shakespeare plays in 1594, but their claims to each of those plays, at least in their canonical Shakespearean forms, is murkier than their claim to *Errors*, and none of their claims are demonstrable. Any claims about which plays the Chamberlain's Men owned in 1594, or about what the 1594 texts of those plays were like, demands intense interpretation of ambiguous and fragmentary evidence. *The Comedy of Errors*, documented as being played on the same night the Chamberlain's Men are documented playing somewhere else, is actually the play to which they have the least ambiguous claim.

Scholars necessarily reconstruct the beginning of the company's history from later testimony. But Shakespeare's partners and fellows in the Chamberlain's Men, the most important witnesses to his career and the providers of most of that later testimony, had deep professional investments in the public perception of Shakespeare and of his canon. The claims of the playing company's leaders constitute the most valuable source for recreating the company's history, but they are not a neutral source. The Chamberlain's Servants, who became the King's Servants after the accession of James I, would go on to become the most powerful and durable acting company in early modern English history, maintaining their theatrical preeminence until the playhouses were closed in 1642. Shakespeare's partners in art and business alike, they became the custodians of his reputation and arbiters of his dramatic canon after his death, most importantly by overseeing the folio publication of *Mr. William Shakespeares Comedies, Histories, & Tragedies* in 1623, the famous First Folio. The King's Men are the closest thing to an authorized biographer that Shakespeare has ever had. But their account of him is naturally colored by their hindsight and by their success. The beginnings of Shakespeare's theatrical life are seen through the lens of his later career; early evidence about him is tested for consistency with the familiar, established figure of William Shakespeare the King's Man, and with the King's Men's narratives about that figure. The formation of the Chamberlain's Men in 1594 is Shakespeare's defining moment; it has come to define everything he did afterward, and everything he did before. Shakespeare scholars, themselves deeply committed to the Shakespeare of the Globe and the Blackfriars, are unsurprisingly comfortable with the tacit teleology that makes young Shakespeare into an image of the mature Shakespeare, and the 1623 Folio into the alpha and omega of his working life.

But the company in 1594 was many years from the dominant position it would later achieve. The Lord Chamberlain's Men formed during major upheavals in London's theater business and faced powerful and competitive rivals. The first years of their partnership were spent consolidating their position; in subsequent years they were committed to the public identity they formed in those years, and to the narratives that supported that identity. The star of the story that the Lord Chamberlain's Men devised for themselves, and adapted to their professional needs, was their colleague William Shakespeare.

Two Households: The Events of 1594

In 1594 the Privy Council reopened London to professional actors after two years of nearly continuous prohibition. The Council had restrained playing in the capital late in June 1592 after some rioting by apprentices,[6] and high death tolls from the plague had subsequently kept the London playhouses closed, with only occasional brief intermissions, until spring 1594. In the meantime, one major playing company fell on hard times; a letter by the playhouse owner Philip Henslowe describes Pembroke's Men "breaking" while in the country, unable to defray their costs, and returning to London in August or September 1593. The professional English playing companies had been designed for touring, as Scott H. McMillin and Sally-Beth McLean point out,[7] but as McMillin and MacLean also demonstrate, the high profits of playing London had led the professional companies first to commission and then to depend upon plays requiring larger casts,[8] so that the economics of urban playing circa 1592 might have proved unsustainable in the provinces. Lord Strange's Men had made precisely this argument when petitioning the Privy Council to lift the restraint: "our Companie is greate, and thearbie our chardge intollerable, in travellinge the Countrie, and the Contynuance thereof wilbe a meane to bring us to division and separacion."[9] This claim was rhetorically motivated, to be sure, and claims made during clients' appeals to patrons should not be taken too literally. The Strange's Men subsequently managed to travel the country for two years without bankruptcy, and dividing a company into smaller touring units seems to have been a well-known practice.[10] But at least some actors believed that the economics of touring with a large company would lead to the dissolution of companies, as was the case for Pembroke's Men. And every major playing company from the era would undergo significant changes (of personnel, of patron, of court privileges) during the long restraint and its aftermath.

The Privy Council did not merely reopen the London playhouses but chose two groups of players as favorites to be promoted. The Lord Admiral, Charles Howard, and Henry Carey, the Lord Chamberlain, allies and kinsmen by marriage, each took direct charge of a company as official patron. Beginning with the Christmas season of 1594, the Admiral's Men and the Chamberlain's Men shared a monopoly on Court performances. While this might seem to be personal favoritism by Lord Chamberlain Carey, Andrew Gurr points out that neither Howard nor Carey had previously given any such advantage to acting companies they had patronized.[11] The restriction of Court performance to two companies was rather favoritism as an official tool of policy. Two companies were to share the privilege of performing for the Queen. The two Privy Councilors' companies would also be given exclusive privileges to perform in London and its suburbs. A Privy Council minute from February 1598 makes that exclusivity official.[12] Gurr proposes that the Council's policy, privileging what he calls the "duopoly" of two companies, was actually instituted in 1594.[13] Whether the shared monopoly began in 1594 or later, the Admiral's and Chamberlain's companies were clearly the leading London companies, and the Court's favorites, from that spring onward. The companies that had dominated the Christmas revels in the preceding years, such as the Queen's Men, the Earl of Pembroke's Men, and the Earl of Sussex's Men, disappear from the Court records entirely after Twelfth Night 1594.

Some of the players from those earlier groups may have joined the newly favored companies, some might have simply changed their names and patrons, and the companies that left London to tour England were not failures on their own terms. The ongoing Records of Early English Drama (REED) Project, which has undertaken the first complete compilation of early English performance records, continues to demonstrate how misleading theater historians' "London bias" has been. The Queen's Men, especially, had a long and honored provincial career even after they lost the privilege of performing before the Queen.[14] But while the touring performers would go on to play an important role in the history of English theater, 1594 marks their exit from the history of English professional drama and its development. They could continue playing and even thriving without access to London. But it was London's unique resources, its enormous and lucrative market for plays, its supply of professional writers, its proximity to Court and access to the book trades,[15] combined with London's unique business pressures, its voracious audiences and close competition, that drove the literary evolution of the drama.

A touring company needed fewer plays in its repertory than a London company offered in a given week, and the playhouses relied on customers returning for more than one weekly show. Pleasing such customers required material that could satisfy the same viewers repeatedly, in enough supply that they not be served the same meal too often. The extant corpus of English professional drama was written for those playhouse audiences. The artistic richness of the surviving plays stems from that audience's extraordinary demands and from the competitive pressure that the London companies exerted upon one another. Neither company could afford to fall behind the other in artistic sophistication; both worked to outdo the other, and their audiences grew accustomed to increasingly better-crafted plays. The rapid flowering of English drama as an art form comes from the hothouse of London.

The leading players in the Admiral's Men and the Chamberlain's Men were collegial competitors, or at the very least had been colleagues before becoming rivals. Five of the leading partners in the original Lord Chamberlain's Men had been performing with Edward Alleyn, the leader and star of the Lord Admiral's Men, throughout the restraint on playing in London. A traveling license from May 1593 lists the sharers of their company as "Edward Alleyn

Figure 1. Title page of *A Knack to Know a Knave*, 1594. RB 62152. By permission of The Huntington Library, San Marino, California.

servant to the right honorable the lord high Admiral, William Kemp, Thomas Pope, John Heminges, Augustine Phillips and George Brian, being of one company, servants to our very good lord the Lord Strange."[16] Many scholars have described this group as the "amalgamated" Strange's and Admiral's company, but the group is better described as Lord Strange's *Men* and the Admiral's *Man*; even though Alleyn had joined the Lord Strange's Men as an actor, he evidently refused to subordinate his personal relationship with his patron to the group's collective identity. Alleyn's stubbornly egotistic fidelity was vindicated when the playhouses were reopened and he once again led a full company of Admiral's Men, stronger than they had ever been.

Alleyn was by far the most famous actor in England and had far outshone his colleagues from Lord Strange's Men. Indeed, he is the only player whose personal name is used to identify an early modern acting company on the title page of a printed play. *A Knack to Know a Knave* was printed in 1594 "as it hath sundrie tymes bene played by ED. ALLEN and his Companie. With KEMPS applauded Merrimentes. . . ."[17] (See Figure 1.) The company in question is the Lord Strange's, with Alleyn as leading man. The oddity of a combined company with two patrons presented a naming problem, but the decision to use Alleyn's name (by no means the only or most obvious solution) positions him as the dominant figure, the public identity both of the company and the play.[18] Alleyn eclipses not only his colleagues and their patron but his own patron as well. Only the clown, Kemp, gets a share of the billing and the authority. Alleyn's star power made him the play's discursive author, and the imagined master, rather than the fellow, of Lord Strange's Men. When the temporary partnership broke up, the play remained Alleyn's.

Most of the other properties that the "amalgamated" group is known to have performed went with Alleyn to the Lord Admiral's Men. Alleyn and his father-in-law, the theatrical landlord Philip Henslowe, were tenacious acquirers of plays. Although scripts were licensed by the Master of Revels for performance by a specific company, and by that company alone, there are repeated examples of Henslowe, Alleyn, or both supplying the same play to multiple companies while retaining control themselves of the playbook and the performance rights. Some plays, such as Greene's *Friar Bacon and Friar Bungay*, turn up repeatedly with various companies at the Rose, evidently provided by Henslowe to a series of theatrical tenants.[19] Whenever Henslowe managed to open the Rose for five or ten days during the upheavals of 1592–94, whichever company was in residence performed Marlowe's *Jew of Malta*; it's a Strange's play, a Queen's and Sussex's play, and eventually a Lord Admiral's play, but in practice it is always a Henslowe play. The *Diary* records sales of playbooks to "the company" (meaning the Lord Admiral's Men) by the retired Alleyn, and two decades later a company of younger actors would denounce Henslowe for charging them two hundred pounds for plays without surrendering the "books" themselves, meaning the master copies signed by the Master of Revels and constituting the play's performance license.[20] Alleyn not only kept *A Knack to Know a Knave* after the rest of the cast became his competitors but kept almost all of the plays he had acted with the Strange's Men at the Rose. Alleyn and his father-in-law kept *The Jew of Malta, Tamar Cham, Friar Bacon and Friar Bungay, Orlando Furioso, The Battle of Alcazar, The Massacre at Paris*, and *The Spanish Tragedy*. Alleyn's former associates took few, if any, of the plays from that joint run into their professional future; at best one of those plays appears in subsequent performance records. Perhaps the Strange's Men owned *Don Horatio*, the prequel to *The Spanish Tragedy*, but they make little mention of it. Only a history play that Henslowe calls "harey the 6" can be identified, not quite conclusively, among the Lord Chamberlain's Men's later possessions.

Alleyn's former partners (Kemp, Pope, Heminges, Phillips, and Bryan) were joined in the new Lord Chamberlain's Servants by Burbage and Shakespeare sometime before March 1595. No list of the company's leading actors before 1598 survives; by that time, William Sly and Henry Condell were important members of the group. Burbage was the son of James Burbage, builder and owner of the Theater playhouse, but his acting career during the playhouse closures is entirely undocumented. For that matter, there is no direct evidence of any of the other leading Chamberlain's Men in any of the playing companies during the restraint of 1592–94. None are mentioned as Queen's Men. The personnel of Pembroke's Men during the relevant years is almost entirely unknown, and scholarship has produced, at best, speculative claims about fairly minor figures.[21] The membership of Sussex's Men is entirely unknown, and even speculation is limited. The lack of evidence here is a sobering reminder of how much is missing from the theatrical record, and of how often the surviving facts simply do not tell theater historians the things we most wish to know. Empirical method and confident conclusions must part ways here.

The temptation of conclusions has proved very strong in the case of the Chamberlain's Men's initial personnel, leading scholars to construct speculative stories about the Pembroke's Men and Sussex's Men by working backward from later evidence.[22] These companies are variously described as having been breakaway factions of some other company, or amalgamations of actors from companies that had dissolved, with far more specificity than evidence: Pembroke's Men are imagined as having split off from the Strange's company, for example,[23] or from the Queen's, and Sussex's Men are imagined as a recombination of actors from disbanded companies. That individual players cannot actually be traced moving between these companies does not serve as a sufficient deterrent to speculation, and when necessary speculative biographies for the players are cobbled together in order to support the speculative company histories. Richard Burbage is commonly presumed to have been the leading actor of one of the companies, for example, because he is known to have played starring roles for the Chamberlain's Men. But nothing of the kind follows. When Burbage began to play the lead is unknown. There is no proof of him acting any major part prior to 1594, and indeed no evidence that he acted at all between 1592 and 1594. The argument that he could not have been trusted playing the lead role unless he had previously done so, an argument upon which all accounts of Burbage as company leader in 1593 implicitly or explicitly depend, depends itself upon an obvious logical fallacy. Clearly, Burbage had to be trusted with the chief part for the first time, and when, by whom, is unknown. What we know about Richard Burbage in early 1594 is that he was twenty-five years old and the son of a playhouse owner. He might have already been a seasoned leading man. But he also might have been an actor used to major supporting roles, moving into the leads for the first time, or a well-connected but relatively inexperienced player finding greatness thrust upon him. To decide among these possibilities without further evidence is to express a preference and to impose it upon history.

Shakespeareans have much preferred to imagine Shakespeare's company as preeminent, and its star as unquestionably capable. Burbage's later success is superimposed on his early career, translated into the domain of the always-already. The unanswerable question is answered satisfactorily, if not forensically, and the resulting pseudo-fact is used both to support further arguments and to foreclose otherwise legitimate questions. Theater historians can base arguments upon Burbage's leadership of, say, the Pembroke's Men, although neither his leadership nor his membership can be confirmed; meanwhile the question of how much Burbage's early career depended upon his father's playhouse is obscured when he is "known" to have led a touring company in the provinces for two years. This operation, preposterous in the literal sense of reversing chronological priority, appeals to consistency as a marker of plausibility; surely, if Burbage was a great actor, is it not unreasonable to suggest that he had been one for some time? But the presumption of consistency, the premise that undocumented periods of an artist's career do not significantly differ from the documented periods, essentially denies that Richard Burbage had a past at all.

The primary tool for the reconstruction of the Pembroke's and Sussex's companies, and occasionally even for the Queen's Men despite the richer positive evidence about them, is the disposition of those company's plays, several of which turned up in the Lord Chamberlain's Men's repertory.[24] The typical method is to presume that plays were transferred from company to company as part of players' movements, rather than by some other method such as simple purchase; should a Pembroke's company play turn up in the Lord Chamberlain's Men's hands, one or more of Pembroke's Men are imagined turning up with it. The underlying assumption here is that possession of a play indicates some legitimate prior claim. If it belonged to the Chamberlain's Men in 1594, the unspoken reasoning goes, it must have already belonged to some of them. In fact, the scholarly narratives are driven by the goal of establishing exactly such prior claims upon each play for the Chamberlain's company.

The notion that Shakespeare's players must have been the legitimate claimants to their plays exerts a powerful influence on scholars, occasionally distorting their methodology in odd ways. In one of the most egregious instances the most prominent Shakespearean theater historian today, writing a major history of the so-called Shakespeare company, grows so intent upon establishing that one of the founding sharers had come from the Queen's Men, bringing a legitimate claim to certain Queen's Men's properties, that he denies that John Heminges had been in Lord Strange's Men in 1593, notwithstanding the company traveling license with Heminges's name on it or the scholar's own previous (and subsequent) citations of that document. "The only newcomer to these groups of former Strange's . . . players was John Heminges," he claims as a preparation for claiming that Heminges "likely joined the new company directly from the Queen's along with several of their playbooks."[25] This strange mistake, made by a deeply learned expert in a work he intended as a definitive history of the company, suggests a profound investment in preserving the Chamberlain's Men's claims to their initial repertory. The presumption of legitimacy is elevated to a tacit first principle, inviolable even in the face of documentary evidence, which is either overlooked through convenient error (as here) or else overruled and pronounced erroneous (as in the court records for Christmas 1594).

The Lord Chamberlain's Man whose earlier career has invited the most speculation, and whose prior claim to the company's plays has been most sacrosanct, is William Shakespeare. One of the great conundrums of Shakespearean biography is the question of which company the playwright acted with before joining the Chamberlain's Men, a riddle because the standard method is to deduce his presence from the presence of plays later attributed to him. The result is a complicated back story which places him in a shifting series of groups, as some kind of Pembroke's/Strange's/Queen's/Sussex's Man. Such stories can seldom be made to work satisfactorily. Terence G. Schoone-Jongen's recent book *Shake-*

speare's Companies ably demonstrates the impossibility of establishing Shakespeare's previous company affiliations.[26] Nor is there any evidence to suggest that Shakespeare kept control of any play he had written, or had collaborated in writing, before joining the Chamberlain's Men. Such control over a script was for the buyer, not the seller, and no evidence suggests that Shakespeare was a sharer in any playing company until 1594. Nor did the other known actor-dramatists in the 1590s maintain control of the performance rights to their plays; the former Queen's Man Robert Wilson, a major star in his day and a prominent playwright, did not carry any such rights with him when he left the Queen's Men. Neither did the young player Ben Jonson retain the stage rights to any plays he might have written for the resurgent Pembroke's Men leading up to 1597. To presume Shakespeare had some special claim upon scripts as their "author," or to suggest as Andrew Gurr recently has that Shakespeare personally retained the freedom to dispose of the officially licensed playbooks,[27] is to impose an anachronistic arrangement upon the past.

But the greatest problem in using this approach is that Shakespeare's name is eventually attached to all of the printed plays which seem to have been part of his company's original repertoire, no matter which company had owned it previously. Shakespeare's name on a play says nothing about which company he came from, because the Chamberlain's Men put his name on everything.

The Kings of Shreds and Patches: The Chamberlain's Men's Secondhand Repertory

Every play that the Chamberlain's Men took over from some earlier company's repertory was eventually, but never initially, ascribed to William Shakespeare. If any version of a play had existed previous to 1594, the company would sooner or later claim it as Shakespeare's or else cease to claim it at all. Such claims came later rather than sooner: the Shakespearean attributions did not begin until four years after the company's formation, and the process of attribution was not completed until a quarter-century later, with the publication of the Folio. Among these retroactively ascribed "Shakespeare" plays are most of the dramas that would be published in widely variant texts: *Hamlet, The Taming of a* (or *the*) *Shrew, King Lear, King John, Richard III, Henry V,* and the second and third parts of *Henry VI.*

No other printed versions of Shakespeare's plays are as drastically at variance with the Folio texts as are the First Quarto of *Hamlet* or the 1594 *Taming of a Shrew* or *King Leir* or the various early iterations of the history plays.

The First Quartos of *Romeo and Juliet* and *The Merry Wives of Windsor* are quite different from those plays' Folio texts, but not nearly as different as the First Quarto of *Hamlet* is from the Folio version, or as *King Leir* is from *King Lear*. The most glaring and puzzling textual multiplicity associated with Shakespeare's plays comes in the works that existed both before and after the formation of the Lord Chamberlain's Men in 1594. And that multiplicity is endemic throughout the texts of the Chamberlain's Men's plays that were printed before the end of 1595. Only one of those plays, the exceptional case of *Titus Andronicus*, has a quarto text closely resembling the later Folio version. All of the other plays belonging to the King's Men in 1623 but predating the formation of the Lord Chamberlain's Men exist in printed texts radically different from the canonical versions.

Nor are there records of the Chamberlain's Men performing any of the other, non-Shakespearean printed dramas that had belonged to earlier playing companies, even if they performed "Shakespearean" plays taken from those companies. They make no recorded claim on *Fair Em*, which had belonged to the Lord Strange's Men, even though the company included all of the Lord Strange's company's sharers. Roslyn Lander Knutson argues that since the Chamberlain's Men possessed some of the Pembroke's Men's plays they would have had Marlowe's *Edward II* as well (which presumes wholesale, rather than piecemeal, transfers of company repertories), yet no trace of it survives.[28] Nor do any printed dramas from 1594 or earlier gain an attribution to the company unless they are also attributed to Shakespeare. *Fair Em* does not become a Chamberlain's play in reprints; *Edward II* remains a Pembroke's play on its printed title page in 1612 and 1625, long after Pembroke's players (and even a later group with the same name and patron) had ceased to exist. The only play known to have been in the company's repertory that was not attributed to Shakespeare is a biblical drama called *Hester and Ahasuerus*, which is now lost to history. Part of this is an artifact of the limited and sporadic performance records of the mid-1590s; surely, the company acted other plays, even if they are now lost. But they did not preserve those plays or accord them the value that they would later attach to the Shakespeare canon. The plays which they still retain in their active repertory during the Jacobean and Caroline periods, when the performance records are comparatively fuller, are those from Shakespeare. The plays that the company took as parts of its long-term identity are those it identifies as Shakespeare's.

This has seldom seemed odd to scholars and critics, who have themselves often been exclusively focused on Shakespeare. Few historians of Elizabethan drama will complain when all the evidence is about Shakespeare's plays. And the idea of an acting company that acts nothing but Shakespeare fits comfortably with twenty-first-century expectations, as such companies have long since become a familiar part of English-language theater. But Shakespeare and his fellows should not be mistaken for the Royal Shakespeare Company; such a singular focus on the work of a single playwright is inconsistent with the practices of the other Elizabethan playing companies, and with the Chamberlain's Men's own later practices. The idea that the 1594 Chamberlain's Men did not possess even a single play that became a long-term success, except for those that Shakespeare had written, suits hagiography better than probability. The thought that only the Shakespeare plays went on to become part of the company's core repertory may confirm the reverential feelings we have been taught to have for Shakespeare. But it is closer to the evidence to say that all of the plays from 1594 which enter the core repertory become Shakespeare's. It might not be that Shakespeare was what the company kept, but that what the company kept became "Shakespeare."

What we know of the Chamberlain's Men's original holdings must be reconstructed from third-party records, primarily from printed copies of their plays. 1594 was a watershed year for the publication of playbooks, with an unprecedented number of commercial plays entering print. The bulk of the properties that can be identified with the later repertory of the Lord Chamberlain's Servants are history plays, the very plays to which an acting company's title would be the least secure in practice. Companies might own plays but could not press an exclusive claim on a historical subject, and it was routine for companies to offer rival dramas about the same Roman statesman or English king. Henslowe hired Ben Jonson to write a "Richard Crookback," obviously meant to match or overmatch Shakespeare's *Richard III*, and paid a consortium of writers to undertake a play titled *Caesar's Fall*.[29] Henslowe also records the Admiral's Men playing a very successful *Henry V* beginning in November, 1595.[30] The particular case of the Admiral's Men's *Sir John Oldcastle*, which staged the same historical figure who had been the original model for Falstaff, will be handled at length in Chapter 4. The Admiral's Men were not always the aggressors; the Chamberlain's Men also commissioned plays on historical subjects similar, if not identical, to Admiral's Men's properties. The Admiral's Men's *Malcolm, King of Scots* did not rule out a King's Men depiction of that king in *Macbeth*, nor did the Admirals' two-part *Cardinal Wolsey* keep Shakespeare and Fletcher from staging Wolsey in *Henry VIII*. Neither were Shakespeare and Fletcher deterred by Samuel Rowley's Henry VIII history, *When You See Me You Know Me*. Both companies would commission a play about Catiline. Famous literary subjects were also fair game; the Admiral's

Servants had a *Troilus and Cressida* before Shakespeare and his fellows did.[31] By the same rule, Thomas Heywood was later free to stage his own *Rape of Lucrece*, freely borrowing from Shakespeare's poem, for Queen Anne's Men.

Duplication of subject matter naturally threatened to blur the boundaries between one company's property and another's. The distinction in the public mind between competing companies' plays could only be maintained by demonstration; a history play distinguished itself in performance. Players needed to maintain a perceptible difference between their historical dramas and their competitors' and needed to maintain their theatrical superiority as well. Otherwise, the rival company's more effective or more sophisticated offering might render one's own play commercially and artistically obsolete. In a business environment where revision and expansion of older plays was routine (and Henslowe's so-called *Diary* indicates just how routine paying for "additions" was) and where competitors were always free to create a newer, fresher version of a historical drama in one's repertory, revising one's own plays was a commercial necessity. Revision, for the players, was the essence of theatrical possession. It was not the theoretical but the practical key to keeping hold of a dramatic property, and to keeping it worth holding.

The new Lord Chamberlain's Men, possessing a number of established historical dramas from previous companies, almost all of which were newly available in print for the reading public, could not ignore the possibility that their plays would be rewritten and improved by a competitor. Indeed, it is by no means certain that the Chamberlain's Men had the firmest or most legitimate claim upon these historical dramas. We have no logical reason to presume them the virtuous party in every potential dispute. They may themselves have chosen to exploit the blurred lines between one history play and another by rewriting older properties whose title they might have imagined lapsed (if, for example, the previous owners were unlikely to perform in London again) or whose previous owners were in no position to press their case. In some cases the Chamberlain's Men's claim to a specific play might have been based not upon provenance or prior transmission but simply upon possession, meaning possession of the most powerful and most theatrically convincing text.

The Queen's Men had acted a number of history plays, demonstrably written by 1594, which resemble the canonical Shakespeare histories printed later, including works about King John, Richard III, Henry V, Richard III, and Lear (who appears in Holinshed's *Chronicle* as a genuine king). The two-part *Troublesome Reign of King John* (not much longer than a standard five-act play) had been printed in 1591 with an attribution to the Queen's Men and was only the second English play published as belonging to a professional troupe.³² *The True Tragedy of Richard III* was entered in the Stationers' Register on June 19, 1594, and printed that year as a Queen's Men's play. *The Famous Victories of Henry the Fifth, Containing the Honorable Battle of Agincourt* was registered on May 14, 1594, but not printed until 1598; it too would carry a title-page attribution to the Queen's Men. *The Chronicle History of King Leir* was also registered on May 14 but not printed until 1605; the 1605 Quarto does not mention Queen Elizabeth's Men, because that queen was deceased, but the play is presumably the same "Kinge Leare" that Henslowe records on April 6 and April 8, 1594, during a short combined run by Sussex's and the Queen's Men;³³ if not, then the multiplicity of plays about Lear in multiple repertories would make the Chamberlain's Men's claim upon the material even more complicated and fragile.

All four of these plays are clearly related to the plays later published as Shakespeare's but share almost none of their language. Scholars have variously imagined these plays as sources, as drafts, and as derivatives of the canonical *Henry IV, Henry V, King Lear, Richard III,*³⁴ and *King John*. The Shakespearean incarnations of these plays begin to appear beginning in 1597, when the First Quarto of *The Tragedy of King Richard the Third* was printed "As it hath been lately Acted by the Right honourable the Lord Chamberlaine his servants," with a text distinct from that of the earlier *True Tragedy of Richard III*. The process of associating these plays with Shakespeare begins in 1598, when the Second Quarto of *Richard III* adds the attribution "By William Shakespeare." *The First Part of Henry IV*, which reworks and expands *The Famous Victories*' material about the Henry V's apparently idle youth, is printed in quarto in 1598 and attributed to Shakespeare on the title page of the Second Quarto in 1599. *The Second Part of Henry IV* is named as Shakespeare's from its first printing in 1600, although *Henry V*, also published that year, is not. The first edition to identify *Henry V* as Shakespeare's, even implicitly, is the surreptitious printing by William Jaggard in 1619, and the first edition upon which Shakespeare's name appears is the Folio. The First Quarto of *King Lear*, prominently attributed to Shakespeare, was published in 1608, and there is no previous mention of the play as Shakespeare's. *King John* is ascribed to Shakespeare by Francis Meres in 1598, along with *Richard III* and *Henry IV*. However, the play is first printed as "Written by W. Sh" in 1611, when this partial byline is attached to a reprint of the twenty-year-old *Troublesome Reign*. A third edition of *The Troublesome Reign* would appear in 1622 as "Written by W. Shakespeare." The now-familiar text of *King John* is first printed in the Folio. Clearly, not everyone viewed the old Queen's Men's play and the later King's Men's play as distinct.

The Chamberlain's Men also possessed or assumed possession of various plays about Henry VI. *The First Part of the Contention of the Two Famous Houses of York and Lancaster*, a version of *Henry VI, Part 2*, was entered in the Stationers' Register on March 12 and printed in 1594. *The True Tragedy of Richard Duke of York and the Good King Henry the Sixth*, a version of *Henry VI, Part 3*, was printed with an attribution to Pembroke's Men in 1595. *The True Tragedy* was not entered in the Stationers' Register before publication but appears in a much later transfer of rights. The texts vary substantially from the Folio versions, and like the plays from the Queen's Men's repertory have been imagined by different critics as source plays, as early drafts, and as hapless or piratical adaptations. However, the quarto texts of the *Henry VI* plays are generally closer to the 1623 printing than the Queen's Men's texts are. The sneer about the "tiger's heart wrapped in the player's hide" in *Greenes Groatsworth of Wit* associates Shakespeare, however allusively, with *The True Tragedy* and with *3 Henry VI*,[35] before joining the Chamberlain's Men; only *The True Tragedy* can be personally associated with him in this way. Yet even that allusion comes in the context of at least an equivocal accusation of plagiarism, against the upstart who had allegedly been "beautified with" other poets' "feathers."[36] No one else would link these plays to Shakespeare until 1619.

The First Part of the Contention, as its name implies, presents itself as the first part of a dramatic sequence, not the second; *The First Part of the Contention* and *The True Tragedy*, taken together, make a self-sufficient ten-act entertainment. They are not dependent upon another play about Henry VI, although clearly at least one other such play existed by 1592. Thomas Nashe's *Pierce Penniless* remarks upon "brave Talbot, the terror of the French . . . triumph[ing] again on the stage,"[37] which clearly recalls the material of *Henry VI, Part 1*. Henslowe notes a play he calls "harey the vj" play (and marks as "ne," an annotation which Henslowe often used for new plays[38]) on March 3, 1592, during the tenancy of the Lord Strange's Men with Alleyn. He lists fourteen more performances for the piece before playing was restrained at the end of June, making it the company's most frequent offering; the troupe acted twenty separate plays over a string of ninety-four performances, during which "harry the vi" appeared fifteen times.[39] The play got two more performances in January 1593, when Alleyn and the Strange's play played at the Rose for a month after their Christmas performances at court.[40] Henslowe never refers to the first or second part of the play, as is his usual custom with multipart plays such as *Tamburlaine* or *Tamar Cham*; whatever Henslowe saw, he did not imagine it to be part of a series. Whether the "Harry the VI" at the Rose was the Talbot play that Nashe mentions or yet another Henry

VI drama is impossible to establish. What does seem clear, however, is that both the Pembroke's company and the Strange's company possessed at least one Henry VI play in the early 1590s. This, again, reflects normal practice; no company could have an exclusive claim to an English king. Some critics have presumed a connection between the companies, because the Shakespeare Folio contains three parts of *Henry VI*, but this is circular; again, the presumption is that if the plays ended up in the same hands, they originated in the same hands. The surviving evidence, however limited, makes it certain that rival Henry VI dramas did exist in different companies' possession and argues against any one company possessing a "complete" cycle of Henry VI plays.

The very few non-history plays that can be confirmed as part of the Chamberlain's Men's initial repertory are found in the scanty performance records for the company that year. The *Comedy of Errors* performance at Gray's Inn on December 28 may well have been the Chamberlain's Men's, although other playing companies might still have been active in London, and whether the play was written before or during 1594 is impossible to establish. But one crucial record gives us a glimpse of the company's original repertory in performance. From June 3 to June 13, 1594, Henslowe records the Admiral's and Chamberlain's Men playing together at Newington Buttes, some distance outside London. Fears about the plague were still keeping the players out of the populous inner suburbs. Whether the two companies performed as a single troupe or gave performances on alternating days, they worked out a rough alternation between plays owned by each group. Henslowe lists a number of staples from the Admiral's Men repertory: *The Jew of Malta*, *Cutlack*, and *Belin Dun*. The Biblical play *Hester and Ahasuerus* is recorded nowhere else by Henslowe and so might have come from the Chamberlain's Men. Henslowe also notes three plays which became familiar Chamberlain's Men properties: "andronicus" on June 5 and 12, "hamlet" on June 9, and "the tamynge of A shrowe" on June 11.[41]

None of these three plays was new, and two had already been sold to printers. *Hamlet* had been around since at least 1589, when Thomas Nashe had poked fun at it.[42] *A Pleasant Conceited Historie called The Taming of a Shrew* had been entered in the Stationers' Register on May 2, 1594, and published by sometime that year "As it was sundry times acted by the Right honorable the Earle of Pembrook his seruants." The quarto text is radically divergent from the Folio's, and the play was not attributed to Shakespeare until 1623. Henslowe had seen *Titus Andronicus* before, as a Sussex's Men's play, in January and February of 1594, before the reorganization of the companies.[43] The book was

Figure 2. Title page of *Titus Andronicus*, 1594. By permission of the Folger Shakespeare Library.

also entered in the Stationers' Register on February 6 and printed sometime that year with a startlingly complete performance history below its title.

The first edition of *Titus Andronicus* describes it "As it was Plaide by the Right Honourable the Earle of *Darbie*, Earle of *Pembrooke*, and Earle of *Sussex* their Servaunts."[44] (See Figure 2.) (The Earl of Derby was the former Lord Strange, who had recently inherited a grander title.) The rest of the list testifies, as does the title page of *A Knack to Know a Knave*, to the theatrical shifts and shocks of the early 1590s, but unlike the *Knack to Know a Knave* it emphasizes the ownerlessness of the play the book contains. If a single owner carried the play, and the Master of Revels' approved copy, from company to company, that individual possessor lacked the authority to impose any discursive identity upon it. The list of companies also makes clear the company to which it does not belong; the play's serialized provenance underscores that Edward Alleyn has no further claim on it. *Titus Andronicus* does not represent itself as having a natural, inherent relationship with any individual (not an actor, a poet, or a patron), or with any group. The list of three companies, by definition, is a list of companies who formerly owned it, and the sheer fact of the list emphasizes the transience of possession. (This is not how things work for other scripts that were played by more than one company; plays performed by several companies at Henslowe's Rose, for example, would be attributed to only one in print.) The title page of *Titus* does not proclaim any intrinsic rights or authority but instead rehearses a history. In doing so, the edition invites the reader to remember just how hard the play is for any group of actors to keep.

But surprisingly, the First Quarto's approach works in securing the Chamberlain's Men's claims to *Titus*. The Second Quarto, in 1600, simply adds the current possessors to the list as a fourth company: "the Earle of Pembrooke, the Earle of Darbie, the Earle of Sussex and the Lord Chamberlaine theyr Seruants."[45] (See Figure 3.) The next time the play appears, in 1611, the title page simply gives it to "his Majesties Servants," although a head-title inside repeats the triumvirate of playing companies from 1594. Subsequently it turns up in the Shakespeare Folio, firmly in the control of the King's Men and now publicly associated with an author for the first time. (It had, however, been listed as Shakespeare's in Francis Meres's *Palladis Tamia*, while its companion pieces from 1594, *A Shrew* and *Hamlet*, were not.) Although there are other plays which only gain an ascription to a playing company in later quartos (*Mucedorus*, which becomes identified as the King's Men's twelve years after its first publication, is a fine example), no play other than *Titus Andronicus* is presented as having this kind of serial ownership; plays published without an attribution might subsequently gain one, and reprints might register a company's changed name, but no other piece is attributed first to one group of adult players and then another. No one in London seems to have disputed the Chamberlain's Men's possession. Yet the *Titus* quartos make no appeal to any sense of authorship or originating authority. Rather, they ground their claim entirely on provenance, on the circumstantial sequence of transfers and ownership; the root question of property is not framed as "Who first made it?" but instead "Who last had it?"

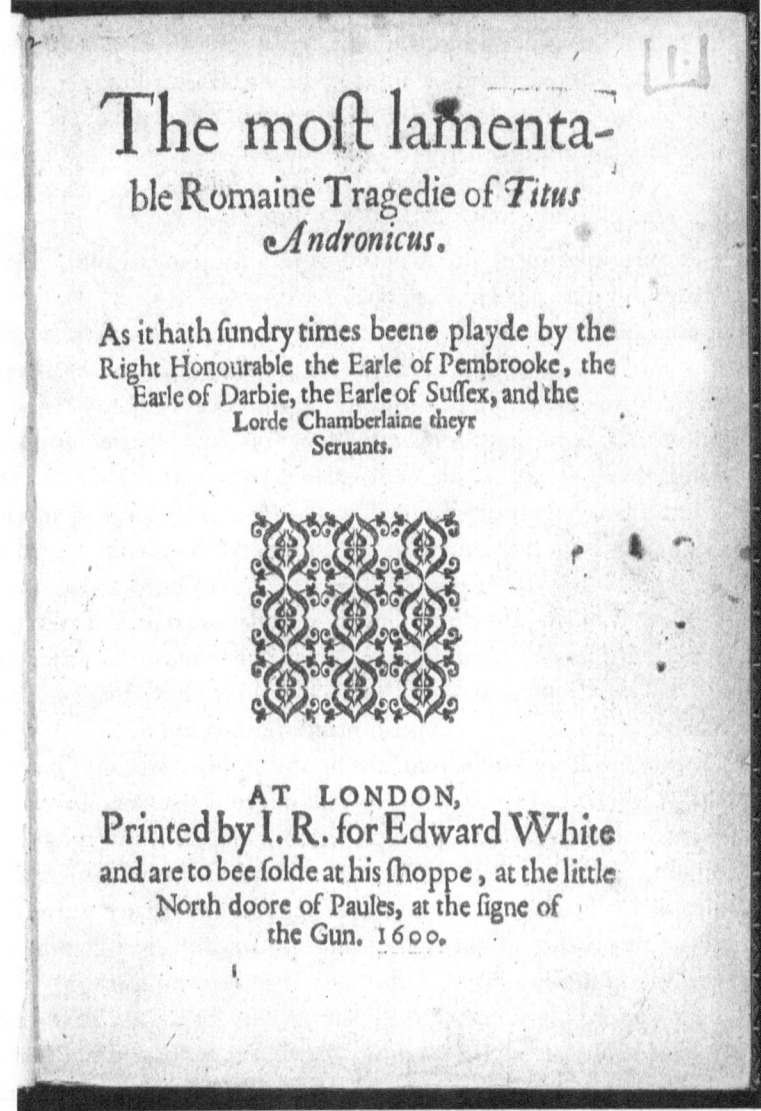

Figure 3. Title page of *Titus Andronicus*, 1600. RB 69369. By permission of The Huntington Library, San Marino, California.

Titus Andronicus is also exceptional for its textual stability. It is the one "Shakespeare" play whose text is relatively consistent from the 1594 Quarto to the 1623 collection (one scene is added in the Folio, and the other variants are relatively minor). This makes the 1594 *Titus* the first so-called good quarto, the first Shakespeare play whose first printing substantially resembles its Folio text, and in fact the only uncontroversially "good" Shakespeare quarto, the only stable text, to be published before 1597. Its textual situation is most like that of *Richard II*, printed in 1597 with a text resembling the Folio's, but, like *Titus*, with one fewer scene than the Folio would have. *Titus* is much more like the plays written after the changes of 1594 than it is like the other plays printed in that year. It is the play whose transfer from one set of owners to another is most transparently legible to outsiders, least liable to misconstruction, whose text moves from hand to hand unchanged.

But even the Chamberlain's Men's custody of *Titus Andronicus* was not necessarily immune to challenge, at least in the provinces. On January 1, 1596, Sir John Harington enjoyed a performance of *Titus* in his country house at Exton in Rutland, about seventy miles north of London.[46] Theater historians have often assumed the appearance of this play to indicate the presence of the Lord Chamberlain's Men themselves, and it is barely possible for them to have made the trip for the performance. The company performed before the Court on December 28 (their third straight evening playing at Court) and again on January 6. They could have made the journey to Rutland and back, if they gave no other performances and spent all of the intervening time on the road. The Chamberlain's Men would have faced a difficult journey in winter, sacrificed other chances for lucrative private performances in London over a full week of the Christmas holidays, and risked missing a performance for the Queen if they chanced to meet bad weather. The obvious difficulties involved have been interpreted to suggest the leading players' serious obligations to Harington[47] or else an unusually "hefty reward."[48] If one presumes that the Chamberlain's Men's theatrical rights were inviolable and therefore never violated, such conclusions become necessary. Otherwise, the circumstances suggest that the actors in Rutland might not have been the Lord Chamberlain's Men.

The play, after all, had belonged to the company for less than two years and had yet to be attributed them to print. Perhaps the performers in Rutland had some plausible claim to it from earlier in the decade; perhaps they were some later version of Pembroke's or Sussex's Men. The performance record notes them solely as "Les commediens de Londres," which could mean any company that could claim a fairly recent London base.[49] And perhaps a touring troupe had simply purchased a printed copy of *Titus Andronicus* and acted it, with the Chamberlain's Men occupied in the capital. The principle of exclusive performance did not hold any strong or necessary sway in the country. An early modern acting company's hold on their plays was seldom self-evident and seldom firm. Ownership had to be exerted.

Upstart Crows, Inc.: Developing the Repertory

There is no way to know how many sets of hands the Chamberlain's Men's plays had passed through before 1594. But certainly none were fresh, and the company's challenge was to forge a new reputation with a repertory of old plays. The task of consolidating their claims to their own repertory would continue to occupy them over the remainder of the decade. Over time, two things happen to the plays that the Chamberlain's Men's inherited or appropriated. Their texts change a great deal, so much that some texts seem to have been replaced completely, and they become increasingly associated with Shakespeare's name. The mainstream of twentieth-century Shakespeare bibliography has obscured these processes by reversing the priority of the texts, denying the evidentiary value of publishing chronology and insisting upon the essential precedence of the Folio texts. During the heyday of the New Bibliography, in the middle of the twentieth century, large numbers of texts were designated as "bad" quartos in order to support a general narrative in which the version of a play first published was almost presumptively treated as a preposterous derivative of a version printed much later. As the hold of that general narrative has been weakened and the methods of the New Bibliography contested, editors have begun to approach each play as an individual case, variously endorsing or denying the twentieth-century orthodoxy in specific editions. In practice, the New Bibliography's preposterous chronology has been demoted from a general principle that hold true in nearly all cases to a principle that holds true in some cases and not others. But if that chronological orthodoxy is put entirely to one side, as a set of yet-unproven hypotheses, and the actual historical sequence of events is considered seriously as potential evidence, another and very different general pattern emerges. The publication and attribution of Shakespeare's plays, considered as a sequence of facts, suggest a coherent approach taken by the playing company toward their initial dramatic properties.

The Chamberlain's Servants employed a double strategy to bolster their claim on their repertory. First, they revised the secondhand scripts, refashioning them into more sophisticated works, better fitted for future seasons in the playhouses. Not coincidentally, these revisions served to distinguish the Chamberlain's Men's versions from their forerunners and to weaken any potential rivals' claims. Others might have shared in the possession of the originals, but no one else could lay claim to what the new partners had made of them. (The sow's rights to her lost ear never expire, but her title to silk purses is more complicated.) Second, the company increasingly used William Shakespeare's authorship as a signifier of possession. Shakespeare's name functions, especially in the early attributions, to cement the company's claims upon plays which they inherited in 1594 or which dealt with an easily duplicated historical subject (thus *Richard II* and *Richard III* come in for two of the first three Shakespeare ascriptions). His name is a distinguishing element between the Chamberlain's Men's plays and any forerunners or rivals, the guarantor of the play as a discrete and coherent property independent of other texts and other claimants. His *Richard III* is, by virtue of being his, imagined as a play distinct from The Queen's Men's old *True Tragedy of Richard III*, just as *Master William Shakespeare his King Lear* is distinct from the Queen's Men's *History of King Leir*. Since Shakespeare was a partner in the Chamberlain's Men, his claim upon the play was by extension his partners' as well. When Shakespeare's name does not appear on a Chamberlain's Men's play in the 1590s, no author is named at all. Not until 1600, with the insistent debut of Ben Jonson's "bibliographic ego," in Joseph Loewenstein's phrase, does a Chamberlain's Men's play appear under any other author's name, and then it is the acting company that goes unmentioned.

The company's evident double strategy, the rewriting of old plays and their attribution to Shakespeare, involves a fundamental tension. The logic of establishing ownership by current possession, by what one has done to the play since acquiring it, is at odds with the logic of authorial possession, the persistent claim of the originator. By 1623, Heminges and Condell deploy the logic of originary possession almost exclusively, with their tales of unblotted papers and surreptitious copies. In 1594, the conceptual foundation of Shakespeare's dramatic authorship is far less clear. Douglas A. Brooks has pointed out that some of Shakespeare's first theatrical attributions refer to the plays as "Newly corrected and augmented" or "emended" by Shakespeare rather than "written" by him;[50] as late as the end of the decade, the emphasis might still be heavily laid upon revision and "correction," rather than upon origination, of the script. Even such cautious and hedged ascriptions are relatively slow in coming; his name does not appear on a play at all until 1598, when it appears upon three: the First (or first extant) Quarto of *Loves Labours Lost* and the Second Quartos of *Richard II* and *Richard III*.[51] Shakespeare's discursive authorship of plays emerges upon a broad front in 1598 and 1599, with testimony from third-party witnesses as well as title pages. Meres gives his list of Shakespeare's theatrical successes in the autumn of 1598, and soon after there are explicit allusions to Shakespeare the stage poet by John Weever and by the students who mounted the satirical "Parnassus" plays at Cambridge; allusions in marginalia by Gabriel Harvey and by a reader named Adam Dyrmonth also associate Shakespeare with various of his plays and date from 1598 or later.[52] While all the previous references to Shakespeare by name had mentioned his nondramatic poems, he is suddenly a widely noted dramatist.

The lapse between Shakespeare's entrance into the new company and the public recognition of his authorship is all the more striking because of his established success as a poet before he joined, the author of the very popular *Venus and Adonis* and of the successful *Rape of Lucrece*, both published with authorial dedications. Joining the Chamberlain's Men, for Shakespeare, initially meant ceasing to be a publishing author rather than becoming one. Shakespeare's public authorship was temporarily eclipsed or submerged, his name kept from new publications for four years, strangely at the very moment that the public was most enthusiastic for his works. *Venus and Adonis* was reprinted three times between Shakespeare's entering the company and his name's first appearance on a printed play. Clearly, readers had an appetite for Shakespeare, not as a dramatist but as a narrative poet. Shakespeare did not attempt to feed that appetite. His entry into the Chamberlain's Men marked a gap in his publishing career, at least as it was imagined by the booksellers in Paul's Churchyard, and he gave up using print to further his individual relationship with patrons. He ceased the nondramatic publications that he might have dedicated to important noblemen, although he still evidently circulated sonnets in manuscript; even when his later nondramatic poems appeared, he did not dedicate them. This marks the end of one career and the beginning of another. Shakespeare forgoes his independent literary career in favor of a public association with the Chamberlain's Men, a joint career in at least two senses: as a poet joined to a group of actors, and initially a joint career as a dramatic poet and an actor.

The challenges of that career, and the extent of Shakespeare's achievement, are oddly diminished by insisting on his originary authorship of the company's original repertory. If one argues from the New Bibliographers' position that the "bad" version of a Shakespeare play first published was always written last, and the "good" text published later was always written first, then the 1594 Chamberlain's Men become owners of a far more impressive set of plays. If one considers that the texts published first might have been written first, then the new company's inventory seems substantially less formidable and their competitive position much more difficult. A company armed with something like the Folio texts of *Henry VI*, *Richard III*, and *The Taming of the Shrew* would be in a far stronger competitive position than a company acting the "bad" quarto and octavo versions of those plays in daily competition against the Lord Admiral's Men and their Marlowe plays. In the standard narrative built around Shakespeare as the originating genius of the repertory, the Chamberlain's Men eventually eclipsed their rivals because they possessed superior plays, and possessed them from the very beginning. But the evidence itself suggests that the Chamberlain's Men actually began with the weaker of the two company repertories and transformed it into the stronger one, competing against rivals with better plays by bettering their own. During the later 1590s Shakespeare extended and complicated the dramaturgy developed by Marlowe and Kyd into something more flexible and subtle, raising the standards of English drama higher than they had been before.

How Shakespeare worked can be illustrated by the case of *King Leir* and the subsequent Quarto and Folio texts of *King Lear*, a case where the Shakespeare texts are almost universally agreed to be the later versions. Shakespeare has adapted the earlier play, in part, by drawing upon more printed sources, making it his own by integrating more of others' work. His most obvious new sources are the episode from Sidney's *Arcadia* (book II, chapter 10) which provides the outline of the Edgar-Gloucester-Edmund plot, and Samuel Harsnett's 1603 *Declaration of Egregious Popish Imposters*, which provides the language and imagery of "Poor Tom's" voice. When Shakespeare revises a play, it gains more sources. And he returns to the main source underlying the play he rewrites. His *King Lear* is far closer to Holinshed, with the spectacular exception of the ending, and far more engaged with Holinshed's language than *King Leir* is. Shakespeare's goal is not to individualize his work by moving it further from its sources but to grow closer to those source texts, better integrating them into his developing work. His revision process, as evidenced by the case of *Leir* and *Lear*, resembles a loop, periodically returning to original sources, and the more Shakespeare works the more fully he inhabits those source texts and the more completely he makes them his. Shakespeare, like most early modern playwrights, typically revises with assistance from a collaborator; in his case, the collaborator is often a printed book.

At the same time, the later *Lear* has a far more developed sense of artistic unity and of thematic coherence than the earlier *Leir* does. The secondary plot which Shakespeare has added (borrowing from a source) reflects upon the main plot in a complicated and satisfying way. The king who misjudges his three daughters is mirrored by an earl who misjudges his two sons, and the two plots are wound together both on the level of narrative and on level of figurative language. The storylines intersect one another at discrete junctures, creating one kind of unifying effect, while threads of metaphor and leitmotif are woven steadily through the entire play, creating a unifying effect of a different kind. Here the impression of dramatic unity is demonstrably the fruit of afterthought.

The verbal and narrative coherence of the play, the intricacy of its structure and of its poetic fabric, stems not from the author's original design but from his redesign of an earlier and structurally simpler drama. The evident wholeness of the play does not arise from some holistic process in the writer's imagination but from the application of artistic craft in distinct stages. Nor, as Steven Urkowitz has ably demonstrated, did Shakespeare cease to revise after transforming *Leir* into the First Quarto of *Lear*; he continued to revise over time.[53] The artistic design in *Lear* is artful design, rather than some natural phenomenon. Art, although this should not need to be said, is an artifice.

Revising History

The process by which the Chamberlain's Men, and their sharer William Shakespeare, transformed four rather disparate plays about the Wars of the Roses into a retroactively cohesive dramatic cycle can stand as an epitome of their approach to the entire repertory they begin with in 1594. The Chamberlain's Men's miscellaneous legacy of plays is revised and retroactively organized into an apparently coherent body of plays just as the secondhand assortment of plays in the so-called First Henriad transformed into something resembling a unified historical cycle. Shakespeare is the key figure in this project of unification and renewal, both as working playwright and as increasingly public author. The four plays in the sequence, the three parts of *Henry VI* and *Richard III*, had originally belonged to three distinct playing companies. The Queen's Men's *Richard III*, suitably revised and transformed, is combined with the Pembroke's Men's two-part *Contention of the Houses of Lancaster and York*, again revised, as Steven Urkowitz has argued,[54] into something resembling the Folio texts of *2* and *3 Henry VI*, and also with *1 Henry VI* and its "Talbot, terror of the French": perhaps a revision of the Strange's Men's *Harry VI*, perhaps a revision of another company's Talbot play. While critics have noticed various inconsistencies between the individual plays in the tetralogy (many typical of the inconsistencies of all serialized drama from the early modern playhouse), it is more remarkable that any coherence appears at all in a "series" cobbled together from elements of three different repertories.

Those who would prefer to imagine Shakespeare as originating the series personally must ask why he would undertake a four-part sequence that would be spread among three different sets of players. The purported unity of dramatic design across the four plays (or even, as some critics would have it, across the eight plays of the two Henriads together), once cited as a sign and guarantee of Shakespeare's originating genius, almost certainly precludes it. Even if the three texts printed in 1594 and 1595 are imagined as reductions or distortions or adaptations of some earlier and superior texts, those ur-texts cannot be imagined as a consciously unified cycle, since not all of the plays belonged to the same actors, and since the plays' new common theatrical owners, the Chamberlain's Men, had barely come into existence when the plays were printed. If Shakespeare wrote all four of these plays, or early drafts of them, before he joined the Chamberlain's Men, then he wrote them for more than one set of actors and without any reasonable expectation of ever seeing them acted together. If the four plays together imply unity of any kind, it reflects a deliberate act of unification achieved by reworking an assortment of history plays. The artistic unity of these four plays and Shakespeare's originary authority over them are mutually exclusive propositions; one may be true, or neither, but not both.

The canonical Shakespearean versions of these four plays do work in various ways to impose a retroactive cohesion upon a "cycle" of histories whose own diverse theatrical histories are concealed by the process of revision. The later printed versions of these plays make more intertextual references to one another, reinforcing the sense that they are parts of a relatively unified whole. These references could not derive from the period when the plays were acted by rival troupes. And in *Richard III* the connections to earlier plays in the tetralogy intensify with each successive version of the text. The 1597 Quarto of *Richard III* refers to the *Henry VI* plays in a way that the 1594 *True Tragedy of Richard III* (a Queen's Men's play with no interest in directing auditors to the Pembroke's Men's works) does not; the 1623 Folio text of *Richard III* has even more references to *Henry VI* than the 1597 text. (Witness, for example, the Folio Richard's extended reminiscences in the midst of wooing Lady Anne.[55]) The later a text from the first Henriad appears in print, the more gestures it makes toward the other Henriad texts.

The Chamberlain's (or King's) Men's texts of the First Henriad also create a sense of literary unity by emphasizing the play's common source texts, most importantly Raphael Holinshed's *Chronicles of England, Scotland, and Ireland* and Edward Hall's *Union of the Two Noble and Illustre Families of York and Lancaster*. Shakespeare revises the plays by grounding them more thoroughly, and more specifically, in their original sources. As he returns to the chronicle source for Lear, Shakespeare digests increasing amounts of Holinshed's and Hall's prose into the text of his plays. This process is at odds with later notions of how adaptation and revision work, notions which figure the source text as a starting place from which the process of adaptation moves steadily away. In such a model, resemblance between the source and the new work is greatest at the first stage of composition and can only diminish during any further literary process. For Shakespeare and his contemporaries, schooled in classical notions of *imitatio* and *digestio*, the relationship of text to source is far richer and far less unidirectional. And for working Elizabethan actors, the process of revision was something ongoing and expected.

But the real fruits of Shakespeare's artistic craft can be seen in two of the plays with which the company began in June 1594, and which continued to evolve and grow over many years. The next two chapters will turn to the cases of *The Taming of a Shrew* and *Hamlet*, whose surviving texts indicate how thoroughly and how frequently the Chamberlain's Men's plays were revised.

CHAPTER 2

Sixty Years of *Shrews*

> All his successors gone before him hath done't, and all his ancestors that come after him may.
> —*The Merry Wives of Windsor*, 1.1

The play registered and printed in 1594 as *The Taming of a Shrew* has two obvious things in common with the text printed as *The Taming of the Shrew* in the 1623 Folio: the basic plot outline and the heroine's name.[1] Otherwise, the texts share little; the wording of the 1594 and 1623 texts agrees roughly as often as the wording of their titles disagrees. The 1594 *Shrew* takes us to Athens, rather than Padua, where a shrewish virgin named Kate is wooed and "tamed" by a stranger named Ferando rather than Petruchio. The Athenian Kate of 1594 has a pair of sisters who have one suitor apiece; the Paduan Kate of 1623 has only one sister who has a different name but three suitors all to herself. The 1623 *Shrew* is verbally superior. It begins with the same frame story that the 1594 *Shrew* does but abandons it inexplicably; a long editorial tradition dating back to Pope has supplemented the Folio text with the additional Sly scenes. Despite their divergent texts and later critics' expressions of surprise, *The Taming of a Shrew* and *The Taming of the Shrew* were evidently thought of as a single play. The Stationers clearly considered Short's 1594 copy valid for the 1623 text, and no one gainsaid them. There is no reference to an old play and a new play, to any "other" *Taming*; the two texts are elements of a single property, a single work.

The two texts present the scholarly reader with two possible versions of theatrical history. If the *Shrew* plays were written in the same order in which they were published, then the Quarto and Folio tell a story of artistic development and growth, as an interesting play is shaped into a more sophisticated and polished play. That may be a story of Shakespeare's own artistic growth, as Leah S. Marcus has argued eloquently and forcefully, and also (as Marcus again suggests) a story of changing artistic priorities as some of the Quarto's most arresting elements are sacrificed in pursuit of other effects.[2] It may also be a story of Shakespeare as adaptive craftsman, transforming an earlier playwright's work. But it is surely part of a larger story in which the Chamberlain's Men's secondhand plays grew more complicated and poetically accomplished through revision. A play which had belonged to Pembroke's Men became a Chamberlain's Men's play.

If, however, the 1623 Folio *Shrew* was actually created before the 1594 Quarto *Shrew*, as most twentieth-century textual criticism asserts, the texts tell a very different story. In that story, Shakespeare has little need of growth and reaches full poetic maturity almost at the outset of his career; even the splendid poetic sophistication of the 1623 *Shrew* was the work of his mid-to-late twenties. If the 1594 text was derived from the Folio text, then the Folio text must logically have been created earlier, and since the London playhouses were closed between 1592 and 1594, the play must have entered the active repertory before 1592; one editor of the play even places the date of the canonical text before 1590.[3] This narrative imagines Shakespeare as serenely masterful from the beginning, a towering figure beleaguered by smaller men who, unable to properly appreciate or digest his brilliant *Shrew* play, reduced it to a far cruder piece. It may not be entirely clear why theatrical pirates or adapters would be so careless in reproducing a comedy which, had it been written in 1589 or 1591, would have represented a major artistic breakthrough. But the story of Shakespeare's early artistic supremacy demands exactly such misunderstanding and interference as the only permissible explanation for the differences between the *Shrew* texts. If Shakespeare is imagined creating the preferred text of the *Shrew* on his first try, with no need for substantial revision or collaboration, then divergent texts can only be signs of corruption. The argument for the priority of the 1623 over the 1594 *Shrew* is an argument for a specific vision of heroic literary authority: vested almost entirely in the individual author, residing in the organic perfection of initial composition, subject to others' interference but not to others' improvement. That vision appeals profoundly to many scholars and leads them to defend the priority of the Folio *Shrew* even when the textual evidence suggests that the Folio text has been revised, not only during Shakespeare's lifetime but after it.

Sincklo Recalls Soto

The First Folio text of *The Taming of the Shrew* has not yet gone a hundred lines when it reaches a serious crux: a single line of type that recalls two distinct and distant moments in the long company history of the King's Men. The Lord in the Induction material, greeting the visiting players, singles one out for praise:

> *Lord.* [. . .] This fellow I remember,
> Since once he plaide a Farmers eldest sonne,
> 'Twas where you woo'd the Gentlewoman so well:
> I haue forgot your name: but sure that part
> Was aptly fitted, and naturally perform'd.[4]

The reply, with its speech prefix, provides the crux:

> *Sincklo.* I thinke 'twas *Soto* that your honor meanes.[5]

The reading of the Folio text itself is not in doubt, and neither Sincklo's nor Soto's name, taken alone, seems mysterious. The puzzle lies in the most obvious readings of those names, which combine to throw the Folio text's *terminus ad quem* and *terminus a quo* into confusion. The line needs to be explicated, or explained away, in order to preserve most theories about *The Taming of the Shrew*'s date and its alleged priority to the 1594 *The Taming of a Shrew*. The treatment of the Sincklo/Soto question reveals how deeply Shakespearean textual criticism remains invested in preserving Shakespeare's individual authority, often to the extent of tacitly altering its protocols when it seems that William Shakespeare's honor is at the stake. More troubling still, the procedures of explication and emendation around this crux demonstrate how profoundly textual criticism remains a project of foreclosing ambiguity and doubt in the service of a definitive and static text.

"Sincklo" refers to the actor John Sincklo or Sincler, a member of the Lord Chamberlain's Men whose name appears in several other dramatic texts.[6] "Sincklo" appears as one of the gamekeepers in act 3, scene 1 of the Folio's *3 Henry VI*, as a beadle in the 1600 Quarto of *2 Henry IV*, and in the Induction to John Marston's *The Malcontent* in 1604 (where Sincklo performs a bit of metatheater with his senior partner William Sly). His name also appears in the manuscript "plat" or plot of *The Second Part of the Seven Deadly Sins*, now preserved in Dulwich College, where one of his roles is again a "keeper" who interacts with

King Henry VI.[7] Sincklo's appearance in the *Seven Deadly Sins* plot has come to be used as a key piece of evidence for assigning *The Taming of the Shrew* a very early date. Sincklo never appears in lists of "principal players" or on the company's royal patents; nor does he figure in any of his colleagues' surviving wills. Some have proposed that "dem kleinen engelender Dinckenclo," who received a payment from the Landgrave of Hesse in 1596, was Sincklo;[8] if so, his only appearance in a household payment book gets his name wrong.

There are records of at least two John Sinclers, Sinckleys or Sinclairs in London during the relevant period, at least two women (an Elizabeth and a Mary) recorded as John Sinckley or Sincler or Sinclaire's wife, and a widow named "Bettrice Sinckloe" who might be the aforementioned Elizabeth, but whose husband's personal name is unknown.[9] None of the court or tax records ties any of these Sinclers to the profession of playing, or to any other figure from the London theaters. The obvious inference is that "Sincklo" was not sharer but a hired player, too low in the company hierarchy to be listed in royal charters or named as a "principal player." This fits with the handful of minor roles to which he can be conclusively linked. Some scholars have tried to cast Sincklo in the company's other plays, based on jokes about his character's stature in *2 Henry IV*, but those attempts are built more on supposition than on fact. The only evidence for John Sincklo's acting career is preserved in the margins of the plays themselves.

"Soto" evidently refers to a character in Fletcher's *Women Pleased*, a servant who dresses in his master's clothing in an abortive attempt to woo a gentlewoman, Lady Belvidere, on his master's behalf. The reference is singularly apt, although its aptness has gone unremarked: the Lord, planning his trick upon Sly, recalls another moment of class-conscious travesty, with another clownish character failing to sustain an aristocratic disguise with appropriate bearing; the players respond to this prompt by offering, as the main of action of *The Shrew*, an entertainment which offers a successful class disguise, with Tranio impersonating Lucentio in order to woo on his master's behalf. However, this bit of intracompany intertextuality links the Folio text to a play whose cast list suggests a date between 1619 and 1623, long after the date most scholars seek to fix for *The Shrew* and clearly after William Shakespeare's death. (There is also a character named Soto in Middleton and Rowley's *The Spanish Gypsy*, but this play is even later than Fletcher's and so presents the same complications in dating the Induction of *The Shrew*.) Few textual critics have been eager to pronounce the manuscript underlying *The Taming of the Shrew* a posthumous text. Moreover, a late Jacobean date for the printers' manuscript undermines claims that the Folio text precedes the 1594 Quarto text.

Inconveniently, the reference to Soto comes in the one line ascribed to Sincklo, a speech heading used as evidence for an early date and often, but mistakenly, for a date of 1592 or earlier. The actor whose presence is taken to bespeak an early provenance speaks evidence for a later one; the speech has an apparent *terminus a quo* much later than the speech prefix's *terminus ad quem*. This moment in the Folio text derives from some period after the King's Men began acting Fletcher's *Women Pleased* but before the end of Sincklo's performing career. Using the currently accepted ranges of dates proposed for those events, this means sometime after 1620 but before 1606 or so. Proper respect for the evidence means some of these accounts must be revised.

"Two Alternatives"

The mainstream approach to the Sincklo/Soto problem was established by Arthur Quiller-Couch and John Dover Wilson in their 1928 *New [Cambridge] Shakespeare Taming of the Shrew*, the first edition of the play to promote Peter Alexander's argument that *The Shrew* preceded *A Shrew*. In part, Quiller-Couch and Dover Wilson work by selectively decoupling the spoken name from the speaker's name. They freely discuss Sincklo, whom they use to support an earlier date, without raising the issue of Soto, but Soto is only discussed in conjunction with Sincklo. The name construed as a sign of "earliness" is not undermined by the "lateness" suggested by the other name, but the evidence of lateness is strictly controlled and limited by the other name's purported earliness. Sincklo's name is treated as evidence in its own right, and Soto's as merely potential evidence, as far as Sincklo's name permits. Quiller-Couch and Dover Wilson use Sincklo as Soto's discursive chaperone.

This one-way uncoupling of Sincklo from Soto is abetted by the standard editorial practice of emending speech-prefixes, so that Sincklo's name does not appear in the text itself, and the two proper names can only be joined in the paratext (where they are always, of course, more than a scant three syllables apart). Although Sincklo is banished from the text, he is prominent in the *Cambridge* editors' textual note, where the bare fact of his name is marshaled as evidence.[10] Soto's name appears nowhere in Quiller-Couch and Dover Wilson's extended note on the text or in their introduction; the name is excluded from their formal discussion of dating and provenance and instead exiled to the endnotes. Quiller-Couch and Dover Wilson do not withhold information about Soto but provide it only to readers following up on the reference. Their note calls the name "important, if puzzling . . . as regards stage history,"[11] but apparently they do not rate its importance highly enough for any more than a marginal discussion.

When Quiller-Couch and Dover Wilson do at last discuss Soto, they are acutely and explicitly aware that the name's obvious reading works against their thesis, and even that "Sincklo" is a relatively weak guarantor of an early date. "The reference to Soto," they write, "points at first blush to a play of Fletcher's which is dated as late as 1620," and they admit that "if the evidence we have about him were taken at its face value" Sincklo "would have been on the stage for over 30 years."[12] The goal of their explication, then, is to exchange the evidence at hand for something other than its face value.

The *New Cambridge* editors' influential but peculiar solution is to supply two mutually exclusive arguments without actually choosing between them, although they favor one over the other:

> The passage, therefore, leaves us with two alternatives: either (i) that ll. 82–87 are an insertion (they could, in fact, be omitted without any injury to the text) made after Shakespeare's death at some revival of *The Shrew* shortly before the publication of F.; or (ii) that *Women Pleased* was itself based upon an earlier text belonging to Shakespeare's company and that Sincklo was playing Soto in this earlier version sometime about 1591–92. We incline to the second alternative.[13]

Quiller-Couch and Dover Wilson's "two alternatives" remain the standard gloss on Soto's name today. The *Norton Shakespeare* footnote on Soto's name, almost identical to that of the *Riverside Shakespeare,* illustrates the persistence of Quiller-Couch and Dover Wilson's dual explanation: "the reference must be a late addition to Shakespeare's text or else refer to a character in an earlier play, now lost."[14] Most editors still propose both of the now-traditional hypotheses, although H. J. Oliver (about whom more below) argues exclusively for the *Cambridge* editors' preferred second alternative. The appeal of the "two alternatives," however diametrically opposed their internal logic, seems to lie in the combination itself. These arguments seem more influential as a pairing than as arguments per se.

Although Quiller-Couch and Dover Wilson clearly prefer one of their hypotheses to the other, they are not confident enough in their hypothetical earlier text to rest the play's date and provenance upon it. Their reluctance is perfectly understandable, since there is no evidence that any such text existed, unless one counts as evidence the very problem that the hypothesized text is meant to explain. The editors suggest that the allusion is not to a known play but to a lost play (similar in many respects to the known play) to which no reference survives except for the case in question. This is hypothesis as scholarly wish, imagining a piece of additional evidence one would like to have in order to make a case one would like to make. And while this specific hypothesis of convenience has now become a traditional gloss, hypothesizing in this way is not widely accepted as editorial practice. Could, for example, a scholar finding a reference to Caliban in the text of an early modern play but hoping to date that play before *The Tempest* postulate a hitherto-unknown source play for *The Tempest*, with a hitherto-unknown ur-Caliban, whose existence is corroborated only by the reference in the undated play itself?

One should not even begin to speculate about lost ur-texts as the *Cambridge* editors do until one knows, beyond reasonable dispute, the date of the reference upon which the speculation is built. But Quiller-Couch and Dover Wilson know nothing of the kind. In 1928, the date of *The Shrew* was not even a matter of scholarly consensus, let alone incontrovertible fact. Indeed, it was a question which had newly been thrown into dispute, and the *New Cambridge* edition is actively furthering the controversy by advocating the upstart position. The previous orthodoxy took the publishing chronology of the 1594 and 1623 texts at face value, presuming that order of publication reflected order of composition unless positive evidence suggested otherwise. Peter Alexander's argument that the 1623 Folio text preceded the 1594 Quarto was still an "explosive suggestion" to Quiller-Couch and Dover Wilson, so recent that they write of Alexander making it "the other day."[15] The very early date proposed for the Folio version was not something everyone knew but something a few energetic people claimed. The idea of quarto texts as derivative reconstructions was still far more of a minority position, and indeed more of a novelty, than the so-called disintegrationist approach which preceded the New Bibliography. The *New Cambridge* editors cannot use an established date of the Sincklo/Soto crux to argue the logical necessity of an early Soto play. Instead, Quiller-Crouch and Dover Wilson need to protect their conclusions from the most obvious implications, the "face value," of Soto's name. They keep Soto entirely out of the discussion on dating and then approach the problem of the *Women Pleased* reference as if the question of the date were already established. The fact is made to fit the theory.

Quiller-Couch and Dover Wilson hedge their fairly shaky bet by leaving open the possibility of a late insertion. If an *Ur-Women Pleased* does not seem persuasive, the editors are willing to concede exactly six lines of revised verse later than *Women Pleased*. The reason for the concession is perhaps obvious; the limit placed upon the concession is merely reflexive. Quiller-Couch and

Dover Wilson trade in exceptions here; the six-line "insertion" is presented as exception to the otherwise integral text. The possibility of "a late addition to Shakespeare's text," in the *Norton* edition's phrase, and the potential for contamination by other agents, is strictly confined to the single, otherwise inexplicable, instance. Why a play which is imagined as being revised around 1620 should be imagined as being altered in only one place, for six trivial lines, is not explained. Rather, the urge to enclose the revised text as tightly as possible arises from an unspoken principle: that Shakespeare's authority is to be assumed everywhere that it is not manifestly disproved. A reference to a play written after Shakespeare has died may be conceded as a single posthumous addition, but the rest of the play is tacitly presumed to be free of tampering. The reasoning here cannot withstand scrutiny; the argument works backward from the desired conclusion, rather than forward from the evidence.

Both hypotheses present serious difficulties: the late insertion theory might lead readers to seek other posthumous revisions, and the lost play is not much more than a wishful tautology. So Quiller-Couch and Dover Wilson present them together, joined in prophylactic uncertainty. The frailty of each argument is cushioned by the existence of the other; as long as neither is dismissed, both can survive and further speculation be avoided. Refusing to commit to one explanation of the Soto remark relieves critics from the need to defend the explanation they have chosen. If the critical discourse is carefully structured as a choice between rival explanations, any exposed flaw in one hypothesis can be presented as implicitly strengthening the others. Naturally, it does not follow that the weakness of one proposition strengthens another, but framing the crux as a binary choice slyly preserves the unexamined and unwarranted premise that only two alternatives exist. As long as the critical focus remains on choosing between the Quiller-Couch and Dover Wilson's two problematic explanations, speculation about other possibilities, including that of taking the evidence at what Quiller-Couch and Dover Wilson call its "face value," is foreclosed.

Editors' discussions of the text generally follow Quiller-Couch and Dover Wilson by presenting both theories, and sometimes more than two, as more or less plausible alternatives, although the ur-play notion is often favored. In fact, the decision to offer multiple theories but not to choose between them intrinsically favors the ur-play argument, which is too weak to stand on its own merits but can be made to seem plausible when presented as one among a number of unconfirmed theories. In this case, the performance of academic doubt serves as a necessary prelude to the promotion of a dubious idea.

The editors of the *Oxford Shakespeare* give the fullest and most painstaking version of this performance, entertaining a wide selection of hypotheses without choosing between them but favoring the idea of a "lost Elizabethan play later adapted by Fletcher."[16] Stanley Wells considers the possibility of the Soto line as a late addition and even takes the unusual step of linking that possible addition to other signs of revision in the Folio text, although elsewhere in the same textual note he expresses a belief that those revisions "were undertaken during composition."[17] He even briefly entertains the notion that the reference to Soto is a mere "hint" of Shakespeare's which Fletcher "expanded . . . into a character" some fifteen years later.[18] This odd hypothesis, which Wells himself dismisses as "unlikely," suggests that the Soto speech is a reference to nothing at all, and that fifteen years later another playwright creates a play to which the earlier text only seems to allude. This, too, would be difficult to defend as a general approach to dating literary allusions; if the principle that an allusion might precede the text, and that the literary work might be a poetic response to the allusion itself, were to be widely adopted, it would swiftly become impossible to use allusions for dating literary works.

Wells thoroughly and rather scornfully dismisses Eric Sams's attempt to coordinate the standard dating of Sincklo and Soto when (in Wells's phrasing) Sams "arbitrarily dates" *Women Pleased* to 1604 and dates *The Taming of the Shrew* to succeed it.[19] Wells finds this "wildly at odds with all the stylistic evidence, which points to a much earlier date of composition," and objects that there is no evidence that Fletcher was writing for the King's Men, rather than for the boys' companies, so early in his career.[20] While Wells's objections have some real merit, the charge of arbitrariness is at odds with Sams's good-faith attempt to reconcile the disparate dates in the crux without hypothesizing new evidence; far more arbitrary expedients, such as Dover Wilson's hypothetical lost play, are treated with more respect.

Like Quiller-Couch and Dover Wilson, the *Oxford* editors lean toward the ur-Soto hypothesis but, like their predecessors, refuse to commit entirely: "We suspect this explanation [the lost Soto play] is correct, but in the nature of the case it could never be proven (or disproven)."[21] The grounds of this suspicion, in the absence of corroboration or even the potential for corroboration, goes unexplained. The evidence underlying the ur-Soto notion is not given the rigorous examination applied to other hypotheses, since no evidence exists to be examined. But Wells's parenthetical appeal to the basic unfalsifiability of the claim, the impossibility of disproving it, shows how thoroughly the burden of proof has been misplaced here. A hypothesis that cannot be falsified, that is not subject to any test or examination, should be suspect for that very reason. Wells seems here to imply, if only equivocally, that an "explanation" remains viable as long as it cannot be "disproven." The logical impossibility of proving a negative, therefore, ensures that the *Ur-Women Pleased* hypothesis will never die. The traditionally favored explanation for the Sincklo-Soto crux is impossible to prove but has been enshrined by editorial tradition. The burden is now placed on challengers to disprove it. Indeed, it has become acceptable to confess the impossibility of proving the hypothesis even as one advocates it. The standards of scholarly proof and disproof have been suspended in the case of the *Shrew* plays, providing an untestable, unfalsifiable foundation upon which the bibliographic orthodoxy can rest.

This superficially prudent hesitance about Soto, the refusal to choose between the unproved and unprovable possibilities, also has the practical effect of excluding the name from evidentiary status. The name "Soto" is not treated as a building block used to construct a larger argument about the provenance of the text. Instead, general accounts of the text are used to divine the proper interpretation of the anomalous fact. Many scholars proceed as if neither of the two standard but contradictory explanations of Soto's name has any implications for the date of *The Shrew* as a whole. The question of whether the Induction refers to an actual play from around 1620 or to a hypothetical play from the late 1580s or early 1590s is treated as irrelevant to the business of dating the play, so much so that modern editors may declare themselves open to both possibilities for dating "Soto" without proposing any adjustment in their dating of *The Shrew*. Textual critics can be publicly agnostic on this specific piece of evidence and firmly convinced of their general conclusion; they may not feel confident explaining how Soto's name got into the text, but they are certain that it doesn't change anything.

Repetition has made Quiller-Couch and Dover Wilson's twin hypotheses seem obvious and commonsensical to later editors; modern textual critics seem to have far less sense than Quiller-Couch and Dover Wilson of their arguments' vulnerabilities. More importantly, the "explosive suggestion" of the 1920s has become now become the standard account of the *Shrew* plays' relationship, and that account allows no space for Soto. Scholars who come to the Sincklo/Soto crux already convinced of the Folio's text's early date, rather than still making the case as the *New Cambridge* editors did, have been trained to expect that "Soto" will fit into the established dating.

Ann Thompson, Quiller-Couch and Dover Wilson's successor as editor of the *New Cambridge Shakespeare Taming of the Shrew*, pronounces that "it is now generally agreed that *A Shrew* is some kind of memorial reconstruction of *The Shrew* itself," vigorously champions that position, and presses for a date "perhaps as early as 1590."[22] Brian Morris begins his discussion of dating with the announcement that "much of the earlier scholarly speculation about the date of *The Shrew* can be disregarded once it is accepted that *A Shrew* is a Bad Quarto and therefore later than its original."[23] Stanley Wells and Gary Taylor profess themselves agnostic about the relationship between the Quarto and Folio texts,[24] but they edit the play as if it had an extremely early date. The *Norton Shakespeare* apparatus firmly endorses the conventional orthodoxy about *The Shrew*.[25] The claim that *"The" Shrew* preceded *"A" Shrew* is presented as a "growing consensus," with Leah Marcus's groundbreaking arguments to the contrary represented as an "interesting" minority position; Eric Sams's infuriated and wide-ranging dissent, "The Timing of the *Shrews*," is ignored. The date of *The Shrew* is limited to 1592 or earlier, on the explicit grounds of its precedence to *A Shrew*; and the Folio text is held to derive, directly or indirectly, from "Shakespeare's 'foul papers'" because of "certain features of the text."[26] Why an authorial manuscript would include a reference to a play written after the author's death is left unexplored; rather, the detailed exploration performed in the *Oxford Shakespeare's Textual Companion* is treated as moot. Moreover the *Oxford* and *Norton* texts arrange Shakespeare's works in "chronological" sequence, placing *The Taming of the Shrew* earlier than any of Shakespeare's work except for *The Two Gentlemen of Verona*, and before the other plays published in 1594. The polemic implicit in the editors' table of contents shores up the establishment position and quarantines the Folio *Shrew* text to a date at least thirty years before its publication, safe from the three intervening decades of its theatrical history.

Inconveniently, one of the "features of the text" upon which the orthodox narrative about *The Shrew* is based is the embarrassing detail of Sincklo's name.

How to Write Foul Papers

The notion that actors' names in printed texts might derive from an authorial manuscript, and that such names might even be construed as positive evidence of the author's hand, dates from the early 1930s, when R. B. McKerrow, "busy generating editorial theory," in Paul Werstine's phrase,[27] invented his influential account of Shakespeare's "foul papers," singling out certain types of oddity in printed texts as reliably legible signs of Shakespeare's drafts. "One of the reasons for the badness of dramatic texts was that they were often set up from the author's original manuscript and not from a fair-copy," McKerrow argues.[28] McKerrow's approach identifies certain kinds of "badness" as merely bad, unfortunate artifacts of the playhouse or the printing house but embraces other kinds of "badness" as good, as Shakespeare's own personal mistakes and hurried orthography, which are to be treasured. McKerrow's assertions naturally cannot be tested by examination of Shakespeare's long-since-lost foul papers themselves, but his detailed and entirely speculative claims about those papers' features have become part of the foundation of Shakespearean bibliography.

McKerrow builds his imaginary model of Shakespeare's "foul papers" by negative definition, carefully enumerating the features of theatrical prompt-books and taking the lack of such signs, or of signs McKerrow finds sufficiently persuasive, to indicate Shakespeare's autograph draft. "It thus seems to me," McKerrow argues,

> that the origins from prompt-books of the texts . . . to which we have been referring is far from being proved, and that until this is done we may continue to assume that they were printed from the author's own manuscript, or at any rate from a rough copy of some sort or another.[29]

The "at any rate" is a nice piece of rhetoric, suggesting McKerrow's openness to other possibilities without actually postulating any other species of "rough copy." Yet McKerrow abandons this caveat by the end of the paragraph in which he makes it, proposing "an author's rough draft much corrected" as the typical printer's copy for plays. Most of McKerrow's followers have embraced the proposed rule and not the equivocal exception; since McKerrow, the editor's rule of thumb has been to construe roughness as authorial.

McKerrow effectively constructs, while purporting to disown, a false dichotomy which allows for only two kinds of copy text: if the copy does not come from the prompter, it must come from the author's rough draft. McKerrow simultaneously (and perversely) shifts the burden of proof onto anyone not embracing the foul-paper hypothesis. The copy text shall be assumed to derive from Shakespeare's authorial manuscript unless proved otherwise. By the same token, Shakespeare's authorial manuscript will be presumed to exhibit certain specific features until proved otherwise, which cannot be done in the absence of any such manuscripts. Assertions which are neither proven nor subject to falsification are presented as necessary starting points for any discussion of the text. Subsequent editing practice has adopted McKerrow's speculative axioms as first principles, and their near immunity to disproof has transformed them into virtually inevitable conclusions.

McKerrow makes a point of claiming actors' names as a sign of authorial rather than theatrical manuscripts, specifically rebutting Dover Wilson's and A. W. Pollard's arguments to the contrary. McKerrow does not deny (and could not deny, in the face of material evidence) that promptbooks included actors' names, but he creates a novel and artificial distinction between the demonstrable ways that such names appear in promptbooks (which can be examined) and the imagined way they appear in Shakespeare's foul papers (which cannot be):

> A third mark of prompter's copies is the mention of actor's [*sic*] names as a *gloss*. This is important. As far as I have noticed, the name of the actor in a prompt copy always appears *in addition* to the name of the character, not substituted for it. . . . I believe that there is no case in any play having the clear marks of being, or being printed from, a prompt-copy, of an actor's name being given *alone* without that of the character whom he was to represent.[30]

McKerrow is having it both ways here. His argument is premised on the idea that bookkeepers routinely removed authorial idiosyncrasies while preparing promptbooks. Therefore, by McKerrow's logic, actors' names are never substituted for characters' names in promptbooks because the bookkeeper would remove any such substitution. McKerrow imagines the prompters removing actors' names from texts and also adding them "as a gloss." Having cast doubt on the objection that actors' names appear in prompt books, McKerrow proceeds to offer, through a vividly imagined narrative of Shakespeare at work, his own hypothesis about how actors' names might enter the authorial draft:

> Even the occasional mention of the name of an actor seems to me far from unnatural in the manuscript of such a dramatist as Shakespeare, who was writing for a particular company with which he was closely connected. Psychologically it is, I think, just what we should expect. To a man with a good power of visualization such as every successful dramatist must have, and who knows in advance what actor will fill each of the more important roles, the actors themselves must have been more or less constantly present in his mind as he wrote. I suspect, indeed, that this fact is responsible for the extraordinary vitality and vividness of some of Shakespeare's minor characters. . . . What more natural than that Shakespeare . . . should momentarily forget the names which he had assigned to the

characters and put down instead the much more familiar names of the actors instead?[31]

McKerrow's gifts for storytelling and characterization carry his argument here. However slyly McKerrow slips in the reference to the "fact" that the actors were "constantly present in [Shakespeare's] mind," this is not a fact but a supposition or, more accurately, a wish. We do not know what was in Shakespeare's mind as he wrote, and for all our scholarly longings, we cannot know; this is simply what McKerrow would like Shakespeare to have been thinking.

For all its air of facticity, McKerrow's argument includes virtually no verifiable facts. While it is true that after 1594 Shakespeare was writing for a particular company with which he was closely connected, there is no way to establish which playing companies Shakespeare belonged to (if any) before joining the Chamberlain's Men, or the identity of his fellow actors in those companies, or the duration of his working relationships with those allegedly "familiar" actors. The use of Sincklo's name to date the play earlier than 1594, as editors from Quiller-Couch and Dover Wilson to Ann Thompson have done, sets McKerrow's fanciful narrative in the years when his story is least plausible. Neither is it established that Shakespeare knew all of the casting of his plays in advance; we simply don't know the details of the casting procedure and don't have enough information about the casts to reconstruct it. The most we can say is that Shakespeare knew his company's casting process, as we do not; to say that he could necessarily predict, let alone dictate, the outcome of that process is to speak more than we know. McKerrow's careful-sounding negative construction, his "far from unnatural," is a rhetorical masterstroke, mimicking scholarly caution while cunningly framing the question so that the burden of proof seems to fall upon any doubters, as if all that it took to support an argument were to prevent it from being proved palpably "unnatural."

By 1935 McKerrow had extended his imaginary reconstruction of Shakespeare's compositional process from the appearance of actor's names in the text to inconsistencies in the handling of character names. McKerrow's influential but unsubstantiated "Suggestion Regarding Shakespeare's Manuscripts" posits that "a play in which the names are irregular was printed from the author's original MS."[32] McKerrow's reasoning has been thoroughly debunked by Paul Werstine, and by the evidence itself.[33] The casual treatment of character names that McKerrow ascribes to authorial drafts is evident in surviving playhouse manuscripts. In fact, John Sinckler or Sincklo's first name is only known to us because it appears in a playhouse manuscript which mixes actors' and characters' names indiscriminately. But McKerrow's ideas have become so integral to

Shakespeare editing that his principles frequently go uncited and unexplained, as if the characteristic features that McKerrow imagines for "foul papers" were as demonstrable as the distinction between octavos and quartos. Thompson, for example, might doubt that the Folio *Shrew* derives from "foul papers," but she takes the model of "foul papers" copy-texts, and the features of such texts, as perfectly straightforward.[34]

It was not always so. W. W. Greg was initially skeptical of taking actors' names as signs of authorial copy. Greg wrote in 1931 that he "should not venture to deny that" such an interpretation "is possible," but that the evidence runs contrary: "In every instance in which an actor's name appears in a manuscript play it is written in a different hand from the text, or at any rate in a different ink and style, showing it to be a later addition and not part of the original composition."[35] By 1942, Greg had largely accepted his friend McKerrow's "foul papers" model, and he confidently repeats the contention that inconsistent speech prefixes, which "would probably be tidied up by whoever prepared the prompt copy," are consequently signs of an authorial draft.[36] In the case of Folio *Shrew*, Greg still refuses to believe that "the parts have been cast in his mind by the author," but he exempts Sincklo from his refusals and considers the name a deliberate, rather than inadvertent, casting note by Shakespeare.[37]

By the time he wrote *The Shakespeare First Folio*, which has served as an important guidebook to subsequent editors, Greg was blandly citing "the substitution of an actor's name" as one of the well-established features "characteristic of foul papers"[38] and carefully distinguishing the way actors' names appear in promptbooks from the ways they are imagined to appear in foul papers.[39] Greg holds up *The Taming of the Shrew*, because of its reference to Sincklo, as an example of a text derived from authorial manuscript,[40] but he remains skittish, if not downright ambivalent, about using actors' names to point to authors' papers. Greg takes Sincklo's name as a clear sign of Shakespeare's foul papers behind the First Quarto of *Henry IV, Part 2*, but also declares that Sincklo's name "cannot possibly be attributed to the author" in the Folio text of *Henry VI, Part 3*, on the grounds that Sincklo's name is also used consistently in the speech headings throughout the scene, and therefore cannot be a slip of the authorial pen.[41] The apparent inconsistency comes from Greg's scrupulous fidelity to McKerrow's original logic; an actor's name suggests foul papers because it is assumed that a prompter would remove the name. When summarizing general editorial principle Greg presents the conclusion of McKerrow's syllogism (actors' names are a characteristic of foul papers), but when applying those principles Greg keeps the original premises of the syllogism in mind.

Greg's caveats and fine distinctions, and for that matter McKerrow's, tend to be simplified away in later practice; the statement of general principle outweighs the discriminating application. The issue is not how delicately McKerrow or Greg or any of the editors who follow them use McKerrow's hypothesis but the elevation of that unproved and unprovable hypothesis into a standard and uncontroversial tool of editing. The caution with which Greg and some later editors apply McKerrow's categories camouflages the profound flaws in the categories themselves.

H. J. Oliver's *Oxford* edition in 1982 confidently asserts the appearance of actors' names in the text as primary evidence, indeed his leading evidence, for the foul papers theory:

> Shakespeare must have had Sincklo in mind when he wrote this part for the otherwise unnamed "Player"—and used the appellation in the speech prefix by an easy slip of the pen. (The name of an actor would hardly thus appear in a prompt-book, in one line and not another, where it could only cause confusion.)[42]

These two sentences rely upon a number of suppositions: about the way Shakespeare composed, about the way promptbooks were organized, and about what would confuse early modern actors or prompters. But perhaps the most breathtaking assumption is Oliver's confidence that Sincklo got more than one line. Here the textual critic takes his own emendation as evidence; the text gives "Sincklo" only one speech, but after Oliver has assigned that line to another speaking character, he points to the "inconsistency" with the other character's speech prefixes.

Brian Morris, who expresses reservations about the unmodified foul papers theory, nonetheless calls the appearance of Sincklo's name "one point . . . at which we can almost certainly detect Shakespeare's hand," and he pronounces it "very unlikely that a book-keeper or prompter could be responsible."[43] The sway of McKerrow's theories can be seen in how even doubters must cede some ground to them. The assumptions here are counterintuitive, contrafactual, and taken as entirely self-evident. It has become a bibliographical truth almost universally acknowledged that the appearance of performers' names in a text excludes the possibility that it is a performers' text.

Sincklo and Nicke

Of course, actors' names do appear in the relatively few surviving texts prepared by book-keepers or prompters. Indeed, the specific actors' names in the 1623 *Shrew* appear in those texts. The "plot" of *The Second Part of the Seven Deadly Sins* lists not only "I Sincler" and "Iohn Sincler" but also the names "Harry," "Vincent," "Saunder," "Will," "Kitt," "Ned," and "Nick." The Folio *Shrew* has a speech for a "Nicke" as well, in act 3, scene 1, after the stage direction *Enter a Messenger*.[44] "Nicke"'s name, like "Sincklo"'s, is used to promote the foul papers idea, but the King's Men's prompter has written "Nicke" into promptbooks as well. A "Nick" appears in the manuscript of *Sir John van Olden Barnavelt* in 1619 (which is to say, around the time the company performed *Women Pleased*) and also figures in the 1631 manuscript of *Believe as You List*. Gerald Eades Bentley, who is strongly committed to the notion of an early date for *The Taming of the Shrew*, nonetheless gives "Nick" his own entry among the actors listed in *The Jacobean and Caroline Stage*.[45] But no critic associates the "Nick" in a King Men's manuscript from 1619 with the "Nicke" in a King's Men's play provided to the printer in 1623; scholars are interested in fixing the date of that manuscript as early as possible.

Nicke's name is inconveniently common, but editors use Sincklo's name to provide a *terminus ad quem*. The curious side effect of this procedure is that the editors must also provide a *terminus ad quem* for Sincklo. But since his career is never documented outside the plays themselves, scholars pronounce an end (or a "likely end") to Sincklo's career on the basis of no documentary evidence whatsoever. The standard technique is to argue from negative evidence: once Sincklo's presence can no longer be confirmed, his absence is assumed. E. K. Chambers's *Elizabethan Stage* puts cautionary question marks beside some of Sincklo's presumed company affiliations but is blandly confident in assigning initial and terminal dates for his career. Chambers lists Sincklo as performing from 1590 to 1604, which is to say from the date Chambers prefers for the *Seven Deadly Sins* plot to the Induction of the *Malcontent*, and not a day later.[46] Andrew Gurr's company history of the King's Men is slightly more generous, extending Sincklo's stage time to "c. 1606."[47] Gurr gives Sincklo the extra years by speculatively casting him as various diminutive characters in plays from 1604 or 1605; this is interesting, but not quite evidence. (Sams's proposed date of ca. 1605 is founded on this consensual date of termination for Sincklo's career.) Ann Thompson even offers Sincklo's absence from the list of "principal actors" in the 1623 Folio as a sign that Sincklo had retired, although there is nothing odd about a minor actor being excluded from the list of "Principals," and the list has nothing at all to do with how recently the actors had left acting.[48] It includes a number of players who had died or retired decades earlier, alongside some of the troupe's current leadership. Thompson also argues that if Sincklo had not retired, he would have been "too old" to play Soto in 1620, but neither Soto's age nor the upper age limit for playing comical servants has been established. And while Sincklo's marginal presence in the Folio is often compared to the appearance of Kemp's name in the Second Quarto of *Romeo and Juliet* (1599) or of Kemp's and Richard Cowley's names in the First Quarto of *Much Ado About Nothing* (1600), those quartos were published soon after Kemp left the Chamberlain's Men, and Kemp's name is a relic of his recent tenure with the group. By 1623 Kemp's name has been removed from the text. Sincklo's name, on the other hand, is cast as a souvenir of the distant past and is presumed to have stayed in the script for three decades, and for almost two decades after he is imagined leaving the stage. In any case, the entire project of using Sincklo to set an end date for *The Shrew*, or indeed for any play, is manifestly illogical. That one cannot prove Sincklo still remained with the company cannot be offered as proof that he had departed.

It may well be, as Hans Walter Gabler puts it, that Sincklo "disappears from the Elizabethan dramatic records after 1604,"[49] but Gabler's account is not quite fair, because Sincklo never figured in those records. Moreover Gabler's formulation, which strikes me as typical for most critics dealing with this question, excludes the 1623 Shakespeare Folio as a "dramatic record." It is more accurate to say that Sincklo's name first appears in print in 1600, turns up again in 1604, and appears for the final time in 1623. Sincklo's appearance in the Folio is taken as a relic of the 1590s, even when "Sincklo" alludes to a play from 1620. But this needs to be proven before it is deployed as proof.

Andrew Gurr rehearses the smoothly circular argument that Sincklo's name in *The Shrew* and in *3 Henry VI* is a survival from those plays' time in the Pembroke's Men repertory and adduces Sincklo's membership in Pembroke's Men from his name's appearance in scripts that Gurr attributes to the Pembroke's Men.[50] There is no evidence, beyond this neat tautology, that Sincklo ever acted with the Pembroke company, and his name does not appear in the quartos which advertise *The Taming of a Shrew* and *The True Tragedy of Richard, Duke of York* as belonging to Pembroke's Men. Sincklo never appears in any version of a play presenting itself as the Pembroke's Men's, but always in versions presenting themselves as the Chamberlain's.

At stake, again, is the precedence of the Folio texts over the "bad" quarto texts from 1594. If *The True Tragedy* and *The Taming of a Shrew* derive from the superior Folio texts, then those Folio texts must have existed prior to the formation of the Chamberlain's Men in 1594. Therefore it becomes necessary to establish that the Pembroke's Men possessed the "good" texts. *The Taming of the Shrew* must be imagined as a text from 1592 instead of 1623. For even the best of scholars, the conclusions begin to drive the evidence. Since the Folio versions must have preceded the quartos, then the Folio versions must have been the Pembroke's Men's versions, and so an actor named in the Chamberlain's Men's versions must have been one of Pembroke's Men.

The critical reasoning on this point sometimes becomes explicitly bardolatrous. To allow for the 1594 text to be an independent source play would be, Richard Hosley argues, "to assume around 1593 the existence of a dramatist other than Shakespeare who was capable of devising a three-part structure more impressive than the structure of any extant play by Lyly, Peele, Greene, Marlowe or Kyd"; Thompson concurs, finding such a possibility "so dubious that it seems wisest to assume that it was Shakespeare who was responsible for the complex structure and interweaving of materials we find in both *Shrew* plays," and therefore that the 1594 play is derivative of the Folio text.[51] Shakespeare's literary superiority is here used as a universal axiom, and the idea of someone "other than Shakespeare" creating sophisticated art treated as presumptively impossible. More strangely, Hosley and Thompson hold up the three-part structure of *The Taming of a Shrew*, with its A-plot, B-plot, and frame story, as radically more sophisticated than the tripartite structure of Kyd's extant play *The Spanish Tragedy*, with its A-plot, B-plot, and frame story. The conviction of Shakespeare's superiority overrides even demonstrable fact.

The most important evidence for locating Sincklo in the early 1590s has been the *Seven Deadly Sins* plot, long considered to derive from the amalgamation between Lord Strange's Men and Edward Alleyn of the Admiral's Men in that time period. (Even this account, however, places Sincklo not with Pembroke's Men but with a rival troupe.) The primary basis for associating the plot with Edward Alleyn has been provenance, because the document comes from Alleyn's archive at Dulwich College. Alleyn's name does not actually appear in the manuscript. However, David Kathman makes the case that the plot entered the Dulwich collection through a bequest from the bookseller William Cartwright, and that no connection to Alleyn is certain.[52] If one no longer presumes Alleyn's participation, the principal actors seem to be a list of principal Chamberlain's Men from the mid-to-late 1590s. Moreover, Kathman has positively identified one of the plot's boy players, "T. Belt," as the Thomas Belt apprenticed in 1595 to one of the Chamberlain's sharers, John Heminges.[53] The playhouse document which has been taken to prove Sincklo's pre-1594 career is in fact demonstrably later than 1594, and all of the surviving documents about Sincklo can now be seen to associate him with the Chamberlain's (and later the King's) company.

Whether by chance or design, Sincklo's name is only printed in plays which have somehow entered the Chamberlain's/King's repertory from that of another company. *The Shrew* and *3 Henry VI* are of course old Pembroke's plays, and *2 Henry IV* is part of Shakespeare's extended reworking of the Queen's Men's *Famous Victories of Henry V*. The Induction of *The Malcontent* explicitly comments on that play's previous ownership by the Children of Blackfriars. "I wonder you would play it," remarks William Sly in the character of a truculent spectator, "another company having an interest in it."[54] If Sincklo's name in a printed text bore any significance, it was diametrically opposed to the meaning scholars have constructed for it. Sincklo's name in a printed play has been taken as a trace sign from a play's existence before the King's Men acquired it; it might be better construed, to the extent that it will bear construction, as a sign of the Chamberlain's Men's possession and the consolidation of their ownership. His name begins to emerge in the same period that William Shakespeare's name first begins appearing on printed plays, in reworked dramas whose prototypes had once been owned by other companies. If Sincklo's name suggests a date for *The Taming of the Shrew*, it suggests a *terminus a quo* in the mid- or late 1590s. Sincklo does not guarantee a pre-1594 text. He raises the possibility of a later one.

Revision Trouble

The same impulses which have led scholars to push Sincklo as far back in theatrical history as possible have also impelled them to try to push "Soto" back even further. Quiller-Couch and Dover Wilson's second hypothesis is preferred to their first. A lost Soto play is more comfortable for many critics than the idea of a nonauthorial insertion, however small, in Shakespeare's text. If *The Taming of the Shrew* must be dated before *The Taming of a Shrew* (and some critics date *A Shrew* to early 1592, arguing that it preserves a reference to the actor Simon Jewell, who died that year),[55] then some form of *Women Pleased* must be dated even earlier than 1592. That all of the other available evidence places *Women Pleased* between 1619 and 1623 is not the point. Gabler summarizes the hypotheses about revisions in Fletcher's play, all founded solely upon the necessity to avoid a late date for *The Shrew* and its Induction, but sees no internal evidence for any such revisions.[56]

The hypothesis that Fletcher might have revised a play three decades old is used to exclude the possibility that Fletcher might have touched up another three-decade-old play, *The Shrew*. The idea that plays by playwrights other than Shakespeare were revised over many years is acceptable, but the idea that Shakespeare's plays were revised to this extent creates uneasiness. Fletcher's plays are moving targets; a Shakespeare play is an ever-fixèd mark. Also excluded is the possibility that plays underwent gradual revision and mutation between their first productions and their later printings. Every revision-centered argument about the purported inconsistencies between Soto's role and the Lord's description of that role posits an earlier version of the play, which had been superseded by 1620 or so.[57] The possibility that the Lord's summary, printed in 1623, might be an accurate statement about *Women Pleased* circa 1623, and that Fletcher's play might have undergone changes between that comment and its first printing in 1647, is excluded entirely. Hypothetical revision is allowed in order to push the date of composition back, not forward. And a variant text which does not exist, the *Ur-Women Pleased*, is conjured out of thin air in order to deny revision as an explanation for existing variants.

In fact, the differences between the 1594 and 1623 *Shrews* are very much like the difference between *King Leir* and the texts of *King Lear*. In each case, the pre-Chamberlain's Men's version of the play has had its B-plot replaced with a new one taken from a literary source. Just as an incident from Sidney's *Arcadia* is expanded into the Edmund and Edgar subplot, the story of Kate's sisters Phylema and Emelia and their respective suitors is discarded for the story of Kate's sister Bianca and her crowd of competing wooers. The Folio subplot is created by returning to the Quarto subplot's sources, Ariosto's *I Suppositi* and Gascoigne's *Supposes*, by using elements in those sources that the earlier staging had overlooked, and by recomplicating the intrigue found in the original source plot.

In the cases of both *Lear* and the *Shrew*s, the earliest printed version of the play provides a bit of key, and explicit, motivation for a leading character which the version published later removes. King Leir articulates a very specific purpose for testing his daughters as he does; the flattery competition is a "policy" which Leir hopes to "beguile" Cordella, maneuvering her into allowing him to choose her husband and "match her to some king within this isle."[58] *King Lear*, of course, leaves Lear's "darker purpose" dark, inviting character's motivations to be read as something far more complicated and more primal than plot mechanics. Stephen Greenblatt has pointed to this change as an example of what he calls Shakespeare's "strategic opacity,"[59] his deliberate stripping of easy and coherent motives from his chief characters in order to produce an impression of psychological depth. *The Taming of a Shrew* likewise allows its Kate to articulate a simple explanation for her behavior as an aside to the audience in scene 3, foreclosing any uncomfortable ambiguity or complexity. The 1594 text's Kate is merely pretending to resist Ferando's wooing, and intends to struggle with him for mastery within the marriage:

> But yet I will consent and marry him,
> For I methinks have lived too long a maid.
> And match him, too, or else his manhood's good.[60]

The questions of Kate's intentions and consent are dispatched within three lines. The 1623 text never addresses them so explicitly but never ceases addressing them implicitly. The 1594 text confines the question of Kate's subjective experience to a single aside, while the 1623 script leaves it an open question. The Folio text does not pretend that Kate's decisions can be explained in three pentameter verses. This, surely, is Greenblatt's "strategic opacity" at work, although Greenblatt himself primarily locates this artful stripping of motivation in the tragedies, and argues that Shakespeare invents the technique (a "crucial breakthrough") in the course of writing *Hamlet* around 1600.[61] While the male hero of a famous tragedy attracts Greenblatt's attention, Shakespeare seems to have used the strategy of selective opacity to complicate the stance of a female character in one of the comedies, and it can by no means be demonstrated that Shakespeare's work on *Hamlet* is earlier than his work on *The Shrew*. The artful mystery of Prince Hamlet may owe something to the complexity of Katherina.

If Katherina's is the only name that survives from *The Taming of a Shrew* into *The Taming of the Shrew*, her name no longer persists in Fletcher's sequel, *The Tamer Tamed*. Petruchio remains Petruchio, and while some other names from the 1623 *Shrew* remain, those names now signify new characters. Bianca is no longer, apparently, Katherine's sister or Petruchio's sister-in-law, and Tranio is no longer a gentleman's servant but a gentleman in his own right. The play's references to Petruchio's deceased "other wife"[62] always specify her difficult personality but never name her. And while Petruchio and his "other wife" have clearly been long-standing fixtures in the play's community, and their histories are personally familiar to the other characters, the community is no longer in Padua or Athens. *The Tamer Tamed* is set in London, or rather in a nonspecific theatrical location that cites London in its clowning scenes. The evident inconsistencies between the Folio Shakespeare play and the Fletcher play have excited a good deal of critical comment, but seldom with any reference to the Quarto *Taming of a Shrew*.

Since the 1594 text has been firmly categorized as derivative and non-Shakespearean, it has been tacitly omitted from the debate. The questions of the 1623 *Shrew*'s relationship with the 1594 *Shrew* and its relationship with *The Tamer Tamed* are generally examined in isolation from each other; the canonical Shakespeare play is imagined in relationship with one other text at a time, but never as part of a group. However, if the Quarto is considered as part of the *Shrew* family, rather than an illegitimate by-blow, it has a great deal to suggest about the relationship between its two siblings or cousins. It, too, gives its characters names that will largely be changed, and a place that will be altered. The inconsistencies between the two later plays are much like the differences between the first one and the second. The "inconsistencies" between any two texts in the *Shrew* group can usefully be seen as part of a larger mutability or fungibility of names and places. That a name or a location has been changed between one text and another is not an exception which requires a discrete explanation but one instance of the larger rule. Local habitations and names are very much in flux in these plays, so much so that one should rather expect them to be revised than to be retained. (The next chapter will suggest how easy character names could sometimes be to revise.) Fletcher's failure or refusal to maintain consistency with Shakespeare's play makes more sense if the Shakespeare play was not itself consistent in these matters. Indeed, it may be consistent with a later version of Shakespeare's play than survives. If the two states of the *Taming* plays are imagined as reflections of the play shortly before the date of printing, and a companion play printed in 1647 (but existing in a very similar form in 1633, in manuscript) seems not to fit with either *Taming* play, there is at least a possibility that the *Tamer Tamed* is consistent with whatever names the *Taming of the Shrew*'s characters had on stage in 1633.

To admit speculation about late revisions, to treat dramatic texts as potentially open until the moment of publication, would flirt with one of the last great taboos of Shakespeare scholarship: the implicitly forbidden hypothesis that Shakespeare's works might have been substantially improved by his collaborators. The Folio text of *The Taming of the Shrew* is published a decade into Fletcher's career as the King's Men's company playwright: in fact near the end of that career. The Folio text explicitly points at another of Fletcher's works. But the notion that Fletcher might have had any significant hand in the 1623 text is tacitly rejected; it is professionally unthinkable. Surely, I would not positively identify Fletcher's as the revising hand; I do not propose to set up any new orthodoxies upon the foundation of negative proof. But the texts of the *Shrew* are not served by ascribing them simple histories or single parents.

Revision of Shakespeare's work by other hands can be admitted as a hypothesis, as in the case of *Macbeth*, if that revision is imagined as a source of interference or inferiority. *Macbeth*'s brevity, its occasionally garbled text, the presence of discrete songs or scenes that can be treated as foreign accretions, are all acceptable signs of another hand. Indeed, this is more comfortable than the idea that Shakespeare himself produced a truncated and sometimes confused play. But textual critics treat *The Taming of the Shrew* far more gingerly, despite elements that might in other circumstances be blamed upon a ham-handed adapter, what the *Norton* edition calls "marks of confusion or incomplete revision," especially in the Hortensio subplot.[63] But the *Norton* is careful to ascribe even the faulty revisions to Shakespeare and to quarantine them to his initial drafts. If mistakes were made, the conventional reasoning goes, they were made in the original composition process and left uncorrected for the next thirty years.

The standard account of *Macbeth* insists that any mistakes or inconsistencies arise from post-Shakespearean tampering; the standard account of *The Shrew* insists that any mistakes are Shakespeare's own, and that they were carefully preserved from tampering of any kind until the publication of the First Folio. I find it difficult to imagine Shakespeare's fellow actors revering his manuscript so slavishly that they would refrain for three decades from correcting even his obvious plot-related errors; only Shakespeare's critics are capable of such uncritical fidelity. Equally mysterious is the idea that Shakespeare's personal manuscript was so treasured that it was hoarded for thirty years before being sent off to serve as disposable printer's copy, which is the essence of the unmodified foul papers hypothesis. (The foul papers story presumes that fair copies, such as the promptbooks, were too valuable to be sent to the printer, so the dispensable foul papers were supplied instead; why the King's Men would still have the foul papers in 1623 but no longer consider them worth keeping has not been made clear. Various modified versions of the foul papers hypothesis, imagining transcripts derived from the foul papers, forget the initial premise upon which the hypothesis is founded, the idea that copyists eliminated the author's idiosyncrasies.) It is also peculiar to imagine Shakespeare leaving his own mistakes uncorrected for approximately twenty years while *The Shrew* stayed in repertory in his own playing company (and even while he presumably acted in it himself).

The reluctance to hypothesize a late collaborator or adapter for *The Shrew*, even as a scapegoat, can be attributed to the existence of the Quarto text. If the superior Folio text was shaped by hands beside Shakespeare's, where does the source of its literary superiority reside? Suppose, as Leah Marcus suggests, that the "burnished, eloquent language" of the "wittier" and "more refined" 1623 text reflects a late-Jacobean emphasis on refinement and wit, and that Shakespeare was not the sole burnisher?[64] Between a Quarto text that many Shakespeareans wish to disown, and a Folio text "tainted" by non-Shakespearean elements, would there be room for Shakespeare at all? Of the two *Shrew*s, one must be assigned solely to him, in order to sustain his literary authority. Otherwise, where could Shakespeare be found among his many sources and partners, between Fletcher's sequel writing and a late collaborator and *A Shrew* and Gascoigne's *Supposes*?

The question is natural but ultimately improper to ask. It is not the task of scholars to defend or advance William Shakespeare's literary reputation. Nor is advocacy for a beloved figure likely to gain us any keener appreciation for his work. The scholar's task is not to create the author we prefer but to read the works as they have been left to us. Shakespeare can stand up for himself.

Against Conclusions

The conventional and expected goal of textual criticism is to provide an overall account of the text, organizing the pesky details into a well-rounded and easily summarized whole. The imagined goal of working with specifics of the text is the ability to speak about text in generalities. By this standard, my criticisms of previous textual critics should culminate in my own revised but complete and encompassing narrative about the text of *The Taming of the Shrew*, elegantly explaining all of its textual variants, or my labor will be turned to no account. A narrative is critiqued, in this model, so that it may be replaced.

I find it tempting to locate all of the differences between *A Shrew* and *The Shrew* in the context of this book's larger argument and offer the need to consolidate the Chamberlain's Men's claim upon the play in the 1590s as the unifying explanation for the metamorphoses undergone by *A Shrew* and *The Shrew*. But I will confess that the violence done to logic and evidence in the case of the *Shrew* plays, always in the service of promoting a coherent general narrative, makes me wary of totalizing conclusions. I would rather tear down a general narrative and replace it with nothing, at least for a while, than offer an all-encompassing narrative that ignores and marginalizes the inconveniences of the actual text. Any tale that scholars tell about these plays must be on some level a story about how little we know, or our story will not be true.

Surely, the case of Sincklo and Soto establishes that these plays were open to revision, and that the 1623 text is not earlier than the 1594 text. And the transformation of the Pembroke's Men's play into a different and superior Chamberlain's Men's play surely cemented the company's hold upon their property. But I would not present this as an explanation for every question about these texts. My argument is that revision asserted and strengthened theatrical possession, not that property was the motivation behind every theatrical revision. The company did not stop revising a play once their claim to it was secure. The post-Shakespearean allusion to Soto has nothing particularly to do with the original revision of the old play for the new company; surely it was not made in 1596 or 1597 any more than it was made in 1592, and certainly this particular adjustment was not made to strengthen the company's claim on an old Pembroke's Men's property. The play had belonged to the King's Men for a quarter century before they played *Women Pleased*. Rather, the Soto reference promotes the play's connection to the King's Men's other, newer properties. It reflects the company's interests at a later point in its history. The actors never ceased revising. There have been more changes to the texts of *The Shrew* than any one story explains. If I part ways with Sams in the matter of the *Shrews* it is here, because I do not accept any single date for this play. This text is not the product of any discrete historical moment. It was not written at one time. It is not an integral text.

While editors have remained agnostic about the Sincklo/Soto crux but convinced about the larger picture, I would prefer to do it the other way around. Evidentiary details are hard to use until they are organized into some theory, but what use is a theory that obscures and distorts the evidence? Textual theories, especially in Shakespeare studies, have driven the treatment of bibliographic facts far more thoroughly, and far longer, than anyone is happy to acknowledge. And the great advantage of such theories is also their great poverty: they serve to make the condition of the text simpler, and more easily comprehensible. If I advocate for anything, it must be the pleasures of textual skepticism. Early modern texts, and especially early modern dramatic texts, are messy, complicated, and puzzling. For scholarship to mitigate that mess and complication is to reject the very nature of the texts with which we work, and to obscure them. I do not purport to understand every aspect of the *Shrew* plays' textual condition, and I harbor deep suspicion of any scholar who does profess such all-inclusive comprehension. The texts in question are far too open, far too promiscuous in their histories, for any simple stemma, and premature conclusions have been the great bane of Shakespearean textual criticism.

What the case of Sincklo and Soto illustrates most clearly is the temptation and folly of the *terminus ad quem*; critics have repeatedly attempted to foreclose textual possibilities, to reduce the number of potential agents, to simplify the account of the text and to shore up the author's authority by placing the earliest limit possible on the text's development, even when that means fixing an artificial boundary three decades before publication. But the reference to Soto suggests, quite casually, that such boundaries are merely academic artifice, premature conclusions in every sense. *The Taming of the Shrew* was evidently open to revision after its author was dead, and until a few years before it was printed. I would be a fool to presume that the latest demonstrable revision is necessarily the last, or that early modern plays had any *terminus ad quem* but publication. Early modern plays were never finished; they were merely sent to the printers.

CHAPTER 3

Hamlet, Part by Part

"What imports the nomination of this gentleman?"
—*Hamlet*, Q2, 5.2

Hamlet Quarto Zero: Imagining the Ur-Text

When the Lord Chamberlain's Men performed *Hamlet* on June 9, 1594, the play had already been famous for so long that it had become a joke. In 1589 Nashe had mocked the "whole Hamlets, I should say handfuls, of tragical speeches" that upstart writers derived from Seneca.[1] In 1596 the play would still be a joke to Thomas Lodge, who sneered at the "ghost at the Theater who cried out like an oyster-wife, Hamlet, revenge!"[2] Those last two words of Lodge's were famous enough to be echoed by other contemporary witnesses as the signature line from *Hamlet* but cannot be found in any surviving texts of the play.

A long-standing critical tradition considers the *Hamlet* that Nashe and Lodge derided to be an entirely different play, the inferior *ur-Hamlet*, which in this account was replaced by the authentic Shakespearean article sometime between 1600 and 1602. What, then, did the Chamberlain's Men perform in June of 1594? And how late did Lodge hear the Ghost crying revenge at the Chamberlain's Men's original playhouse? Elizabethan and Jacobean witnesses, who do not distinguish between *The Taming of a Shrew* and *The Taming of the Shrew*, also make no distinction between Shakespeare's play and any forerunners. There is no evidence for any contemporary sense of two separate *Hamlet*s. Yet *Hamlet*'s texts had clearly changed enough by the time they reached print that the Ghost's famous exhortation, the entire surviving text of the *ur-Hamlet*, had gone.

The *Shrew* texts and the *Hamlet* texts present very different problems. A

Shrew and *The Shrew* present a play in two radically different states, and at least one of its texts must date from the outset of the Chamberlain's Men's joint career. *Hamlet* exists in a number of texts whose tangled relationship with one another can not be established beyond doubt.[3] Two of the texts, the Folio and the Second Quarto, are considered "good" and the First Quarto "bad" (an additional German text is considered even worse, when it is considered at all), but critics disagree about the precedence of the "good" texts, and any conclusion involves elements of speculation. The *Hamlet*s, "good" and "bad," reveal the text in various states, none of which can be identified with the play the Chamberlain's Men possessed in 1594, let alone the play as it existed beforehand. Indeed, none of the extant texts can persuasively be put forward as the *ur-Hamlet*; Lodge's famous catchphrase is not here. If the two *Shrew*s give us two disparate texts with no sign of intermediary stages, what the *Hamlet*s offer most of all is intermediary stages. What they do not offer is a clear beginning point, or for that matter a conclusive final state.

Although *The Taming of a Shrew* and *Hamlet* were both performed at the outset of the Chamberlain's Men's career, the mainstream of twentieth-century scholarship has approached them in diametrically opposed ways. In both cases the first printed quartos are considered "bad," and Shakespeare is held to have already written a superior, canonical text before those quartos were published. But the same conventional wisdom that insists Shakespeare did *not* revise *The Taming of a Shrew* also insists that he *did* revise *Hamlet*. While critics from Peter Alexander to Ann Thompson have claimed that one play the Chamberlain's Men acted in June 1594 was, in essence, the Folio version of *The Taming of the Shrew*, critics have also assumed that the *Hamlet* they acted that week was the un-Shakespearean *ur-Hamlet*. Indeed, Thompson and Neil Taylor, editing the *Arden Three Hamlet*, take it as established that the 1594 performance was not *Hamlet*. They identify "the first performance of *Hamlet* of which we have a specific record" as taking place in 1607 aboard the ship *Red Dragon* and conclude that "it seems . . . despite the lack of hard evidence, that Richard Burbage originated the role of Hamlet for the Chamberlain's Men at the Globe."[4] Thompson and Taylor's formulation reflects a belief in the absolute distinction between *Hamlet* and any predecessor; even if the *ur-Hamlet* had been in the company repertory for years, with Burbage acting the lead, Thompson and Taylor imagine him "originating" Hamlet as a new role sometime after 1599. Although they concede the possibility that Shakespeare could have written "an earlier version" of the play, even that is imagined as a separate work.[5] The *Textual Companion* to the *Oxford Shakespeare* actually gives the *ur-Hamlet* its own entry on the list of "Works Excluded from This Edition."[6]

It is certain that there are topical references in two of the three extant *Hamlet* texts which date from the beginning of the seventeenth century, and certain that the "Hamlet, revenge" catchphrase does not appear in those texts. But these facts alone do not suffice to establish the existence of "a lost English play" distinct from the later *Hamlet*.[7] The *Hamlet* of 1589 and 1594 may have been differed enormously from the *Hamlet* of 1604, as indeed the *Hamlet*s of 1589 and 1594 may hypothetically have differed from one another, but the so-called *ur-Hamlet* might also have resembled the later versions too closely to be treated as a separate play. All that can be established is one variant line of dialogue, and some topical references minor enough to be added or removed through very simple revision; indeed, some of those references are lacking in the Second Quarto. Although the standard critical narrative holds that *Hamlet* was revised once (but only once) so radically that it became a fundamentally different play, creating two *Hamlet*s (but only two), there is no hard evidence to establish the proposed "source" play's difference from the extant play. The evidence for the *ur-Hamlet* hypothesis is itself a hypothesis. Peculiarly, many of the editors who insist that *The Taming of a Shrew* could not be a source or forerunner for the 1623 *Taming of the Shrew* also insist that *Hamlet* did have a predecessor that the bore the same rough resemblance to it that the 1594 bears to the 1623 *Shrew*. *The Taming of a Shrew* is not a source play, this logic runs, and *Hamlet* had a source play just like it.

This contradictory position is partly about biographical convenience. While a reference to a post-Shakespearean play in *The Shrew* complicates any sense of Shakespeare's personal authorship, the theatrical allusions in the texts of *Hamlet* point to events "at the midpoint of his playwriting career," as Harold Jenkins says, strengthening the sense of that authorship and conveniently putting "Shakespeare's most famous play" at the apex of his working life.[8] The idea that Shakespeare wrote the play in or after 1601 also facilitates biographical readings of *Hamlet* which, whatever their other merits, make the author the central figure of literary interpretation. *Hamlet* must be imagined as a substantially new play after September 1601 for it to be imagined as an artistic response to the death of Shakespeare's father.[9] Critics have been far less interested in the death of Richard Burbage's father in 1597, although Burbage played Hamlet.[10]

But most importantly, the *ur-Hamlet* argument saves Shakespeare from the embarrassment of having written a work which some of his literary contemporaries despised. The *Hamlet* or *Hamlet*s Nashe and Lodge saw cannot be reconstructed. But critics have been unwilling to identify the play those witnesses scorned as Shakespeare's. The scholarly belief in the *ur-Hamlet* is not primarily based on textual evidence but upon evidence of reception. When an early witness dispraises *Hamlet*, this is interpreted as a sign that he has seen the ur-*Hamlet*. When an early witness mentions *Hamlet* approvingly, this is taken as a sign that he has witnessed Shakespeare's *Hamlet*. The implicit logic is that the ur-*Hamlet* had to be different from *Hamlet*, indeed so different that it was a mere ur-*Hamlet*, because some early modern critics disliked it. And modern critics have managed to be quite voluble about the imagined defects of a play that does not, to put the matter simply, exist. The hypothetical ur-*Hamlet* is a sheerly potential text and as Emma Smith puts it "no verifiable traces of its plot or language can be recovered" except of course for "Hamlet, revenge."[11] Smith has admirably demonstrated how the lack of evidence about *Hamlet*'s hypothetical ghostly predecessor has not deterred critics. "In the absence of the play itself," she writes, "textual bibliography wrote it, situated it among its putative sources, and discussed its relationship to the extant *Hamlet*."[12] While the urge to maintain Shakespeare's undiluted authority creates pressure to date *The Taming of the Shrew* early, it creates the opposite pressure in the case of *Hamlet*, motivating editors to date the play later, maintaining a safe distance from Nashe's and Lodge's bad reviews and the postulated ur-*Hamlet*.

In fact, the discussion of *Hamlet*'s date centers almost exclusively on the ur-*Hamlet* hypothesis; when critics ask when the play was written they are in fact asking when it was rewritten, when it ceased to be the ur-*Hamlet*.[13] This sometimes leads to odd critical detours, as when Francis Meres's failure to mention *Hamlet* in *Palladis Tamia* is construed as a sign that the play had not yet been written,[14] or when Gabriel Harvey's praise for *Hamlet* in some marginalia leads to intense efforts to ascertain the date that marginalia in order to date Shakespeare's *Hamlet*. Documents written nine years or more after the first explicit mention of a work do not generally figure in the discussion of its dating; the attention to Meres's and Harvey's allusions is focused on dating Shakespeare's revisions. But the Meres and Harvey references, however slippery and problematic they may be, are evidence of attribution rather than of revision per se. At best, they help to indicate when readers began to associate *Hamlet* with Shakespeare; critics have construed such identifications as signs that the play had already been substantially transformed into some version of the extant *Hamlet*. But such constructions rest upon the assumption that the revision of *Hamlet* was a singular event, with all or nearly all of the changes that constitute the text as Shakespeare's being made at one time. The ur-*Hamlet* hypothesis imagines one moment of sharp and entire rupture in the play's history, one moment when the text as it had been was discarded and a radically new play, a "Shakespearean" version, took its place. Although scholars find it either impossible or unpalatable to deny that *Hamlet* ever underwent revision, imagining *Hamlet* as two distinct plays permits them to maintain belief in an original and integral authorial manuscript. If there were an *ur-Hamlet* which Shakespeare rewrote once and for all, that means there would have to be a singular, original *Hamlet* which replaced it, the first text after it stopped being someone else's play and began being Shakespeare's.

But there is no evidence that Shakespeare rewrote *Hamlet* at one time or from top to bottom. There is no reason to believe in any moment of radical substitution, when the play ceased to be the *ur-Hamlet*, nor any proof that Shakespeare created a new manuscript for the play as a whole. Changes to *Hamlet* could easily have been made incrementally, and many might have been made on the working texts in the playhouse rather than on fresh sheets at the poet's desk. The only textual changes that we can confirm, the alteration of a catchphrase and the inclusion of topical material,[15] require fairly simple adjustments to actors' performing texts, and even more wide-ranging changes to the script, if there were such changes, could have been undertaken in a number of stages rather than in a single, authorial draft. The premise upon which the *ur-Hamlet* hypothesis depends, and which it materially and tautologically supports, is that *Hamlet* was substantially revised only once in its long history. But the surviving texts of the play belie that premise. They show the marks of continuing incremental revisions, and of revisions centered on the partial working texts used in the playhouse rather than on a master text. Scholars may wish to reconstruct Shakespeare's final draft of *Hamlet*, but it is not clear that Shakespeare ever finished *Hamlet*, or that *Hamlet* is finished.

The First Quarto and Its Discontents

The greatest focus of scholarly controversy and puzzlement is *Hamlet*'s "bad" First Quarto from 1603. The greatly adapted and abbreviated German text, *Der bestrafte Brudermord* (Fratricide Punished), has attracted less attention because its late date makes it impossible to reconstruct its English original or to isolate changes made later.[16] *Der bestrafte Brudermord* is no help as a copy-text and cannot hope even for the authority editors allow to the "bad" First Quarto, but it must nonetheless be included in any count of *Hamlet*'s extant texts, especially when considering the First Quarto. The *Brudermord* has a plain genealogical relationship to that text, most obviously because both texts name the King's advisor "Corambis" or "Corambus" rather than "Polonius." However, the *Brudermord* also includes a number of parallels with the "good"

Second Quarto, implying a lost precursor which combined features of both the First and Second Quartos.[17] This inferential *ur-Brudermord* tangles the three English texts into what Vinson Dearing calls a "ring" of filiation, and a particularly incestuous one at that.[18] The "good" Folio and Second Quarto texts share so many readings that they have traditionally been conflated into a single text, but the Folio and First Quarto also share some elements not found in the Second Quarto, and the *ur-Brudermord* demonstrates some relationship between the two quartos. Rather than displaying a clear lineage of authority and derivation, the *Hamlet* texts are surprisingly interdependent.

The New Bibliography, following G. I. Duthie, consigned the 1603 *Hamlet* to a double badness, as a product both of a reporter's theatrical larceny and of an unscrupulous stationer's piracy (the play was registered to James Roberts but printed for Nicholas Ling and John Trundle, with no formal transfer of rights recorded).[19] Twentieth-century Shakespeare bibliography often conflated these two categories of "badness" and used each notion to reinforce the other although there is no logical connection between the two. A printer who obtained a hypothetical "reported" manuscript of a play had no reason to trespass on his neighbor's registered copy, and a hypothetical publisher bent on stealing a play belonging to a brother stationer had no special need for a memorized text.[20] The glue binding the "Bad Stationers" and the mercenary reporters into one book is critical sentiment, chiefly a conviction that dishonest characters stick together and that every thief will seek out others of his kind. Fredson Bowers's confident pronouncement that *Hamlet*'s First Quarto is a "memorially reconstructed pirate text"[21] is in fact two separate claims, both of which need to be examined carefully. The memorial reconstruction argument has been disputed in recent scholarship, cast into doubt by Laurie E. Maguire and others, and I will return to it later in this chapter.

The stigma of unlicensed publication is dispensed with more easily. While it is true that *Hamlet*'s original registrant, James Roberts, is not mentioned on the 1603 title page, he is the printer of the Second Quarto in 1604/5. (See Figures 4 and 5.) Both quartos had the same publisher, Nicholas Ling. As Gerald D. Johnson and David Scott Kastan have recently explained (advancing a line of argument originated by E. K. Chambers), James Roberts was not himself a publisher. Rather, he habitually registered copies as "a way of reserving work for himself without risking the capital that publication would involve" and sought investors who would publish the book and employ him to print it.[22] Roberts made his living from his printing fees, rather than from the return on long-term investments in books. Ling, as Johnson has established, ran a business that neatly complemented Roberts's. Ling, a bookseller, functioned

Figure 4. Title page of *Hamlet*, 1603. RB 22275. By permission of The Huntington Library, San Marino, California.

primarily as an investor and backer, who bought and published manuscripts brought to him by other stationers.[23] Part of the price of acquiring a book, for Ling, was reserving the printing job for the finder (no terrible hardship, since Ling would pay someone to print it in any case). It should be no surprise that Roberts did not publish the 1603 Quarto. The sole oddity is that he did not print it. But Kastan hypothesizes that Roberts, who was having one of his busiest years in 1603, could not find time to schedule the *Hamlet* job when

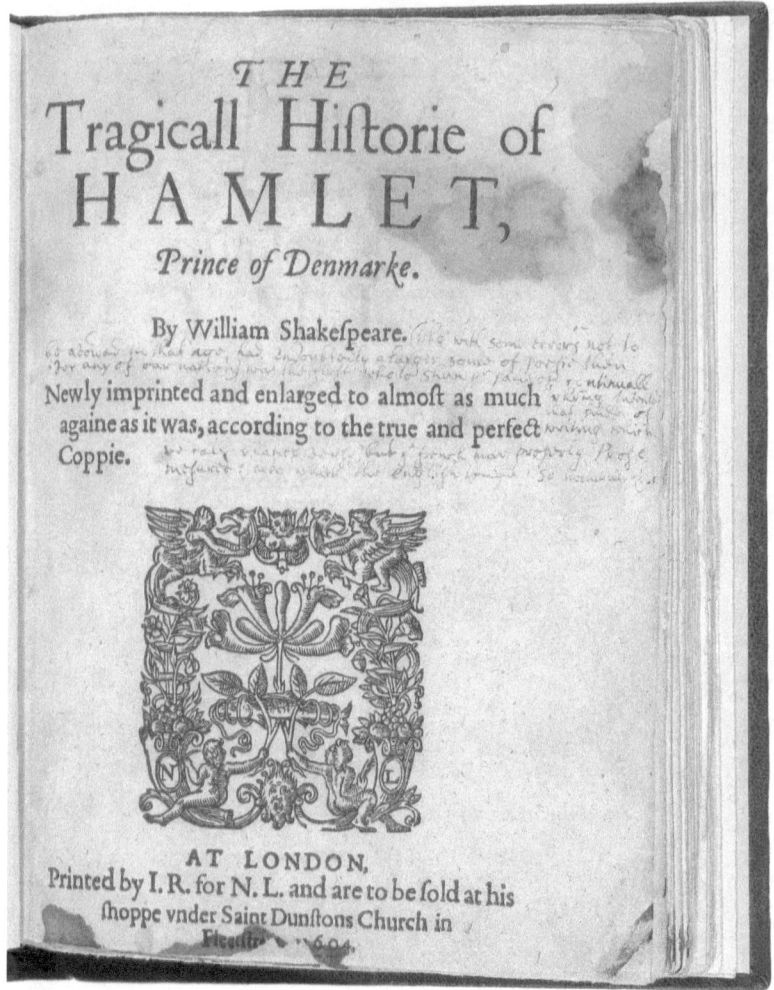

Figure 5. Title page of *Hamlet*, 1604/5. By permission of the Folger Shakespeare Library.

Ling and Trundle asked.[24] Roberts's purpose after all was to ensure himself work, not to keep it out of other men's hands. As long as Roberts maintained to right to print subsequent editions, he had more to gain by allowing another printer to take on the initial job and by taking on the work of reprinting it later, when he might need the business.

Any differences between the 1603 text and its successor in 1604/5 meant nothing at all in terms of the Stationers' notions of ownership, or to the conti-

Figure 6. Printer's ornament of Nicholas Ling. Detail of title page of *Hamlet*, 1604/5. By permission of the Folger Shakespeare Library.

nuity of title to *Hamlet*. Roberts seems to have made no complaint about the first edition (and need not have accommodated himself with Ling or Trundle if they had actually contravened his registration). However the language of the two quartos differs, their title pages display a conspicuous sign of bibliographical consistency: the publisher's mark. The ornament in both cases is McKerrow's device #301, a personal monogram of Nicholas Ling. (See Figure 6.) The pleasingly intricate device includes Ling's initials, a blossoming honeysuckle, and a fish, specifically a ling, as a visual pun on the bookseller's name. Ling is clearly the unchallenged owner of both quartos, however much the second might be "enlarged," and Roberts clearly accedes to that ownership.

It is Roberts who printed the ornament Ling supplied to him, Roberts who physically places the mark of Ling's possession upon *Hamlet*. While no transfer of the rights from Roberts to Ling is recorded, the next owner of the play, John Smethwick, receives it from Ling. Kastan takes this transfer as a sign that "title to *Hamlet* seems to have settled unproblematically on Ling,"[25] but even that phrasing implies (as Kastan otherwise does not) a previous moment when the title was temporarily unsettled or problematic. *Hamlet* seems instead to have been Ling's property, securely and consistently, from at least 1603.

It is easier to define the many things that the 1603 Quarto is not than it is to establish firmly what it is. It is not the play given on June 9, 1594, not an irregularly printed book, not the rumored *ur-Hamlet*. Scott McMillin's study of its casting requirements severely undermines the notion that it is a script cut for touring with a reduced troupe; McMillin finds that the First Quarto requires at least as many actors as the other texts, and he must search for an expedient to keep it from requiring a *larger* minimal cast.[26] As McMillin points out, shorter texts make doubling parts more difficult, rather than simpler, both in general and in *Hamlet*'s specific case.[27] The First Quarto is also not the preferred copy-text for later editions of *Hamlet*, and its failure to fill that role has been a central element of its poor critical reputation. But if the First Quarto is relieved from the demands of editing, from the question of its viability as *the* text of *Hamlet*, and is instead considered as one among a group of texts under consideration, it sheds light on a number of questions about the play. No text of *Hamlet*, nor indeed all of the *Hamlet*s together, can allow us to reconstruct all of the changes the play underwent over its years in repertory; we will never be sure exactly what the Chamberlain's Men did with the play they started with. But a close examination of the *Hamlet*s as a group reveals a good deal about the company's methods of revision; even if we cannot recover all of what the actors did, we can still learn much about how they did it.

The Dead Father: Corambis and Polonius

What we know of early modern stage practice does not suggest that the playing companies limited their methods of revision to a choice between minor adjustments on one hand and global rewriting on the other, or that they limited the occasions of revision to special events or altered venues. Instead, the players had a wide range of options for revising their plays, and frequent occasions to revise them. The methods that were used to change characters' names in the various texts of *Hamlet* suggest the variety of rewriting techniques applied to those texts at different times and show how easily a seemingly global feature, the name of a famous and pivotal character, might be susceptible to very localized revision. Moreover, the changing name of the King's counselor in *Hamlet* suggests how the playhouse's working texts, the "parts" and "plots" into which a play was divided for acting purposes, could both facilitate and impose obstacles to changes in the text.

Most critical attention to the use of "Corambis" in the First Quarto and "Polonius" in the Second Quarto and Folio has been focused on unpacking the possible meanings of these not easily explicable names, and on finding reasons for the change. I am not interested in why the names were switched, but how. The speech-headings give readers the illusion that this person's name is a persistent and global feature of the script, and the character has become so famous that many people know his name even before reading or seeing the play, but the actual name is quite marginal in the performance text.[28] Indeed, only one character in any given text of the play seems to know this old man's name. Which character, like which name, depends upon which text one reads.

Corambis's name is used only by the Queen, and even then only after his death. The name is never used in address but only within short narratives, in the Queen's explanation of the old man's murder to the King at the end of the closet scene, and later in her summary of the mounting problems in Elsinore since his death (11.108, 13.6).[29] No one else calls Corambis anything. In the two later texts, the Queen never uses the old counselor's name, but the King does. He addresses Polonius directly just before the old man's first lines, in a doubled question designed to explicitly identify him as Laertes' parent: "Have you your father's leave? What says Polonius?" (1.2.57).[30] (Only the first question is in the First Quarto. The King simply asks if "Leartes" has his father's permission, and the permissive father speaks.) The remaining uses of the name, like the uses of Corambis's name, are posthumous. The King uses Polonius's name while giving Rosencrantz and Guildenstern instructions to search for Hamlet (4.1.33), twice while interrogating Hamlet about the corpse (4.3.17, 32), and once again while summarizing the recent troubles at court (4.5.79), a summary which replaces the Queen's parallel account in the First Quarto. The King's and Queen's expositions of the two names differ, but only slightly. Corambis goes entirely without a name until the Queen takes his murder as an expository opportunity, simultaneously telling the King what has happened and the audience to whom it has happened. The King manages to drop Polonius's name at the character's first appearance, but the name is then forgotten until the aftermath of the closet scene, when the King reminds the spectators what the old man was called, using the same basic technique the

Queen uses with Corambis; he recounts what has just happened on stage to a third party, in this case Rosencrantz and Guildenstern, and lets the audience overhear the victim's name.

Although the stage directions for all of the printed texts repeatedly impress Corambis's or Polonius's name on the reader, this is an illusion of the literary artifact: the old man's name is spoken very little in performance. Compare the frequency with which Fortinbras's name is used during one short speech by Horatio in the first scene. In the "good" versions Horatio says "Fortinbras" four times in fewer than fifteen lines (1.1.81–94), while the word "Polonius" is spoken only five times in the entire performance. In the First Quarto, Horatio says "Fortenbrasse" only three times (1.71–80), but this is still once more often than anyone in the play says "Corambis." For contemporary playgoers, the old man's name would have been a minor detail, easily overlooked or forgotten. The intervening four hundred years of circulation and reception have made Polonius an archetypical character, so famous that his fame is to some degree independent of the play itself. No one needs to say his name on stage now, because we all know it already. But by supplying the name, we mask the effects of its sparing use.

Every character in *Hamlet* except the King or else the Queen resorts to a variety of circumlocutions in order not to speak the old man's name. When Hamlet wants to address his uncle's adviser he calls him "my lord," "sir," or else, mockingly, "Jephthah" (in a theatrical reference to which I will return; 2.2.204, 196, 392), and when the man is dead Hamlet apostrophizes him as "thou wretched rash intruding fool" (3.4.30). When Hamlet wants to ask Ophelia about him, he simply says "your father" (3.1.130). Otherwise, when he wants to discuss Ophelia's father with anyone other than Ophelia, he must resort to indicating him. In 2.2, the counselor is "that great baby you see there" (365) and "that lord" (521). After the old man is dead he is "this man," "this counsellor," and, most bluntly, "the guts" (3.4.185, 187, 186). Hamlet, a character famous for his enormous linguistic resources (or rather a famous character composed of enormous linguistic resources), neither initiates nor sustains any discourse about the old man outside his (or else his daughter's) presence. At best, he responds to questions about the corpse. To speak about the old man, Hamlet always relies on a pronoun, relative, possessive, or otherwise, because he cannot or will not name him.[31]

Hamlet's incapacity or refusal provides the actor a range of performance choices, some consistent with current stage practice and others which would seem novel or strange, a spectrum of possibilities running from disdain to playfulness to aphasia to conscious depersonalization. But such acting possibilities are not necessarily rooted in the character's psychological motivations, nor primarily an expression of Hamlet's character. Any psychological explanation for Hamlet's reticence would have to explain why the rest of the play's characters, excepting either the King or the Queen, avoid the old man's name as well. Rosencrantz, for example, seeks "the dead body" rather than a person with a name (4.2.4; 4.3.12). But the King's and Queen's respective evasions are most striking, particularly when contrasted with each character's ability to speak the name used in other texts. The First Quarto King, like Hamlet, must lean heavily on relative pronouns when he wants to find the dead Corambis, asking, "Where is this body?" and "Where is this dead body?" (11.134, 11.125). The Folio and Second Quarto Queen, trying to explain how Hamlet has killed Polonius, can only call the dead minister "the unseen good old man," (4.1.11) requiring an ever so slightly clunky trio of adjectives where the First Quarto Queen could simply use "the good old man" as a complement to "Corambis" (11.111). One name has not simply been replaced by another. Instead, the switch has been accomplished by removing the earlier name from one actor's lines and adding the newer name, which scans differently, to another actor's part. At some point one speech, the catalog of political woes from act 4, has been transferred from the first actor to the second (it is always the "naming" actor who speaks it in the surviving English texts) and thoroughly rewritten. The evidence of *Der bestrafte Brudermord*, the only extant text in which both the King and the Queen speak the counselor's name, suggests that the change happened in at least two stages, with the name initially being added to a second part and then removed from the first, or else removed from one part and then changed in the other. The *Brudermord*'s King delivers a single line ("Alas! One hears nothing but downright sad and unhappy news!"), without the old man's name, in place of the catalog of woes.[32] The two actors whose parts have changed are a man and boy, one of the leading actors and one of the apprentices. The actor playing the Queen would need to be replaced every few years, and a new actor taught the lines, in any case. Changing both parts at once would be quite simple; the sharer in the company got a rewritten part and a boy's part was rewritten at the same time.

This revision of the old man's name is too exactly specific, and indeed too odd, to be the result of memorial reconstruction. Someone made and scrupulously sustained a decision to limit the old man's name to one speaker. The supposed reconstructor would have no reason to reproduce that limitation; that he would reproduce it in the wrong actor's part, with the wrong name, entirely by chance, is improbable. There is no reason for a theatrical pirate, if there were such pirates, to refrain from using Polonius's or Corambis's name wherever convenient.

The complication of transferring the old man's name from one actor's part to another also weakens the idea that the name was changed to avoid giving offense on some particular occasion. One version of this idea is the "Pullen hypothesis," which argues that an original text using the name Polonius was altered for a performance at Oxford so that the company would not seem to be mocking the twelfth-century theologian Robert Pullen, one of the University's founders.[33] Every narrative of this kind, whether centered on Pullen or some other figure, argues that the First Quarto text preserves a change made for a single performance, like a textual fly in amber. But if the name needed to be changed for only one day, why go to the trouble of changing two actors' lines? Why not substitute the inoffensive name for the potentially offensive one without making any other changes?[34] Whatever led the Chamberlain's Men to alter the old man's name, the alteration is bound up with other changes in the text, seemingly irrelevant to the issue of the name itself. (It would be hard to explain the transfer of the lamenting speech from the Queen to the King as a response to censorship concerns.)

Whatever the reasons for old adviser's new identity, the change would be relatively easy to make using the working texts of the early modern theater. Elizabethan and Jacobean plays were copied into individual parts for each actor, containing that performer's lines and brief cues. To supply all of the actors with complete texts of the work would have required at least eleven copies of each new play, an expensive and labor-intensive proposition, especially in a rapidly changing repertory.[35] The existence of such actor's parts in the Elizabethan professional theaters is confirmed by the survival of several such parts (many Continental, many from after 1660, and some from academic performances), and by literary evidence, including a number of jokes and references in *A Midsummer Night's Dream*.[36] Simon Palfrey and Tiffany Stern's *Shakespeare in Parts* is the definitive study, and Stern's earlier work has enormously enriched readers' understanding of theatrical parts and of their uses. The most famous of these manuscripts, and the one most germane to the study of professional Elizabethan theater, is Edward Alleyn's part in *Orlando Furioso*, in which he played Orlando.[37] The document is incomplete but bears notes and minor revisions, including some that appear to be in Alleyn's hand. The *Orlando* part plays a crucial role in the rise of the New Bibliography, and W. W. Greg's analysis of it is, in Laurie E. Maguire's words, a "foundation-stone" in his developing narrative of memorial reconstruction.[38] But the existence of such parts opens possibilities that Greg and his later followers would be loath to acknowledge.

The various "parts" were coordinated in performance by a "plat" or "plot," a sheet or two of paper bearing an outline of the play. Taken together, the "plot" and "the parts" constituted a working performance text. There were complete copies of the text, to be sure, most importantly the "allowed book" approved by the Master of Revels or his deputy and bearing the censor's signature; the signed text represented the company's license to perform that particular play. The "book-keeper" or stage manager held a copy, which may or may not have been identical with the allowed book, and companies sometimes had presentation copies made for various patrons. But the plots and parts are what the actors themselves used. The censored manuscript, and even the book-keeper's control text, represents a plan for a performance, the play in theory; the parts and plot, the performers' texts, were the script put into practice.

If they chose, the players could make some revisions on the parts themselves. Alleyn's *Orlando* part has emendations and changes, which Greg argues are all in the actor's hand: "I incline to believe that all the alterations and corrections in the part which are clearly not by the original scribe are by Alleyn. Only I must suppose that as he worked at his part he had on his standish several quills and more than one ink."[39]

This unlikely supposition, especially surprising from a scholar of Greg's profound technical expertise, reveals a great deal about the possibilities Greg was unwilling to accept. Greg not only forecloses the idea that more than one person has made changes to the part but arbitrarily rejects the possibility that Alleyn might have made changes on more than one occasion. If all of the writing really is in Alleyn's hand, but not all in the same ink, the common explanation would be that Alleyn worked on the text at different times. But accepting that explanation would be to accept the potential for ongoing changes in the performance text, a prospect Greg refused to entertain. Instead he chose (quite concretely) to imagine Alleyn sitting at his "standish" correcting his work-text once and forever. (He also imagines Alleyn working alone in his study, rather than with his colleagues in a playhouse.) Cluttering the hypothetical standish with Greg's multitude of pens and ink would require Alleyn to laboriously cut and sharpen several quills with a pen knife and to mix more than one ink by hand, a surprising expense of effort for the task before him. Clearly, this scenario argues a powerful motivation on somebody's part.

Greg (who is seen here in one of his weaker moments) preferred to imagine the part as entirely dependent upon the promptbook as a whole, as strictly derivative rather than potentially constitutive. The evidence Greg can see he uses as a tool to reconstruct a document he cannot find, and whose existence he cannot prove. But there is no reason to exclude the possibility of revisions being made to the part before being transferred to the book-holder's copy, or the possibility of the part deviating from the whole. It would always be necessary that the actor speak the appropriate cues for his fellows, but whether improvements made to an actor's speeches were always copied to the "book" is an open question.

Hieronimo Is Made Again

Minor though Alleyn's changes are, they suggest that the parts were at the very least available as a tool of revision. And Tiffany Stern, the leading scholar on acting parts, has pointed out that the Folio and Second Quarto texts of *Hamlet* have undergone part-based revisions: the middle lines of several speeches have been added or subtracted, without altering the cues.[40] Stern counts eight characters whose parts were revised, leaving their colleagues' lines unchanged: Hamlet, the King, the Queen, Laertes, Horatio, Rosencrantz, Guildenstern, and Osric.[41] There are also very minor changes to two of Polonius's lines. The Second Quarto's "tragedy, comedy, history, pastoral, pastoral-comical, historical-pastoral" extends further in the Folio with "tragical-historical, tragical-comical-historical-pastoral" as well (2.2.379–81), before Polonius's speech continues. The Second Quarto's "That's good," is the Folio's "That's good. 'mobbled queen' is good" (2.2.484), preserving the final cue through a kind of echo.[42]

A play could be significantly expanded by altering only a few parts, with the practical division of the play into component parts governing the way expansions and revisions were done. The additions to *The Spanish Tragedy* published in 1602 are a very good example of part-centered revision. The five additions are primarily an expansion of Hieronimo's already large role, giving him longer and more elaborate mad scenes, and would obviously require copying out a new part for the lead. Beyond that, the new material is carefully designed to minimize the number of actors who will need new parts.

One addition, the third, is a soliloquy, which is simple enough. In fact, after his forty-five or fifty lines of introspection, the Hieronimo of the additions comes to himself and gives the same cue to the next player which the Hieronimo of the earlier version gave, so the actor playing the "First Portingale" doesn't have to change a thing. The little gap on the First Portingale's page that represents Hieronimo's speech is the same little gap, no matter how the speech is extended. The second addition, an expanded bit of byplay with Lorenzo, is brief enough for Lorenzo to make marginal or interlinear changes on his old part instead of receiving a new one. Lorenzo's new lines are "All's one, Hieronimo, acquaint me with it," and "How now, Hieronimo?" and while he does have three new cues, the Alleyn part suggests that a cue of a word or two sufficed. The first and fourth additions, which are most substantial, involve eight new speeches for Isabella, ranging from one to three lines apiece and most likely requiring a scribe to prepare the actor's part again. As with *Hamlet*'s King and Queen, the revisions involve an important adult actor and a boy with whom the adult works closely throughout the play.

These additions also introduce three new characters: Hieronimo's servants Jaques and Pedro (a character distinct from the Portuguese viceroy's brother, "Don Pedro," a nonspeaking role), and the Painter with whom Hieronimo interacts in the long fourth addition. These minor characters would have been doubled by actors who already played other roles, and the additions allow a good deal of stage time for those actors to change from one role to another. All three new characters have substantial amounts of dialogue to learn, but existing parts did not need to be rewritten. The actors could simply be given the fresh pages in addition to the ones they had. The first four of Hieronimo's new scenes deliberately minimize the changes needed to other players' assignments, and the necessary adjustments are primarily required from junior members of the company: three supporting actors get additional roles, and the boy playing Isabella gains some new lines. The additions surround Hieronimo with these actors whenever possible.

The fifth addition, which expands and supersedes part of the final scene, breaks with this pattern, giving new lines to the King, to the Viceroy, and to Castile, three large and substantial roles which may well have been played by shareholders in the company. However, the need for scribal labor is still minimized. The changes to these parts are confined to the end of the text, so that only the last few pages of these players' parts will need to be rewritten. (This is especially important since professionals typically joined the individual sheets of their part into a long scroll, as Alleyn did with his *Orlando* part; an actor's "rôle" was a literal "roll," which complicated insertions into the middle of their texts.) Here is the principle of thrift, in the most literal sense. The reviser has expanded the leading role while incurring something close to the minimum of scribal effort and expense. Few if any changes are made to most of the leading parts, and important roles like Horatio, Balthazar, and Bel-Imperia go completely untouched.

The Spanish Tragedy's reviser clearly imagines the play not as a single organically united text but as a number of component parts, and this conceptual model of the play governs his approach to revision. The longest addition by far, the Painter scene, is carefully inserted so that the scheme of entrances and exits on the company's plot will be minimally disturbed. What is substantially a new Hieronimo scene is made a prefix to one of Hieronimo's existing scenes, so that the established alternation of plotlines and characters will not have to be adjusted. Rather than having Hieronimo make his famous entrance with a book after the King and his kinsmen have exited at the end of act 3, scene 12, the new characters Pedro and Jaques enter to prepare for Hieronimo's entrance, Hieronimo enters for his scene with Isabella and the Painter, and then Hieronimo exits in order to reenter immediately with his book and his famous line, "*Vindicta mihi!*" The so-called law of re-entry is broken, which is particularly noticeable because the immediately preceding scene goes out of its way to let Hieronimo exit with a reasonable stretch of time before his next entrance, but the awkwardness of the new exit and immediate return permits a less complicated revision than a wholesale rejuggling of the plot sequence would require. The decision to add and alter material is always balanced against the practical requirements of making changes in the playhouse texts.

Not all revisions to early modern plays were part-based, and the additions to *The Spanish Tragedy* provide a particularly straightforward example of discrete and narrowly focused revisions. But revising some parts independently of others was one among the players' several methods, and any revision would eventually have to take the practical texts into account. Revision should be imagined not as changing one text but as changing a collection of independent performance texts which were needed for any production. The two texts of *Dr. Faustus*, for example, show a heavy emphasis on plot-based revision, with the insertion of new clown scenes. But including new scenes involving new characters is relatively easy when the script is divided into acting parts. The players who aren't involved in the new scenes don't need anything changed. An actor's part represents everything the actor himself doesn't speak, whether a short line or an extended soliloquy or a long additional scene, with the same small blank space on the page. A gap is a gap, no matter what fills it in performance. In fact, it is very easy to run two of an actor's scenes together into a longer one by removing some intervening scene. The player's part wouldn't need to be adjusted, because parts make no distinction between a brief pause for another actor to speak and a long rest while the clowns improvise.

The technique used to rename the old man indicates that the *Hamlet* texts, including the First Quarto, have undergone significant part-based revision, although this is by no means the only kind of revision that has been made. Clearly the plot has been restructured, and changes in the order of scenes would demand new parts be written out for a number of the leading actors, certainly including Hamlet. His lines are not only different but they are arranged in a different sequence. This does not mean, however, that all of the parts had to be rewritten when the plot was adjusted, or that all the parts which have clearly been revised were revised at one time. The players had an interest in keeping some lines the same.

When one imagines a reviser or reporter beginning at the first line of an integrated text and working his way through the complete manuscript, then the relative lack of changes to certain minor roles such as Marcellus in *Hamlet* or the Host in *Merry Wives of Windsor* seems quite significant. If the reviser is making a complete new manuscript from scratch, changing one character's lines is as simple as changing another's. Kathleen O. Irace, championing the memorial reconstruction argument, writes, "If Shakespeare revised Q1 . . . he must have carefully avoided altering the lines spoken and heard by the actor playing Marcellus, while expanding and changing the remaining roles—a very unlikely pattern of revision."[43] If, however, the reviser is preparing a number of shorter component texts which will need to be copied out by hand for the actors, then leaving certain parts relatively unchanged makes sense. The strategy Irace describes is not "unlikely" at all but standard procedure. The benefit of improving a character's lines must be balanced against the cost of preparing an additional text. The memorial reconstruction hypothesis for First Quarto *Hamlet* presumes that Marcellus's part would be altered in any general rewriting of the play, but there seems little clear advantage in improving this minor character's role. Conversely, once substantial changes have been introduced to a major character's part, requiring a scribe to make a new copy, the reviser incurs no further expense by making as many improvements to that part as come to mind, as long as the changes don't alter other players' cues or the sequence of the plot. When two characters share a great deal of dialogue, revising one may provide an opportunity to make extensive revisions for the other. The transfer of the summary-of-woes speech from the Queen to the King probably required that both parts be copied anew. Early modern acting texts are peculiarly tolerant to revisions of this kind and would permit such discrete revisions to be made on different occasions over the life of the play. Some changes, like the change in *Hamlet*'s plot sequence, are more drastic and require a number of consequent changes, while other adjustments are more local and convenient to make. The Chamberlain's Men could have made all the changes between their texts of *Hamlet* at one time, if they chose, but there is no special reason to insist that they did so.

More interesting perhaps than the "goodness" of Marcellus's part in the First Quarto is the unusual "badness" of Hamlet's part, the one role in the

1603 text that is marred not only by pedestrian verse but by garbled syntax. The "To be or not to be" soliloquy has been a prime focus of critical attention, a kind of touchstone for comparison between the 1603 Quarto and the "good" texts. Some of this attention has been misguided: the inferiority or perceived inferiority of phrasing cannot be taken as evidence of fraud, or indeed of anything except inferiority. The lack of the famous words "That is the question" may disappoint readers but does not prove textual corruption. However, the soliloquy also exhibits syntactical problems. Such lines as "The undiscovered country at whose sight/The happy smile and the accursed damned" (7.121–22) are not simply unimpressive but also nonsensical. Almost all such mangled lines go to Hamlet. When Hamlet says, "Ay, there's the point" (7.114), he speaks more or less like the other characters; when he says "in that dream of death, when we awake/ And borne before an everlasting judge" (7.117–18), he speaks quite differently. The First Quarto is a play in which a single part, the largest, has undergone significantly more corruption than the rest, or in which the leading actor pays far more attention to the rhythm of his speeches than to their literal sense.

Somewhere behind the First Quarto may lie a text cobbled together from actors' parts of varying quality. I do not propose to offer any final explanation for the 1603 Quarto's provenance here, nor to replace any current theory of the text with another. Any such theory rightfully stands as the endpoint of a project which has hardly begun; the First Quarto of *Hamlet* and other early dramatic quartos need to be examined thoroughly with fresh eyes before any conclusions about provenance can be reached, and historically such conclusions have functioned more as an obstacle to study than as an aid: the texts have been explained, and the explanation taken to obviate closer examination. The text must be studied without giving priority to any particular notion of its provenance (touring adaptation, garbled reconstruction, early draft by Shakespeare or by someone else). Everything the First Quarto has to tell us lies in its details, in its many small puzzles and clues, rather than in a single conclusion about its mystery. I propose the 1603 *Hamlet* as an unexplained and perhaps inexplicable text, full of useful information about stage practice but offering no easy key to its own identity.

Loose and Tight

Formal analysis has become associated with the idea of a fixed, transhistorical text; if everything depends upon a particular word or line in a close reading, then the existence of variant readings is imagined to undermine the critical enterprise, and the establishment of a "correct" singular text becomes a fundamental necessity. But this does not necessarily follow. Elizabethan and Jacobean dramas invite us to formal analysis of a different kind. What are the formal characteristics of a text which changes over time, of a text designed to accept and absorb modifications, even if those modifications were not originally foreseen or foreseeable? The Corambis/Polonius problem, and the decision to restrict his name to a single speaker, reveals a real formal distinction between various names in the *Hamlet* texts, a distinction which can only be made when considering the texts as a group.

We can distinguish between names that are loosely or tightly bound into *Hamlet*'s texts, names which are amenable to ready substitution or which can only be changed with real difficulty. Since the play is divided into actor's parts, the work and inconvenience of changing a name increases with each actor who speaks the name in performance; each character's use of the name includes that particular word in another performance text, all of which need alteration if the name is replaced. And while the change of a name would require only simple interlineation upon the parts, it would also require every actor whose part was changed to recall the change in performance, a tricky proposition for actors who had to perform five or six distinct dramas each week. The more characters speak a name, the more risk is involved in changing it, and the more likely a player is to accidentally say the old name rather than the new. But when only one actor speaks a character's name, the risk of changing that name is nonexistent; if the King slips and calls Polonius "Corambis," no one else on stage will contradict him. The more performers speak a character's name, the more tightly that name is bound into the script, and the harder it is to change.

The old counselor is the easiest example of a loosely bound name, confined deliberately to one player's part in every text. Whatever their reasons for changing the senior courtier's name, the players kept the option of changing it again as open as possible. When one considers the number of parts in which each character's name appears, the Queen's name, Gertred or Gertrard or Gertrude, also appears very loosely bound. Since only the King uses her personal name, that could be changed or eliminated very simply if needed. The King's personal name, such as it is, is perhaps the most loosely bound of all, entirely unspoken and thus appearing in no one's part but only in a stage direction. If any of the potential missing texts of *Hamlet* used the King's personal name, then it has been erased from performance in all the texts we have. None of these loosely bound names can be found in Hamlet's part; changes could be made without touching the longest and most complicated role in the play. If

Hamlet speaks a character's name, at least two or three other actors will also speak it, but names meant to be changed are kept out of the leading part.

By contrast, some other figures' names are spoken by a wide range of characters and would require revision of many actors' parts to change. Changing Hamlet's name would obviously be extremely difficult. But Ophelia's and Laertes' names are also frequently spoken by a wide range of characters, and consequently resistant to any easy revision. It would be easier to change three quarters of Ophelia's lines than it would be to change her name. Rosencrantz and Guildenstern's names are used by four different characters, binding those names relatively tightly into the text, because their combined names make a kind of running metrical joke; Shakespeare makes a virtuosic show of the various ways to work "Rosencrantz and Guildenstern" into five iambic feet. Moreover, Fortinbras's name is bound very tightly into the piece, spoken repeatedly by a large number of characters. One easy explanation for the persistence of Fortinbras's name is that because he exists largely offstage he must be usually discussed in third-person narrative, just as Ophelia's father must be called by name once he is dead.

On the other hand, Fortinbras is seldom discussed through paraphrase; he is not typically "the Prince of Norway," or "Norway's nephew," just as the King is never "King Claudius" and the Queen is never "Queen Gertrude." By and large, members of the play's older generation rely little on personal names but are identified almost completely by their place in the political structure, while the younger generation (Hamlet, Laertes, Fortinbras, Ophelia, and the young courtiers Rosencrantz, Guildenstern, and Horatio), whose future places in Denmark's polity are still far from any permanent determination, are identified by their personal names. Here a name is a sign of still-unfulfilled potential, either for good or ill, while those who have achieved their final position in the court hierarchy have ascended beyond personality, identified almost entirely with their titles. The namelessness is also, to some degree, a sign of status and of completion; Peter Stallybrass has pointed out the degree to which successful or triumphant Shakespeare characters shed their personal name for a generic one.[44] That the King has no name but is only "the King" is his greatest accomplishment; his murdered and defeated brother has gone from regal anonymity back to having a personal name, back again to being "Hamlet."

The tightly bound names are so resistant to change that they survive even in the text with the most complicated transmission, *Der bestrafte Brudermord*. Hamlet is still Hamlet and Ophelia Ophelia. Laertes has mutated slightly into "Leonhardus." But the King and Queen, now "Erico" and "Sigrie," have new names altogether, and Osric, who was merely a "Braggart Gentleman" in the

First Quarto, has been expanded into a character named "Phantasmo." But Osric's name, as a metatheatrical reference, opens another set of questions and shows a quite different set of revision techniques being brought to bear on the play.

Hamlet and His Siblings

In the final scene of *Hamlet*, the Prince and Horatio encounter a character whom Horatio does not recognize and Hamlet does not deign to identify. The First Quarto identifies this newcomer only as "a braggart Gentleman," the Second Quarto's stage directions call him merely "a courtier," and Hamlet never calls him anything but "sir" and "waterfly." In the Second Quarto, a second messenger enters shortly after the first has left in order to announce, among other things, what the first messenger was called: "young Osric." Later, the King will almost casually confirm (or, in the Folio, introduce) the waterfly's name, using it twice, and Laertes uses it as well. Osric's name is relatively tightly bound into the "good" texts, considering how small his role is, but the fact that he enters late would make revision simpler; any changes to Laertes' or the King's part could be made on the last few sheets of their rolls. It's worth noting that the King first calls the fop "young Osric," just as the superfluous messenger has, so that both the Folio and Second Quarto texts ensure that the audience first hears Osric's name in that particular phrase. The name is withheld for over a hundred lines and then revealed to be not merely Osric but "young Osric." The character doesn't really need a name at all, as both Hamlet and the First Quarto agree, but the name this supernumerary gets would be familiar to the audience at the Globe.

The name "Osric" is unique in Shakespeare, but not to Shakespeare. It is a stock theatrical name, albeit not an overwhelmingly popular one. An Osric appears, as the father of the love interest, in *A Knack to Know a Knave*, the same play that Kemp and the Lord Strange's Men had performed with Alleyn. Three sharers from *A Knack*'s original cast were leading members of the Chamberlain's Men at the beginning of the seventeenth century, but Kempe had left the company during the construction of the Globe. (His name appears on the initial partnership documents, but he quickly sold his share of the playhouse back to his partners and left the group entirely.)[45] The name "Osric" connects a comedy that three of the leading Chamberlain's Men (Heminges, Phillips, and Pope) had performed with the charismatic Alleyn and Kempe to a tragedy, *Hamlet*, which they acted with both stars as direct competitors.

After the Globe was built, Alleyn emerged from his two-year retirement to lead the Admiral's Men at the new Fortune, which he had helped to finance. Kempe, after a famous but financially unsuccessful morris dance to Norwich[46] and some touring on the Continent, returned to London by 1602, borrowed money from Henslowe and joined Worcester's Men at the Rose, offering particularly close competition to his old mates at the nearby Globe. The leaders of the Chamberlain's Servants had just sunk a good deal of their own personal capital into a building venture, whose now-famous thatched roof bore witness to their stretched and strained funds.[47]

In the short term the partners' investment had earned them increased theatrical competition: a third adult company playing in London's suburbs, the return to their main rivals of the only star more famous than Burbage, and the roundabout defection of their own star clown to an upstart company in their own quarter of the city. Two new companies of boy actors, suddenly back in fashion, formed around the same time, one playing in Paul's Cathedral and another renting the Blackfriars from the Burbages. Where a few years before there had been only two companies licensed to perform in the capital, each occupying its own suburb on its own side of the Thames, there were now five allowed companies, and the Chamberlain's Men had to share Southwark with Worcester's players. Meanwhile the Admiral's Men took sole possession of the northern suburbs by building the Fortune, a playhouse conceived as a grander counterpart to the Globe.[48] Alleyn and his father-in-law Henslowe stood to profit from both the Admiral's and Worcester's companies, while the Chamberlain's Men faced more commercial competition than they ever had.

One moment of widely acknowledged topicality in the Folio text of *Hamlet*, the "little eyases" passage has been used to date all the extant *Hamlet* texts to this period in theatrical history.[49] The "eyrie of children" is traditionally glossed as a reference to the revival of Paul's Boys and the Children of the Chapel, and often to the Poet's Quarrel that Jonson, Marston, and Dekker waged on the boys' companies' stages.[50] The passage is not in the Second Quarto, but the First Quarto's Gilderstone gives a more succinct version of the account Rosencrantz makes in the Folio: "Novelty carries it away, for the principal public audience that came to them are turned to private plays and to the humour of children."[51]

The allusion to the children's companies, and the complaint about their effect on the adult "tragedians of the City" was part of *Hamlet* by 1603. The "City" of course, is exactly the territory from which the adult players were excluded but which the boy players, who were technically student amateurs, could enjoy freely: the precincts of the City of London. The theatrical reference here is so explicit, and so necessary if the lines are to make any sense whatsoever, that even critics and editors disinclined to recognize intertextuality have been forced to acknowledge it. The usual presumption is that the Chamberlain's Men had to be hard pressed by the children indeed to resort to such public comment. However, the boys were not necessarily the company's chief business worry, and there are more theatrical references in the *Hamlet* texts, particularly in the "good" texts, than modern editions suggest.

The connection between the name Osric and *A Knack to Know a Knave* might serve, in a small way, as a metatheatrical reference, for the players themselves if not necessarily for the audience, pointing to the sharers' old fellows, Alleyn and Kempe. Osric's name would have a more obvious referent for auditors at the Globe, however. "Osric" was also the title character of at least one play, now lost, played by Henslowe's companies at the Rose. Henslowe notes receipts from a play called *Osric* as early as 1597, when the Admiral's Men gave it twice, and he paid three pounds apiece to Wentworth Smith and Thomas Heywood in September 1602 for a book he variously records as "marshalle oserecke" or "oserecke."[52] The combined sum of six pounds is Henslowe's usual price for an entire play, rather than additions, so Smith and Heywood probably delivered a new work, possibly associated in some way with the Admiral's Men's older piece. In any case, *Marshal Osric* was worth enough to Henslowe and to Worcester's Men for him to pay out twenty-six shillings for the title character's costume.[53] The name of the well-dressed waterfly in *Hamlet* would be instantly recognizable to Shakespeare's audience, an unmistakable intertextual reference to a property playing at the Rose.

Osric is not the only name from Henslowe's play lists to make an appearance in *Hamlet*. Hamlet shows a marked propensity to drop the names of leading characters from the Admiral's and Worcester's Men's repertoires, especially during scenes involving the visiting players, strengthening the notion that the traveling players are meant to suggest the competitors rather than the home team. Ophelia's father, announcing the arrival of the players, is greeted by Hamlet as "Jephtha(h),"[54] the title character of the biblical play which Henslowe commissioned for the Admiral's Men in May of 1602, and for which he lent sums over several months for costumes, licensing, payment to the authors (in this case, Munday and Dekker), and the expense of wine for a company reading of the script.[55] Interestingly, the "Jephthah" reference persists in *Der bestrafte Brudermord* as well as in all three of the English texts, making it far more durable than either "Corambis" or "Polonius."

A few lines earlier, Hamlet has mocked the old counselor by beginning a story, "When Roscius was an actor in Rome" (7.262; 2.2.373–74); the Elizabethan player most firmly and consistently associated with Roscius, the favorite of Cicero, was Alleyn, who was compared to the great Roman actor by Nashe, Jonson, and Fuller, among others, over a period of many years.[56] Later, after the play within the play has driven the King offstage, the exultant Hamlet sings "O Damon dear," a reference not only to the legendary Damon and Pythias but to the Admiral's Men's *Damon and Pythias*, which Henslowe commissioned from Henry Chettle in late 1599 and had licensed in 1600.[57] And just a moment before the Damon and Pythias allusion Hamlet has managed to pack the names of both Henslowe theaters into one sentence: "Would not this, sir, . . . if the rest of my fortunes turn Turk with me, with two Provençal roses on my razed shoes, earn me fellowship in a cry of players, sir?" (3.2. 253–55) This line not only associates "fortunes" and "roses" with "a cry of players" but manages to evoke one of the staples of the Admiral's Men's repertory, their stock of plays such as *Tamburlaine, Tamar Cham, Mahomet*, and *The Battle of Alcazar*, all of which feature charismatic Muslims as figures of the ranting stage "Turk." None of the individual phrases in this sentence would, by itself, seem overwhelmingly persuasive as a reference to the Admiral's Men, but clustered together as tightly as they are, "Turk" and "fortunes" and "roses" and "players," spoken only four lines after a company of pseudo-Marlovian players has left the stage, make the cumulative indication of Henslowe's theatrical tenants strong indeed. Even Hamlet's badinage with Corambis/Polonius about acting Julius Caesar, just before the play within the play, points both to Shakespeare's *Julius Caesar* and to *Caesar's Fall*, a play which Henslowe, following the established strategy of competitive imitation, commissioned from Munday, Drayton, Webster, and Middleton in May of 1602.[58] These allusions are all highly localized within a single part, Hamlet's, in conversation either with Ophelia's father or with Horatio, immediately before the entrance or after the exit of the traveling players. If Hamlet's part were being revised, these in-jokes could have been added very easily. Moreover, the theatrical allusions mutually reinforce one another through their proximity, coming in quick bunches which invite topical reading from the audience.

Hamlet is not the only character in the Chamberlain's Men's repertory with a penchant for referring to Admiral's Men's plays. In *Satiro-Mastix*, Thomas Dekker's riposte to Jonson's *Poetaster* which both the Chamberlain's Men and Paul's Boys acted between 1600 and 1602, Captain Tucca habitually conjures with the names of popular characters from the theater, and the Admiral's Men's characters are by far his favorites. Dekker's Tucca is Dekker's reinvention of another Captain Tucca in *The Poetaster*; Jonson's captain has a knack for antinomasia, addressing other characters with such grandiloquent phrases as "venerable cropshin," "Minotaurus," "Neoptolemus," "my fine Phrygian fry," and "you whoreson cantharides."[59] Dekker's version of Tucca retains the same verbal habits but draws on the public playhouses for his epithets. He calls various characters "Mephistopheles," "Ieronimo," "my smug Bel-Imperia," "my faire Angelica," "Sir Tristram," "Frier Tucke," "Maide-marian," "mad Tamburlaine," "my Long Meg a Westminster," and "royall Tamar Cham."[60] These characters, of course, are prominent in the Admiral's Servants' *Dr. Faustus*, *Spanish Tragedy*, *Orlando Furioso*, *Tristram de Lyons*, and *First* and *Second Parts of Robin Hood*, as well as the eponymous *Tamburlaine*, *Long Meg of Westminster*, and *Tamar Cham*.

Satiro-mastix's Tucca alludes to plays by other companies as well, and to amateur drama. He thunders the names of "King Gorboduck" and "King Cambises," for example, and calls a prospective bride "Gammer Gurton."[61] And he makes one unmistakable reference to *Hamlet* and its history, declaring, "My name is *Hamlet reuenge*: thou hast been at Parris garden hast not?"[62] The famous tag line from *Hamlet*, now removed from the text, is grouped with the musty staples of popular drama that fill Tucca's mouth. But even this *Hamlet* is oddly hung upon the Admiral's Men; the Paris Garden area of Southwark was not around the Globe but on the far side of the Rose. Tucca's references concentrate on the Admiral's Men's repertory to an extent which is both overwhelming and surprising in a play which is explicitly concerned with Jonson and the boy players for whom he wrote *The Poetaster*, rather than with Alleyn or Henslowe. Tucca alludes to *Alexander and Lodowick*, an Admiral's Men's play, and to their *Damon and Pythias*;[63] examples could be multiplied further. In case anyone has missed his meaning, Tucca makes the Admiral's Men's old playhouse into a term of insult: "th'ast breath as sweet as the Rose, that growes by the Beare-Garden."[64] The Rose by the Bear Garden is, of course, Henslowe's. Whatever their business with Jonson and his children, Dekker and the Chamberlain's Servants also have their adult competitors very much in mind. The kind of theatrical references *Hamlet* makes are standard practice for the Chamberlain's Men in the last few years of Elizabeth's life.

Almost all of Hamlet's references to Henslowe plays have other possible connotations. Jephthah is the hero of a popular ballad, which Hamlet quotes; Damon is a character from classical mythology as well as a stock pastoral name; Julius Caesar is of course the subject of a Chamberlain's company play, and a famous historical figure. These are the glosses typically used by an editor such as Harold Jenkins, and none of the glosses is wrong in itself. But the standard preference for nontheatrical over theatrical explanations of these lines is curious. Surely the staging of a *Jephthah* play shortly before *Hamlet* is published makes for as interesting a footnote as the existence of a ballad does. The play's existence has not been a secret; it can easily be found in Henslowe's *Diary*. And yet Jenkins, preparing exhaustive notes for his monumental *Arden* edition, consistently privileges the nondramatic rather than dramatic texts while explaining these references. The Jephthah ballad, rather than the Jephthah play, goes in Jenkins's footnote; the play is mentioned only briefly in a long end note.[65] Most editors, with less spacious and formidable apparatus, ignore the Admiral's Men's play altogether. Similar situations apply in the case of the *Damon and Pythias* reference, for which Jenkins has no place, and the *Osric* reference, mentioned in a note on the dramatis personae but not in the notes of act 5. If I single out Jenkins here, it is in part for his virtues, because he is exemplary in his kind: his annotations are scrupulously complete, with no concessions made to space, so that Jenkins's decision to include or exclude a possibility is almost always determined by his critical judgment rather than by the demands of format, and for this reason among others his *Arden Hamlet* is a landmark, a prime example for a particular school of editing. Exactly because Jenkins's edition is so authoritative, so clearly governed by the critical intelligence which every page displays, it makes a useful index of twentieth-century editors' working agenda. It is very clear that Jenkins does not want to see Henslowe anywhere near *Hamlet*.

When references to *Hamlet* appear in other plays, of course, they are considered unmistakable allusions to Shakespeare's play. Consider for example the Hamlet in *Eastward Ho!*, a footman to Gertrude the goldsmith's daughter, who grows so overwrought calling for his lady's coach that he prompts the question, "'Sfoot, Hamlet, are you mad?"[66] Lest anyone mistake the name for coincidence, the rest of act 3, scene 2 provides a short barrage of *Hamlet* references, as Gertrude sings parodies of Ophelia's songs and several characters enter toting rosemary. The play, written for the "little eyases" at the Blackfriars by Ben Jonson, George Chapman, and John Marston after the "War of the Theaters" had finished, was published after the first two quartos of *Hamlet* and cannot be read as an "influence" upon *Hamlet* but only as evidence of reception. Read in isolation, the topical references to the Chamberlain's Men's play have been used to reinforce the positions assigned *Hamlet* and *Eastward Ho!* in the English literary canon, maintaining a hierarchical relationship on which a "minor" text tweaks but simultaneously pays tribute to the cultural power of a "major" work.

Richard Horwich, writing about *Eastward Ho*'s various allusions to *Hamlet*, construes them as both "parody" and "borrowing," which "call attention to [*Eastward Ho*'s] weaknesses, and at the same time . . . enable it to borrow some of the earlier play's strengths."[67] Horwich's chief hope is that "the spectators at Blackfriars . . . may have glimpsed the majestic figure of Hamlet behind the comic figure of Touchstone (Gertrude's goldsmith father), investing him with a measure of the pathos with which Shakespeare's tragedy is filled."[68] In a sentence such as this, intertextuality seems to be imagined as a kind of rent or tear in the fabric the text, exposing its weakness by disturbing the illusion of coherence. In Horwich's words, such referentiality is "gratuitous," without "pretext or dramatic reason" and "in no way organically related to the action of the play."[69] The assumptions at work here (and I choose Horwich as an example of a mainstream critical tradition) favor the notion of a coherent, self-contained work of art which refuses to undermine its illusion of verisimilitude (if Jacobean playgoers can be presumed to have had such illusions) with any reference to competitors. However, eruptions of intertextuality can be ceded a compensatory virtue if the rent in the play's fabric shows the audience a superior, more canonical text, if the audience is allowed to glimpse Hamlet, and *Hamlet*, "behind" the less exalted play they're viewing. *Hamlet*, presumably, can be forgiven or praised for alluding to other prestigious works, to the classics, to the Bible, or to Montaigne, but cannot be imagined as deigning to acknowledge such "lesser" texts as *Marshal Osric* or *Jephthah*.

If *Eastward Ho!*'s theatrical jokes confirm its subservient place in the canon, for being a parasite upon *Hamlet*, and its inferiority as an artwork, for interrupting the theatrical "illusion" with an outside reference, what then of *Hamlet*, muttering and joking about Damon and Pythias? One school of criticism would preserve Shakespeare in a pose of lofty disregard for his competitors, imagined in retrospect as his hapless inferiors. For Shakespeare to be self-referential is acceptable, and admirable. For him to refer to his rivals is a far harder sell. Any reference to a "globe" in Shakespeare's plays can be plausibly cited as an allusion to the Globe; indeed, that has become the presumptive interpretation. A reference to fortune or to a rose is certainly not generally presumed to mean the Fortune or the Rose playhouses, and such interpretations are held to a higher standard of proof than potential references to the Globe.

Hamlet Delayed

Part of the reluctance to accept the references to the Admiral's Men involves dating. Allusions to Henslowe's *Jephthah* and *Osric* plays, written in 1602, would give all of the *Hamlet* texts a very late date indeed, close to the publication of the First Quarto and after James Roberts's registration of the play on July 26, 1602. *Jephthah* seems to have been first staged sometime that June, and *Marshal Osric* was not commissioned until that September, after *Hamlet*'s entrance in the Stationers' Register. Unless the references to *Jephthah* and *Osric* can be dismissed as coincidence, with Henslowe happening to commission entire plays about characters of those names shortly after Shakespeare's play was performed, then the *Hamlet* texts (particularly the "good" ones, which name Osric) must have been composed after Roberts's entry. If the composition of a Shakespeare play is imagined as a discrete event, with the entire text created at a single historical moment, this seems to be an impossibility. But if the *Jephthah* and *Osric* references were added through small acts of revision at different moments, those additions could have been made at any time before the plays went to press. Osric's name could have been added as late as 1604. James Roberts, whose monopoly on printing playbills led him to do frequent business with all of the acting companies, may have acquired the text from which he set the Second Quarto after he entered his claim with his guild. Even in the narrative of publishing piracy founded by A. W. Pollard, Roberts has long been cast as the proverbial "good" stationer, cooperating with the actors and solicitous of their rights. It seems *Hamlet* continued to be revised between registration and printing, and there is no reason to believe the revisions stopped after publication.

A *Hamlet* open to revision as late as 1602 or 1604 (or 1623) leaves Shakespeare himself open to charges of imitation and influence. Rather than creating a singular masterpiece on a singular occasion, and thereby influencing his lesser competitors, William Shakespeare occupies one station in an intricate network of literary exchange, responding to other writers as they respond to him. Rather than being purely his own, *Hamlet* is contaminated with all manner of verbal traces from the works of other people, both predecessors and peers. For example, a *Hamlet* as late as 1602 would be subject to the influence of the revised *Spanish Tragedy*, with its mad scenes, or of John Marston's *Antonio's Revenge*, a Paul's Boys play entered in the Stationers' Register in 1601. *Antonio's Revenge* has only a few ghostly verbal resemblances to *Hamlet* but both plays share a great many plot elements and basic motifs. In each play, the son of a murdered ruler is goaded to revenge by his father's ghost and feigns mental incompetence to throw the murderous usurper off the scent. If *Antonio's Revenge* is allowed chronological priority, the usual conclusion is that Shakespeare owes a "debt" either to Marston, whose plot he has imitated, or to the author of the *ur-Hamlet* whose plot both Marston and Shakespeare have imitated; neither option has appealed to conservative critics.[70] Chronology is taken to imply a hierarchical relationship, a literal and figurative precedence of one text over another.

The idea of composition as a discrete event promotes a corollary notion of literary influence as unidirectional. Each particular text is imagined as composed, completed, and thereby closed to all further influence from subsequent texts. However, plays which remain open to ongoing revision have the capacity for mutual influence, in which each text leaves its mark upon the other. This model places *Hamlet* firmly in its theatrical context at the outset of the seventeenth century, speaking and listening to *Antonio's Revenge*, inspiring and considering the June 1602 additions to the *Spanish Tragedy* and prompting Henslowe to commission a *Danish Tragedy* from Chettle in July 1602.[71] The three existing texts of *Hamlet* are results of a competitive revision process, reiterated over many years of repertory existence, under the pressure of rival tragedies like *Antonio's Revenge* and *The Spanish Tragedy*. Indeed, the variances between *Hamlet*'s surviving texts suggest its necessary mutability over decades of rewriting and performance. The play's survival in the theatrical marketplace is predicated on the evolution of its text during an era of breathtakingly quick development in dramatic technique, an era in which even landmark works, like Kyd's revenge tragedy, could seem outdated after less than a decade.

Hamlet's revision should not be imagined as a single, easily confined moment of rewriting, in which a hypothetical ur-play is discarded for a new, distinct and "Shakespearean" *Hamlet*. No evidence for such a radically disjunctive moment exists. To argue against the *ur-Hamlet* hypothesis is not to deny that the *Hamlet*s that Thomas Nashe saw in 1589 and Thomas Lodge saw in 1596 were different from the *Hamlet* printed in the Folio of 1623. But there is no reason to believe that Nashe, if he had seen a later *Hamlet* at the Globe, would not have identified that play, however revised, with the one he had derided a decade earlier. The *ur-Hamlet* was *Hamlet*; the play maintained a continuous identity over its long life, even as it expanded and matured. The fantasy of an *ur-Hamlet*, a text discarded and replaced completely after a single act of heroic composition, is only a corollary to the dream of an idealized definitive text, a dream which *Hamlet*'s divergent texts consistently frustrate. But no such text, and no such clean substitution, is likely to have ever existed. In fact, *Hamlet* was never entirely Shakespeare's play, and early modern drama does not easily conform to the binary divisions of outside and inside, posterior and anterior, reception and influence upon which traditional criticism depends.

Whether *The Spanish Tragedy* was revised to give Alleyn's Hieronimo more of what Burbage's Hamlet enjoyed, or *Hamlet* was revised to maintain the Prince's parity with Hieronimo, hardly matters. In neither case would the impetus for revision arise from an individual author but from the imperatives of changing theatrical tastes. Who was the imitated and who the imitator makes little difference, since the logic of the theatrical marketplace demanded a significant convergence of stage technique. Ultimately, theatrical competitors were collaborators, adapting and absorbing the innovations of their rivals. The rapid maturation of English drama in the early modern period is the result of ferociously competitive labor directed into what was essentially a joint enterprise. The Admiral's and Chamberlain's Men were of each other's party, but did not know it.

CHAPTER 4

William Shakespeare's *Sir John Oldcastle* and the Globe's William Shakespeare

> And what judgement
> Would step from this to this? What devil was't
> That thus hath cozened you at hoodman-blind?
> —*Hamlet*, F1, 3.4

The Tell-Tale Thistle

The Chamberlain's Men revised the old plays from their original repertory in many ways, and for many reasons. They updated and upgraded them. They added references to other plays within their own repertory, such as *Women Pleased* or *Julius Caesar*. They added and deleted topical references to their rivals' plays and to the rivals themselves. The jokey quotations from *Doctor Faustus* in the 1594 *Taming of a Shrew* are no longer found (and would no longer be topical) in the 1623 Folio text; during *Hamlet*'s long life it picked up references to Admiral's Men's plays, to the so-called War of the Theaters and to the revival of the boys' companies in London. These revisions served the company's interests in various ways, not least by manifesting and reinforcing their ownership of plays that had originally belonged to earlier companies. By the latter half of James I's reign the company, now the King's Servants, enjoyed clear and unchallenged possession of those old works in London's playhouses. But many of those old plays were also considered properties in the very different system of ownership maintained by the booksellers, printers, and publishers in London's Company of Stationers, a system in which the ongoing revisions of earlier plays could seem suspiciously destabilizing. The occasional, perhaps inevitable, conflicts between the players' and the printers' notion of ownership can best be illustrated by a group of bibliographically anomalous playbooks printed in 1619, playbooks which have previously been the cornerstone of a very different and anachronistic narrative of literary property. These notorious 1619 quartos reveal some London Stationers' response to the King's Men's aggressive business strategies and to the ways the King's Men deployed Shakespeare's name to secure their property claims. The Stationers would also use Shakespeare as a figure to defend their own proprietary claims, as part of a struggle that culminated in the printing of the 1623 Folio.

In 1619, William Jaggard reprinted *The First Part of Sir John Oldcastle* with a falsified date, 1600, and added a new byline: William Shakespeare. Had this addition been intended as fraud, it would have been remarkably unconvincing, since Jaggard also reprinted the phrase "acted by the Right honorable the Earl of Nottingham Lord High Admiral of England his Servants," which clearly identifies the play as belonging not to Shakespeare and his company but to their professional rivals.[1] The desire to trade on Shakespeare's reputation cannot explain the false date. Moreover, Jaggard's reasons for falsifying the date would deter him from adding Shakespeare's name unless he considered the addition valid; his deception was not aimed at the reading public, nor even at his fellow printers and booksellers, but at Shakespeare's acting partners, whom no false attribution would be likely to fool, and at the Court authorities.[2]

But since Jaggard knew his copy text had come from the Admiral's Men, he must have known that the words he printed had not been written by Shakespeare. The authorship that Jaggard asserted for Shakespeare was not a claim about the composition of a specific text but Jaggard's recognition of "Shakespeare's" claims upon a property in which *Oldcastle*'s 1619 publisher also had rights. The imagined property was not confined to a single text, nor were early modern printers bound to later notions about what Margreta de Grazia and Peter Stallybrass have called "the self-identity of the work," the idealized singularity of the verbal artifact.[3] Early modern players and stationers had competing, and often incompatible, notions of what constituted an intellectual property and what claims might be made upon it. A property, or a play, might under some circumstances be construed not as one text but a group of texts or as a distinctive element within a text. Jaggard's *Oldcastle* and the plays with which it was bound show the actors' and printers' rival models of property in contest and illuminate the King's Men's struggle to maintain and extend control over the pre-1594 plays that they identified as Shakespeare's.

No printer's name appears upon the reprinted *Oldcastle*, but Jaggard re-

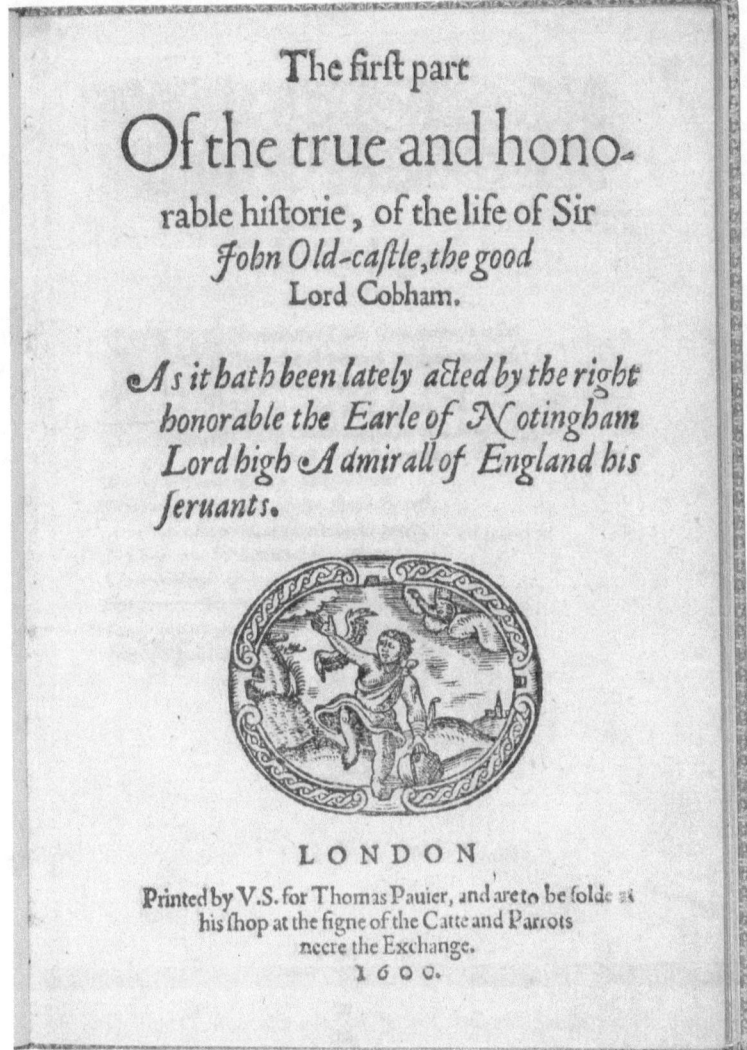

Figure 7. Title page of *The First Part of Sir John Oldcastle*, 1600. By permission of the Folger Shakespeare Library.

placed the original printer's ornament on the title page with a unique ornament from his own shop, an image now cataloged as McKerrow's device #283,[4] effectively signing the book for his fellows in London's Company of Stationers. William Jaggard had been using this particular ornament, with the motto "Heb Ddieu, Heb Ddim," since 1610.[5] (See Figures 7 and 8.) If he

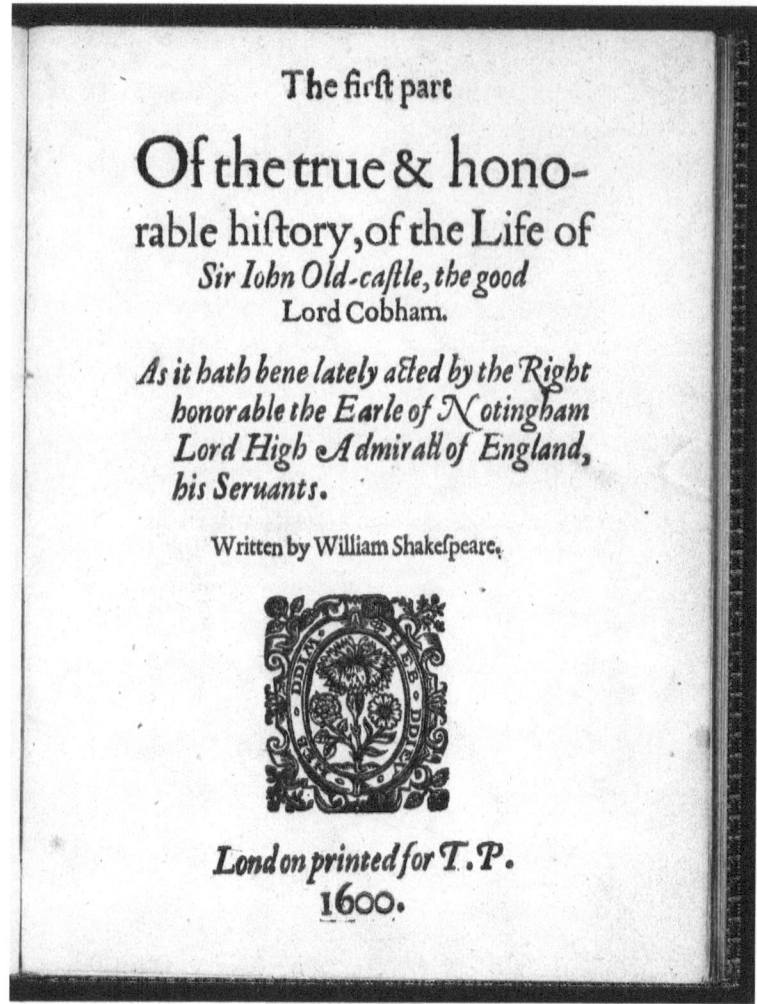

Figure 8. Title page of *The First Part of Sir John Oldcastle*, "1600" (1619). RB 62783. By permission of The Huntington Library, San Marino, California.

had really wanted to conceal what he had done from other printers, he could have used the kind of generic, impersonal devices found on truly anonymous publications of the time, the books whose makers remain unidentified still. Instead, Jaggard leaves a mark of his handiwork, a quite literal trademark, for any of his fellow craftsmen to read.

Jaggard's sign remained illegible to editors and critics for hundreds of years, until the beginning of the twentieth century, when A. W. Pollard, W. W. Greg, and William Neidig uncovered the deceptions of the 1619 *Oldcastle* and nine related dramatic quartos printed with Shakespeare's byline in the same year.[6] Beside *Oldcastle*, Jaggard reprinted two Jacobean King's Men plays (*Pericles* and *The Yorkshire Tragedy*); four chronicle plays derived from the Chamberlain's Men's initial stock of properties (*King Lear, Henry V*, and *The Whole Part of the Contention Between Lancaster and York*, which combined *The First Part of the Contention* and *The True Tragedy of Richard, Duke of York*); and three comedies from the latter half of the 1590s (*The Merchant of Venice, A Midsummer Night's Dream*, and the play now known as *The Merry Wives of Windsor* but always known in quarto publication as *Sir John Falstaff and the Merry Wives of Windsor*). Jaggard printed these quartos to be bound and sold as a single volume, a fact first established by Pollard.[7] The Jaggard title pages bear a variety of dates, most misleading although a few were accurate. Since Greg and Pollard were committed to a narrative of literary "piracy" (and used these quartos as a crucial example), they emphasized the involvement of Thomas Pavier, who held six of the relevant copyrights, rather than the embarrassing participation of Jaggard, who printed all ten plays but who also helped produce the First Folio, the central volume in the Shakespeare canon.

Thomas Pavier is still imagined as the primary agent behind the reprints of 1619, so much so that the 1619 reprints are known to critics as the "Pavier Quartos," but it is impossible to determine the actual scope of his involvement, let alone identify any party as the prime mover behind the deception. Pavier's initials are on several title pages, and he did in fact hold the rights to those titles, but other stationers are similarly named on the title pages of plays to which they had perfectly regular claims. If Pavier was a conspirator, they are equally likely to be his co-conspirators; if they were victims of a conspiracy, Pavier was equally likely to be a victim. Although Pollard and Greg asserted that Pavier had pirated the four plays that he did not own, there is no more reason to believe this is so than there is to believe that Nathaniel Butter conspired to pirate six of Pavier's plays. (In each case, the evidence is nonexistent.) Nor can the party who first proposed the deceptive title pages be identified at this remove.[8] The traditional name "Pavier Quartos" implies a conclusion about ultimate responsibility for the scheme, but that conclusion, like the name, is mainly traditional. Rather than attempting to allocate ultimate responsibility for the 1619 quartos among a number or likely or possible participants, I will refer to these quartos by the name of their printer, whose connection to the books is known beyond dispute; the quartos are unquestionably the work of William Jaggard's shop.

The discovery of Jaggard's falsely dated playbooks was an important early victory for the movement in which Greg and Pollard became leading figures. Gerald D. Johnson calls the discovery of the false dates "one of the triumphs of modern bibliography."[9] The debate over the 1619 reprints vindicated the New Bibliographers' critical practice, their detailed, analytic study of early printing methods, and resolved long-standing arguments that the false dates had caused. Previously, there had seemed to be two editions of *The Merchant of Venice* from the same year, two separate *Midsummer Night's Dream*s from 1600, and a pair of 1608 *King Lear*s, and scholars had been unable to distinguish Jaggard's imposters from the genuine first editions.[10] Moreover, the discovery of the false dates was used as a foundation on which to construct the New Bibliographical narrative of textual piracy. Pollard and J. Dover Wilson, arguing in 1919 for the existence of a class of "pirated" Shakespeare quartos, begin their argument by appealing to the discovery of the falsely dated playbooks.[11] Although there are few strictly logical connections between the kind of "piracy" Pollard and Greg allege in 1619 and the "piracies" that Pollard and Dover Wilson assert in the 1590s, being able to prove some actual forgery in the printing house emboldened Pollard and his colleagues to assert further and more pervasive deceptions in other early playbooks.

Greg, Pollard, R. B. McKerrow, and their followers were bibliographers of almost miraculous skill, able to read the traces that Jacobean printing had left upon a book nearly as well as the Jacobean printers themselves. Their hubris was to imagine that the Jacobean printers had been unable to read the same signs, that the entire guild of Stationers could be deceived while Pollard and Greg were not. It was not enough, apparently, to be William Jaggard's co-conspirator and decode the secret messages that he had left for the proper sets of eyes, not enough to recover meanings that had been left obscure for three hundred years, not even enough to make such a famous belletristic scholar as Sir Sidney Lee seem a fool. Jaggard and his contemporaries had to be made fools as well. As Laurie E. Maguire has observed, Greg tended to use the language of detective fiction to articulate his critical methods,[12] and his instincts for the mystery narrative show keenly here. Not content to play Jaggard's fellow spy, Greg had to cast himself as a detective, reading Jaggard's coded signals as clues, signs left unwittingly and unwillingly by a criminal whom Greg would unmask. For this story to work, the original crime needed to have been secret, and the criminal needed to have worked alone or with a handful of confederates. Greg points his finger at Pavier, whom he makes responsible for the copy:

One thing seems pretty certain, namely, that what [Pavier] wanted to avoid was the charge of having printed plays, to the copyright of some of which at least he had no conceivable right. . . . He had, on the other hand, no reason to make his reprints facsimiles . . . ; the date and imprint, together with a general typographical resemblance perhaps, was enough. If we may suppose some impertinent bibliographer to have pointed out that the edition of "Lear" dated 1608 which he was selling differed from that known to have issued from the Pied Bull that year, Pavier no doubt replied: "That is certainly so, sir; but have you any reason to believe that there were not two editions printed in that year? . . ." And considering that the world has accepted this answer for just on three centuries, I fancy our bibliographer would have gone away satisfied.[13]

Some elements of Greg's account have already been adjusted. Pavier was certainly the owner of most of the "copyrights," if copyright is taken as synonymous with the Company of Stationers' system of registering "copies" in various texts. But many of the larger outlines of Greg's narrative have gone unchallenged, and here he labors mightily to anticipate and dismiss important questions which threaten to undermine his entire account: why are these quartos not facsimiles? Why, indeed, are they less perfect facsimiles than Jaggard, using less personal ornaments, might have made them? Why did Jaggard leave the clue by which his handiwork has been identified?

Greg's initial assertion that the printer of 1619 "had no reason to make his reprints facsimiles" does not make sense if the reprints were meant to fool other stationers, the rightful holders of the "copyrights." The rightful printers and owners would immediately recognize the difference between the false edition and their own, and Greg's hypothetical question, "have you any reason to believe that there were not two editions printed in that year?," would be laughably ineffectual. How could the holders of the guild copyright possibly be persuaded that they had pressed a second edition of their own book, borrowed Jaggard's device to do so, and then promptly forgotten about the entire thing? Greg covers this impossibility by conjuring up "some impertinent bibliographer," long before there were any bibliographers, to swallow the lie and go away "satisfied." But the people likely to ask Jaggard questions were not disinterested academics from a later century but living, interested parties, not scholars but working printers and booksellers who could tell Jaggard's books from their own.

The question is not whether the rest of the guild could recognize Jaggard's device but how easily. How likely were his fellow stationers to recognize the "Heb Ddieu, Heb Ddim" device on a casual inspection? The best answer to this question is another: how often and how prominently had Jaggard used the device before 1619? Greg, having established that Jaggard was using the ornament by 1610, omits mention of how many times the device appeared under Jaggard's hand.[14]

From 1610 to 1618, Jaggard used device 283 on at least eight books of the forty-odd he produced in that period.[15] It appears on plays by Nathan Field and Thomas Heywood, on a reprint of Marlowe's *Edward II*, and various non-dramatic works on such subjects as religion, Ireland, and the English herring fishery. Most significantly, the device is on Jaggard's 1618 "Catalogue of such English Bookes, as have lately bene, and now are in *Printing for Publi*-cation," a comprehensive list of works currently in press which Jaggard evidently hoped to make a semiannual institution. (See Figure 9.) This is a professional industrial publication, apparently taken on Jaggard's personal initiative, requiring the cooperation of the entire guild (who had to furnish their information to Jaggard), and with the guild as a primary audience. So, nine months or a year before Jaggard undertook his deceptive quartos, he gave the "Heb Ddim, Heb Dieu" ornament a prominent place on a catalog distributed to his brother stationers. Then, when he began falsifying the title pages of those quartos, he used the one device in his inventory that the entire London book industry had most recently seen attached to his name. Either Jaggard was recklessly unconcerned that his peers would discover his deception, or he was deliberately inviting them to see what had been done. Jaggard may have intended to deceive readers outside his profession, but he marks these books with the device most likely to identify him within the circle of his trade. Jaggard's quarrel is not with the Company of Stationers or its members or its notions of bibliographic ownership, and he expects no quarrel from members of the Company.

If anything, the Jaggard who printed the 1618 catalog was thoroughly invested in the notion of printing rights, listing the owners of new or forthcoming works, publicizing and reinforcing their titles to yet-unpublished works. The *Catalogue* works as advertising for the book buyer, and especially for the bookseller looking to purchase copies for resale, but it also serves notice that the listed titles have been claimed and are not to be printed except by the rightful company claimant. William Jaggard is fighting against piracy, shoring up the Stationers' protocols of ownership. William Jaggard was the same man in 1619, and the plays he printed in that year were not part of any conspiracy to undermine Stationers' copyright. The Jaggard quartos are in fact a defense of the printers' intellectual property customs against the incursions of play-

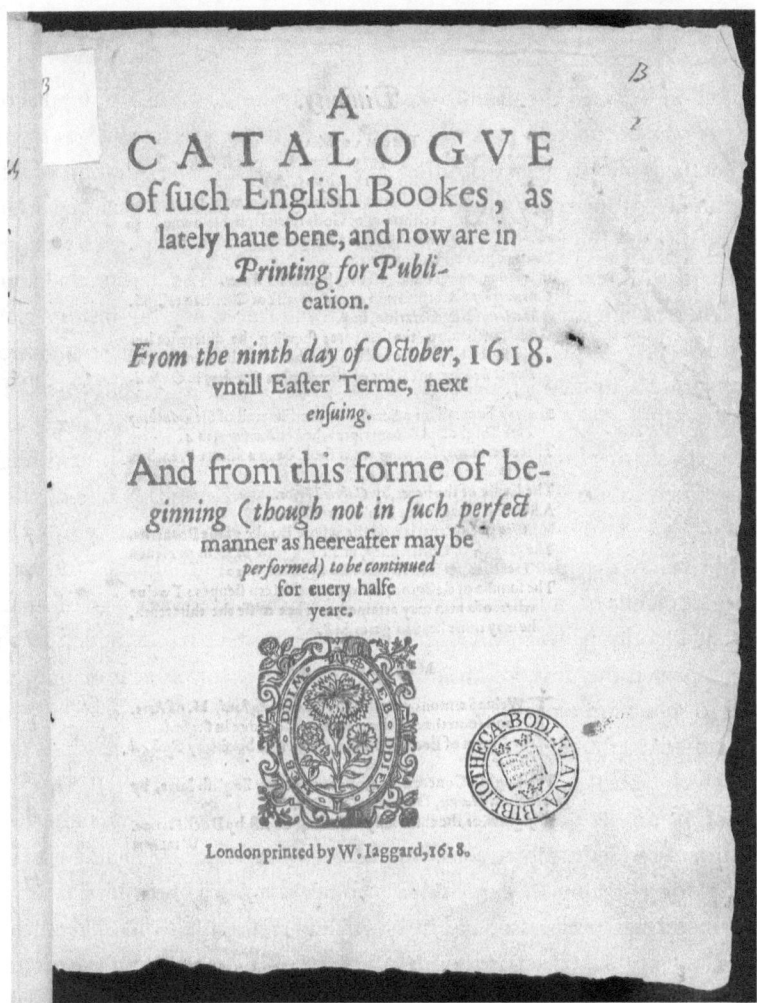

Figure 9. Title page of *A Catalogue of such English Bookes as lately have beene, and now are in Printing for Publication*, 1618. Shelfmark 2585 e.168. Courtesy the Bodleian Library, University of Oxford.

ers and courtiers with their rival models of intellectual possession. The 1619 playbooks violate the Court's rules, and the actors', as a form of protest and to defend the booksellers' notion of their rights.

"Works" and "Plays"

The friction between the printhouse and the playhouse models of intellectual property was not merely over who owned a work, or what privileges ownership entailed, but over the definition of a "work" itself. The question of what constituted a property, of where one property ended and the next began, had no easy answer. The problem of distinguishing between properties was especially hard with texts from the commercial playhouse. The Stationers habitually identified multiple plays on the same topic (most notably history plays) as a single play. Congruities of title and plot, or shared characters, sufficed to constitute a unified property as far as print rights were concerned. The actual wording of the texts was largely irrelevant; one play might have two or more texts, sharing little common language, or none. The multiple texts might be attributed to a single writer, even if he had only composed one of them. The writer's authority was not imagined as preceding or originating the work, which is to say that the writer was not imagined as a generative "author" at all. Any principle of "authorship" was applied retroactively, as a sign of shared, coherent identity between divergent texts. The writer's name, added to title pages, affirmed the unity of an intellectual property (or, in at least one case, served to split a property in two). Such retroactive ascriptions allowed a writer who had adapted an older play to be identified as the author of the source from which he had borrowed.

Actors, on the other hand, deployed writers' names to deny, rather than to affirm, any identity between similar texts. The King's Men had a vested interest in construing their revisions of older dramas as new plays, distinct from any textual predecessor and free from any rival claim. And Shakespeare's name had repeatedly been used upon printed drama as a trope for the interests of the playing company as a whole, forestalling or dissolving any rival claims on their property. His name had worked as a marker of possession but also as a marker of property boundaries themselves, sometimes identifying variant texts as a single play and sometimes creating a distinction between plays that resembled a single property. The attribution of *Oldcastle* to Shakespeare rises from stationers' attempts to anticipate, and counter, the King's Men's use of "Shakespeare" to claim dramatic properties.

Seven of the ten Jaggard quartos bear false dates, to circumvent a May 1619 edict by the Lord Chamberlain which banned any further printings of the King's Men's plays without the company's permission.[16] The Lord Chamberlain's letter to the Company of Stationers is no longer extant, but the Company's official response on May 3 survives in the Company's Court Book C:

"It is thought fitt & so ordered That no playes that his Ma^tyes players do play shalbe printed w^thout consent of some of them."[17] This prohibition has no roots in the Stationers' custom of registering individual stationers' "copy" and more closely resembles the grant of a royal monopoly, which legally superseded the guild rules. (The London Stationers' charter gave them a company monopoly on printing books, and their copy registration system represents their collective strategy for exploiting that monopoly and minimizing conflict among company members. Directly granted monopolies to individuals from the Crown took precedence over these guild arrangements.) While the Lord Chamberlain's letter was not quite a patent from the King, the combination of a highly placed courtier's command and the players' special status as the King's Servants combined to imply a good deal of force, and the Stationers clearly did not opt to oppose the Chamberlain directly or to demand more official backing for his order, which might well have been counterproductive.

Notably, the Stationers' interpretation of the Chamberlain's letter makes no distinction between new and reprinted plays; "no plays ... be printed" does not limit the prohibition to previously unpublished drama. Royal patents and monopolies in the book trade were effective retroactively, to the Stationers' evident frustration, and could override a claim that a publisher had established years or decades before. In 1618 Samuel Daniel had received a royal patent for his *History of the England*, which the stationer Nicholas Okes had registered in 1612, and the rights to which Daniel had agreed to cede, after some initial difficulty, in 1613.[18] Another patent granted in 1619 gave one Mrs. Ogden a monopoly in a book by her deceased father, although that book had been duly registered by its original publisher in 1588; Lord Chancellor Francis Bacon upheld Mrs. Ogden's privilege at trial.[19] Neither prior publication nor prior claim was defense against claims based on royal privilege; the retroactive force of such privileges was routine and well understood. Since the restraint on printing King's Men's plays derived from the Court authorities, and since the Stationers remarked no limitation of the restraint, it must have been understood as applying to the players' entire repertory. Republication of the King's Men's plays, some of which had been in print for more than twenty-five years, had been effectively forbidden, preventing the stationers who held those copyrights from making any further profit without license from the actors. In effect, the players had used their ongoing performance rights to their plays, and their favor with the Chamberlain (William Herbert, the Earl of Pembroke, to whom they would later dedicate the First Folio) to regain control over print rights that had been alienated long before.

The Chamberlain's ban was a measure imposed arbitrarily from above, without even a pretense of even-handedness. Only one playing company was protected, and the investments various stationers had made in specific plays were disregarded entirely. Certainly, no compensation was offered to those who were restrained from publishing books they had owned, at least as the Stationers understood ownership, for years. Neither was the Lord Chamberlain asserting any general principle about actors' ownership of plays. He simply bestowed control of certain plays upon certain actors, as a privilege granted to favorites. The Earl of Pembroke's family had a long tradition of interceding on the behalf of favorite poets, actors, and stationers, not least in the interest of William Herbert's uncle, Sir Philip Sidney. The King's Men themselves had a traditional relationship with Herbert, Sidney, and Dudley patrons. The connections were older than the company itself; James Burbage, father of Richard and Cuthbert Burbage, had been a leading player for Herbert's great-uncle, the Earl of Leicester, in the 1570s.[20] Nor was the connection confined to the past. On May 20, 1619, two months after Richard Burbage's death, Herbert excused himself from watching a play at court, "which I being tender-hearted could not endure to see so soon after the loss of my old acquaintance Burbage."[21] Pembroke's language reflects the inequality of his relationship with Burbage but also the sentimental affection (not merely a death but a "loss") and, more to the point, the partiality. It was seventeen days before Herbert wrote that sentimental remark that the Court of Stationers noted receipt of Herbert's letter restraining them from publishing the company's plays.

Although Herbert's decree had more legal force than the internal arrangements of the Stationers Company, it was precisely the kind of privilege which the stationers tended to resent and to resist. The tension that Joseph Loewenstein notes between "privilege and [guild] copyright"[22] had grown especially intense beginning in 1617 and 1618, "when the number of such [monopolistic] grants suddenly began to increase, and this seems to have provoked the stationers to less equivocal resistance."[23] Pembroke's command in 1619 should be understood in terms of a larger conflict in which James I's court repeatedly encroached upon the Stationers' sense of their own traditional prerogatives. Those encroachments by individual monopolists were often bitterly resented, although the Stationers were themselves dependent upon the principle of Crown privilege. One paradox arising from this tension was that many printers were far more likely to "pirate" a work with the fuller legal protections bestowed by a royal monopoly than they were to violate the unofficial sanction of company regulation. Even a printer such as John Wolfe, whom Joseph Loewenstein characterizes as a "scoundrel" given to various kinds of bibliographic deception,[24] seems never to have transgressed against copy registration, although he openly defied the patent-holders of books such as the primer and ABC. Violating Stationers' copy was a transgression against a guild brother; resisting a royal monopolist was defending oneself against an interloper, and that resistance might be open, or, to borrow Loewenstein's phrase, more equivocal.

Put simply, if a printer invested in the production of a book, acquiring the copy, casting off and setting the type, and printing hundreds of copies which would take years to sell, he expected his investment to be protected. Further, he extended a reciprocal protection to his fellow printers. However, when the Crown granted a publisher the exclusive rights to print every psalter in England (which in practice meant not that the monopolist would print the Psalms but that he would exact a fee from everyone who did), the owner's rights to the text might have seemed less evident, and less explicable. Some more noxious patents covered whole classes of books, such as books with musical notation, and others might void existing guild copyrights. Many privileged works were "pirated" by the same jobbing printers, such as the young John Wolfe, who printed the "authorized" editions at other times. Violating a monopoly could mean simply printing a book you'd printed before but not paying for the privilege of doing so. Early modern plays fell into the class of books that were protected only by guild registration, and those clear titles to guild copyright were overwhelmingly respected. The Lord Chamberlain's extraordinary grant of a categorical monopoly to the King's Men, abrogating previously established claims on many of the works included in the privilege, was precisely the kind of galling measure against which stationers tended to rebel. If Jaggard took few measures in 1619 to hide what he had done from his fellow printers, it may well be because he expected them to sympathize.

The Earl of Pembroke's edict forced Jaggard and his colleagues to exercise their traditional rights through deception, disguising most of the 1619 quartos as copies left over from earlier editions. *Pericles*, *The Yorkshire Tragedy*, and the play we now call *The Merry Wives of Windsor* are dated 1619, suggesting that they had been printed before the Lord Chamberlain's ban. *Oldcastle* kept the date from its first quarto in 1600, and its theatrical owners were still called the Admiral's Servants although that company had since changed its name several times.[25] But there would be no reason to back-date *Oldcastle* if the printers did not believe the King's Men had some claim on it; there was no edict against publishing any other company's plays. Neither did the 1619 printers put Shakespeare's name on any other plays without some reasonable basis for the attribution: all the rest had either been ascribed to Shakespeare already or would be claimed as his in the later Folio. And "piracy" of playscripts, in A. W. Pollard's imagination of the term, was hardly the booming criminal enterprise he supposed. (Peter Blayney has dismantled Pollard's narrative most thoroughly and convincingly in his essay "The Publication of Playbooks" in *A New History of Early English Drama*.) The profits of piracy would have been particularly underwhelming to substantial and respected stationers like Jaggard, or his friend Pavier, who had been promoted to high guild office in 1619 and therefore, as Gerald D. Johnson argues, had far more to lose than gain by any fraud.[26] The evidence suggests that Jaggard (and Pavier, to the extent of his involvement) did consider *The First Part of Sir John Oldcastle* Shakespeare's in 1619, even if it had not been in 1600.

What now seem the oddities of Jaggard's collection, its bibliographic deceptions and apparently miscellaneous contents, are traces of the labor which would produce the First Folio, a volume which displaces the 1619 quartos and obscures their role in the formation of the Shakespeare canon. The false dates are signs of the King's Men's struggle to control the texts which later became the Shakespeare canon; controlling the rights was a necessary prerequisite to the codification of that canon in 1623. Until that work was done, using Shakespeare's authority as a ruling idea to provide "unification and integration" for a set of "heterogeneous plays," as Margreta de Grazia has written, "the Shakespearean corpus had not yet been defined."[27] The collection of 1619 has been acknowledged as one attempt to define that nascent canon, an attempt contingent upon circumstance and the control of rights but not much more contingent on those factors than the production of the Folio would be.[28]

Typically, the ten plays from 1619 are imagined as seven canonical plays (eight including *Pericles*), authorized in every sense of that word by their inclusion in the First Folio, and three (or two) apocryphal plays, excluded from that work and its textual authority. But only hindsight makes these categories visible or meaningful. There was as yet no Shakespeare canon against which the collection could be measured. It is at least as valid, and a far better representation of the printers' circumstances, to classify the plays as six works previously ascribed to Shakespeare and four newly attributed to him. But the six attributed to Shakespeare before 1619 are not exactly the same as those attributed to him in the Folio.[29]

Four Jaggard plays are approved as Shakespeare's by both previous and posterior authority: *A Midsummer Night's Dream*, *The Merchant of Venice*, *King Lear*, and *Sir John Falstaff*. Two plays previously published as Shakespeare's, *Pericles* and *The Yorkshire Tragedy*, were to be excluded from the Folio. The four newly attributed plays are *Oldcastle*, *Henry V*, and *The First Part of the Contention between Lancaster and York* and *The True Tragedy of Richard, Duke of York* (combined, as noted above, under the title *The Whole Contention of Lancaster and York*). *Sir John Oldcastle* is clearly the odd play out here, never cited as Shakespeare's before or again, but its condition is far closer to the histories' than to the apocryphal plays'. By including *Pericles* and *A Yorkshire Tragedy*, Jaggard merely preserves earlier attributions, but printing *Oldcastle* and the other histories requires him to assert Shakespeare's authorship and contribute to the public sense of his emergent canon. The assignment of the three *Henry* plays and of *Oldcastle* to Shakespeare, the "correct" and "incorrect" attribution, must be considered part of one process.

If *Oldcastle* is the singular error in the collection, the one mistake made without precedent, the question must be: What connection to Shakespeare's work did Jaggard and his confederates perceive? The obvious link is with Falstaff, who had once been called "Oldcastle" himself. To understand how the stationers of 1619 thought of that connection, one must consider Oldcastle's and Falstaff's relationship on the stage, and the importance of disputed titles and blurred identities to the Jaggard collection as a whole.

Of Knights and Names

Considering the play's content, it may be difficult to believe any reader would mistake *Oldcastle* for one of Shakespeare's Falstaff plays. Its Sir John, "the Good Lord Cobham" as proto-Protestant martyr, is a stark contrast to Shakespeare's comical scoundrel, and the texts insist on the distinction explicitly. *Oldcastle*'s prologue doesn't want its saint mistaken for the fat rogue at the Globe: "It is no pampered glutton we present,/ Nor aged counselor to youthful sins."[30] Meanwhile, the epilogue of *2 Henry IV* is just as afraid of its fat rogue being taken for the Rose's saint: "Oldcastle died a martyr, and this is not the man."[31] Yet conflation of the characters persisted.

Eight performances of a play identified as *Oldcastle* or *Sir John Oldcastle* appear in the records: three by the Admiral's Men, two by Worcester's, and three by the Chamberlain's or King's.[32] Unless the Chamberlain's-cum-King's Servants acquired the Admiral's Men's text, or, as Roslyn Knutson believes, commissioned their own Oldcastle play (which might amply justify confusion in 1619), at least two witnesses, decades apart, identified a Falstaff play as *Oldcastle*.[33] The first reference to *Oldcastle* is in October 1599, when Henslowe pays Anthony Munday, Michael Drayton, Robert Wilson, and Richard Hathway for the script and, unusually, adds a ten-shilling bonus after the first performance.[34] The Admiral's Men repeated their successful new history in

November 1599 and March 1600, at their soon-to-be-abandoned Rose theater, which had, in 1599, acquired a new, uncomfortably close neighbor, the Chamberlain's Men's Globe.[35]

The prevailing view of *Oldcastle*, championed by Andrew Gurr, sees it as an attempt to renew the Chamberlain's Servants' embarrassment over *Henry IV, Part 1*, whose depiction of Sir John Oldcastle, Lord Cobham, had so offended the incumbent Lord Cobham that the character had to be renamed Falstaff.[36] The close proximity between the Rose and the Globe serves, in this view, to maximize the Chamberlain's Men's discomfort.[37] And certainly, *Oldcastle* was in some powerful sense a Rose play, peculiarly connected to its theater. The play, and the Rose, were eventually given to Worcester's Men, who acted *Oldcastle* twice near the start of their tenancy, in August and September 1602.[38] Indeed, Henslowe opens his accounts with the new company by listing a payment to Dekker for additions to *Oldcastle*; readying that particular play was apparently the first order of business for occupants of the Rose.[39]

The Chamberlain's Men, however, are described in a letter by Rowland White as playing "Sir John Old Castle" on March 6, 1600, at the Blackfriars address of their patron George Carey, the Lord Chamberlain, just when the new, rival history play is supposed to have been embarrassing them most.[40] Of course, an even better time to embarrass the Chamberlain's Men would have been during the brief tenure of William Brooke, Lord Cobham, as Lord Chamberlain, from 1596 to 1597. But Henslowe did not commission *Oldcastle* until autumn 1599, when Brooke had been dead for more than two years.[41] *Oldcastle* was written well after the furor over Sir John's name but fairly soon after the Globe was built, and the Chamberlain's Men seem perfectly comfortable with their Blackfriars "Oldcastle" within six months of the Rose play's debut.

If the play performed for Carey had been lifted from their competitors' repertory, and such transgressions were rare, Shakespeare's company could not have picked a better occasion; the Lord Chamberlain's pleasure would outweigh any niggling complaints from rival players, and the Chamberlain's servants would have demonstrated their proper reverence for the Lollard martyr. If, on the other hand, the Chamberlain's Men put on one of their Falstaff plays, which White identified as "Oldcastle," some auditors must have continued to identify Falstaff with his original prototype.[42]

This double identification long outlived the original controversy over *1 Henry IV*. David Scott Kastan cites various writers from the Caroline period and the Commonwealth who, in his phrase, "saw through Shakespeare's fiction" to Falstaff's initial identity as Oldcastle.[43] Moreover, Sir Henry Herbert,

Master of the Revels, who would have been an infant when *1 Henry IV* debuted, records the King's Men's performing "Old Castle" at court twice, in 1631 and 1638.[44] If Herbert saw *The Merry Wives of Windsor* or a *Henry IV* play, Falstaff and Oldcastle were still sharing their identities two decades after Jaggard reprinted *Oldcastle*.

That identification has led to a rich critical debate over the last fifteen years, beginning with Gary Taylor's "Fortunes of Oldcastle" and still far from resolved. The relationship between the characters was more complicated than simple equivalence, where one could be reduced into merely an alias for the other; one might "see through" Falstaff and remember his original identity without losing sight of his new. Indeed, the newer version was in no danger of fading from memory. As Kastan notes, there are far more references to Falstaff in the early modern period "than to any other Shakespearean character."[45] Clearly, the fat knight had appeals beyond his historical or religious identity, and the widely circulating discourse about him allowed him to be understood, as least sometimes, as distinct from his original. Falstaff never precisely ceased to be Oldcastle, but neither was he strictly confined to that identity.

Nor should his reception be understood in the terms of any single text. Most of the debate Taylor has generated has been grounded in one intertext or another. Taylor, "restoring" the character's name to Oldcastle for the complete *Oxford Shakespeare*, appeals to the uncensored ur-text of *1 Henry IV*, before external conditions forced the name change; David Bevington, having retained the Falstaff name in Oxford's stand-alone *1 Henry IV*, writes of the continuity between the fictional creature of *1 Henry IV* and those in *2 Henry IV* and *Merry Wives of Windsor*. Kristen Poole illuminates Oldcastle/Falstaff's place in a tradition of satire upon Puritans, particularly in the Martin Marprelate tracts. Foxe's *Acts and Monuments* and John Bale's *Brief Chronicle* of Oldcastle's examination and execution loom as intertexts, as does *The Famous Victories of Henry V*.

Falstaff/Oldcastle is fundamentally intertextual: derived from a character in an earlier play, and a still earlier set of stage traditions, engaged in what Bakhtin calls a "hidden polemic" with the literature of Puritan hagiography, carrying his multiple names and multiple histories with him through a series of heterogeneous texts and inconsistent narratives. And the question of "Falstaff"'s relationship to "Oldcastle" should not be limited to a single play. Although the character should not be fetishized as a consistent or "real" individual, part of Oldcastle/Falstaff's theatrical power is the persistence of his recognized identity from play to play, an identity which presents itself as extratextual to some degree because confined to no single script, nor indeed to any single chronology or genre. The imaginary character and his imaginary personality, like the imagined personality of the writer-as-author, serve as a unifying principle for disparate performances in a miscellany of texts, some written by William Shakespeare and some by others; the continuing associations between those performances enrich the figure on the stage. Oldstaff, or Falsecastle, is a series of allusions to himself. If viewers associated the Falstaff in *1 Henry IV* with Sir John Oldcastle, it would be difficult not to bring that association to *2 Henry IV* or to *Sir John Falstaff and the Merry Wives of Windsor*. Nor would the boundaries between one text and another, so important to literary critics, strike the early modern playgoer as more real or significant than the persistence of their theatrical memory.

The durable entanglement of Oldcastle and Falstaff suggests a reason for Henslowe's commission of *Sir John Oldcastle*, and for the peculiar advantages of playing it at the Rose. If *Oldcastle* was designed only as polemic, or theater criticism, the Admiral's Men might have polemicized freely from either side of the Thames. They chose not to. Instead, they used *Oldcastle* in ways likely to exploit Falstaff's popularity. The closeness of the new Globe and old Rose was apparently an advantage to *Oldcastle*'s owners. Part of the play's value lay in its proximity to the Chamberlain's Men and the Globe, making it more valuable to the Rose's tenants than to anyone else. The Rose *Oldcastle* was intended for Falstaff's audience, the playgoers who were now frequenting Southwark and the neighborhood of the Globe. Oldcastle, returned to his original name, was offered as an alternative Falstaff, or indeed as a new development in the evolution of a character who had been treading the stage, in one form or another, before Shakespeare had gotten hold of him. By reforming Oldcastle, in every sense of that verb, transfiguring him from low comedy to pious historical tragedy, the Admiral's Men simultaneously appealed to the popular taste for Protestant patriotism and assumed the greater cultural weight afforded tragedy. A collaboration that included both the stage populist Munday and the courtly nationalist Drayton suggests the company's aesthetic goals, and their sense of how the playgoers' tastes would develop. The goal was not simply to critique Falstaff but to supersede him and create the Falstaff of the future.[46] Success would not have ended conflation between the Sir Johns, of course; revision could not induce cultural amnesia in the audience and was not meant to. But one stage knight, having defeated his rival on the grounds of theatrical sophistication, would occupy the other's theatrical space and be enriched by the audience's memories of his predecessor. The eventual victor was called Falstaff.

Repertories

The King's Men had maintained theatrical control of the plays that predated their company through revision, producing new and superior texts of *King John*, *Taming of a Shrew*, *Hamlet*, and the *Henry VI* plays, among others. However, the actors' revision-centered notion of literary property was not universally embraced by printers and booksellers, as Jaggard's 1619 quarto of *Henry V* demonstrates. Thomas Pavier had acquired the rights to *Henry V* from Thomas Creed, who had come by them on the basis of his rights to the Queen's Men's *The Famous Victories of Henry V*.[47] *The Famous Victories*, most recently edited by Peter Corbin and Douglas Sedge, features such familiar set-pieces as the Dauphin's gift of tennis balls, the French King's and Dauphin's disparate evaluations of the English, Henry's byplay with a French herald before Agincourt, and Henry's final courtship of Princess Catherine. Moreover, it features a decidedly Falstaffian Sir John Oldcastle, a jocular "Jocky" who plots highway robberies with Prince Henry, feuds with the Lord Chief Justice, and finds himself exiled by the new king on much the same terms Falstaff will suffer. *The Famous Victories* in fact provides the basic narrative arc which is developed at greater length and detail in the two *Henry IV* plays and in *Henry V*, with the king's complete progress from Eastcheap to Agincourt.

The Stationers' Company seems to have considered *The Famous Victories* not merely analogous to *Henry V* but identical.[48] Creed's 1594 registration of *The Famous Victories*, and his 1598 quarto, apparently sufficed as copyright for the Chamberlain's Servants' *Henry V* as well, which Creed printed for the first time in 1600, with an attribution to its current theatrical proprietors.[49] On August 14, 1600, "the history of Henry the Vth with the battle of Agincourt," which might legitimately describe either the Queen's Men's or Chamberlain's Men's production, was "set over to the said Thomas Pavier" among several other "things formerly printed."[50] Although the 1600 *Henry V* was printed for Thomas Millington and John Busby, it was Creed's rights which were "set over" to Pavier, and neither Millington nor Busby asserted further rights to the text. Their subsequent lack of control over the play suggests that the unified *Henry V* title lay with Creed.[51] It was the Chamberlain's Men's version which Pavier had printed by Creed in 1602 and again by Jaggard in 1619. Pavier never published a copy of *The Famous Victories* and Creed printed neither play after 1602.

W. W. Greg speculates that the transfer in the Stationers' Register refers to *The Famous Victories*, which Pavier used to gain control of the Shakespeare text instead, an action Greg considered "shady."[52] If so, Pavier must have been a skillful confidence man indeed, since he got Creed, the defrauded owner, to print the text for him. What seems more likely is that Creed and Pavier conceived both texts as a single intellectual property, and that the Stationers' Register does not indicate which play was transferred in 1600 because the Stationers did not distinguish between the Queen's and Chamberlain's versions.

The Famous Victories reappears in 1617, after Creed's death, when Bernard Alsop, the junior partner who inherited his business, printed a quarto of the play, with some copies to be sold by Timothy Barlow.[53] Alsop's edition might suggest that he considered *Henry V* and *The Famous Victories* as separate properties, one of which had been sold by Creed and the other bequeathed to him, except that he attributes *The Famous Victories* to "The King's Majesty's Servants." Clearly, Alsop identifies his text with the play in the King's Men's repertory. Although *The Famous Victories* had once belonged to another troupe, if the King's Men had the current performance rights to *Henry V*, Alsop presumed that the earlier versions must belong to them as well.

Alsop was not alone in his reasoning. Several printers would retroactively ascribe Queen's or Pembroke's playbooks to Shakespeare and his company, many years after the first edition. *The Taming of a Shrew* gained a King's Servants ascription only in 1631, after the First Folio had established its provenance,[54] and *The Troublesome Reign of King John* gained the full "W. Shakespeare" byline only after work on the Folio had already begun.[55] *Romeo and Juliet*, too, gets a belated ascription to "W. Shakespeare," in an undated quarto which R. Carter Hailey has persuasively dated to 1623.[56] The holder of *Romeo*'s copyright, John Smethwick, produced two undated quartos around this time, the other being *Hamlet*, which Hailey dates conclusively to 1625.[57] Smethwick, who was a junior member of the consortium of stationers who published the Folio, takes an approach less spectacular than Jaggard's, withholding dates rather than forging them, but his apparent goals are the same: to continue asserting his right to publish King's Men's plays, including in individual editions, without the King's Men's leave or perhaps without that of Smethwick's partners in the Folio. Although it would seem late in the day for subterfuge, with the Folio already in print, Smethwick seems to have kept the date off the title page of *Hamlet* very deliberately; Hailey establishes that the title page of Q4 *Hamlet* was printed from the same standing type as the title page of Smethwick's 1625 *Usurie Arraigned*; the only differences between the two pages are the changed titles and the lack of a date on *Hamlet*.[58]

The late ascriptions to Shakespeare were not ineffectual; the publishers of the First Folio had to acknowledge their validity. When, on November 8, 1623, Isaac Jaggard and Edward Blount registered "so many of the said Copies" of Shakespeare's plays "as are not formerly entered to other men" their list omitted both *The Taming of the Shrew* and *King John*,[59] although nothing resembling the texts Jaggard and Blount used for those plays had previously been published. As Peter Blayney and others have shown, Jaggard and Blount had to accept *A Shrew* and *The Troublesome Reign* as identical with the canonical Shakespeare plays and secure the copyholders' permission to include the canonical texts in the Folio.[60] They also had to register *1 Henry VI* as the "third part" of *Henry VI*, because the plays which the Folio calls *2* and *3 Henry VI* had been published earlier as *The First Part of the Contention* and *The True Tragedy of Richard, Duke of York*; registering their new first part as the "third" kept their title from intruding on existing rights. The Stationers did not necessarily consider a literary property as a "text" in our understanding of the word, as a specific, unique literary artifact. At least one viewpoint saw a "play" as a title, plot, and set of characters and construed any revised texts as part of the original work. And a character who had achieved extratextual recognition, like Falstaff or Oldcastle, could itself become the principle which bound various properties together, in some sense becoming the "author" of a whole cluster of plays: a fictive personality that organizes texts into a visible bibliographic category. Falstaff is the text, personified. He is the book's public identity, its name. He is not the writer, but he is very plausible as the author.

The Stationers' position on intellectual property is not only logically consistent but quite reasonable. If a printer or bookseller paid a playwright or some actors for the rights to a play, and some years later another group of players (or perhaps, more provokingly, the same players) began to hawk about a "new" play on the same subject, with substantially the same title, it would be natural for the publisher to suspect chicanery. A claim that the play had been put into new words (in effect, paraphrased, no matter how gloriously superior that paraphrase might be) and had thus become a new property could not have seemed overwhelmingly persuasive. The new version's glorious superiority would only make matters worse. In Blayney's words, the Stationers' Company guaranteed a copy registrant "not only the exclusive right to reprint the text, but also the right to a fair chance to recur his costs," and the guild intervened to block publications which would compete too closely for another book's readers.[61] Certainly, a new *Henry V* or *King John* would compete directly with earlier editions and bring direct economic harm to the original publisher (particularly in a business which required long-term investments in inventory, because a single printing might not sell out for years). And a vastly improved *Henry V* or *King John* would provide more powerful competition, making the earlier version worthless. Indeed, the plays were designed to do precisely that. The King's Men had specifically intended their revised scripts to compete with and displace older texts. Their business methods were, by necessity, antithetical to the Stationers'.

Enter Shakespeare, Dressed as an Author

The publishers who ascribed *The Famous Victories* or *The Troublesome Reign* to Shakespeare did not necessarily believe Shakespeare had penned the precise assortment of words that went onto their pages, nor would they need to believe so, as their interest was not in the precisely assorted words. Rather, the phrase "by William Shakespeare" signals a property to which he, and his company, might assert some claim; the words "William Shakespeare" themselves can be taken as a figure for the interest of the King's Men.[62] That interest might not have arisen until long after the original text had been written and set in print; the issue was how the claim might affect control of the property. To place Shakespeare's name on a text was to assert identity between the play one owned and the play the King's Servants currently performed. Asserting that identity protected the stationer's interest in the work and forestalled attempts to displace one's text with a newer, more "authentic" version.

Claims of authorship could be deployed for the opposite purpose as well. Before *King John* or *Oldcastle* gained their ascriptions to Shakespeare, Nathaniel Butter registered and published a new version of the old chronicle play *King Leir*, which had been registered in 1594 and printed in 1605 by Simon Stafford for John Wright.[63] Butter's name for his text, both in the Register and on the title page, was *Mr. William Shakespeare His True Chronicle History of the Life and Death of King Lear. . . .* ,[64] the one occasion in Shakespeare's life as a dramatist when his name went above the title. In fact, Shakespeare's name is an integral part of this title; Butter, and his occasional partner John Busby, were specifically registering Shakespeare's version of the play, as distinct from the text that Wright owned. Stallybrass argues that Shakespeare's name is not placed above *Lear*'s title to herald the "arrival of the 'author' in his most heroic form" but to prevent Lear from being "mistaken for . . . *Leir*," and Kastan considers the authorial name a tool to "individualize and protect Butter's property," a "mark of distinction" to "differentiate" it from the early play.[65] In fact, Shakespeare's name differentiates *Lear* from *Leir* in the most literal way, not merely avoiding confusion between two existing titles but creating the perception of difference where none had been.

Butter's title page goes on to mention the Gloucester plot and the royal favor the play has received: *with the unfortunate life of Edgar, son and heir to the Earl of Gloucester, and his sullen and assumed humor of Tom of Bedlam. As it was played before the King's Majesty at Whitehall upon St. Stephen's night in Christmas Holidays. By His Majesty's Servants playing usually at the Globe on the Bankside.* All of this is to some extent advertising for the book buyer, but it also functions as a property claim, specifically listing the elements which set this text apart from its predecessor. The addition of the Gloucester material is the most obvious difference between the two plots, and the royal pleasure is a valuable imprimatur. (What could be dishonest, if the King approves it? And if *Lear* were simply an old play, would the Master of Revels have scheduled it first in the Court's Christmas season?) *Lear* is being identified as the version performed by the King's Men, the version given at Court, the version with Edgar, and, first of all, as the version written by Shakespeare. The claim begins with the author, and a separate right to copy was asserted, although the economic competition could hardly have been more direct.

Here is the author as creator: Shakespeare's name creates two plays as individual properties, where there had been only one. The author's name, his authority, becomes the distinctive element which differentiates the text from its predecessor and provides the new work an independent existence. Just as Heminges and Condell use Shakespeare's name "synecdochally," in de Grazia's formulation, as a "bibliographical rubric" to make the "heterogeneous printed and scripted textual pieces" collected in the Folio "coalesce," so Butter uses the author's name as a synecdoche for a whole generation of development in dramatic technique.[66] The difference between *Leir* and *Lear* is the 1590s and the artistic growth that English theater saw in those years. The change, however rapid, was collective, and in many ways incremental, the work of dozens of actors and poets in the London playhouses, but Butter reduces that activity to the achievement of an individual personality, the author, whose labor transforms an old play into something new and different. *Lear* will no longer be identified with its previous self but with its new "author," and so Butter uses the principle of authorship to dissolve previous claims on his property. His stratagem must have taught the other stationers how tenuous their rights to "Shakespeare's" works really were and given a strong incentive for adding Shakespeare's byline to new editions. If the existing print rights to a play could be abrogated by adding an author's name to a new imprint, the current owners had to make that addition themselves, before an interloper did. Attributions were not added to plays like *The Famous Victories* and *The Troublesome Reign* with an intent to defraud buyers; rather, they were meant to block an anticipated fraud against the legitimate owners.

Most of the 1619 quartos had vexed ownerships or murky provenances, or both. *Henry V* and the *Henry VI* plays have been discussed. *Pericles*'s print rights had changed hands several times, but the terms of the transactions are lost. Blount had registered the play in 1608 but not printed it, and after Pavier's death in 1626 the successors to his copyrights seem to have believed they owned *Pericles*.[67] In the mean time, two 1609 quartos were printed by Henry Gosson, Pavier's partner in a ballad-publishing combine, while Simon Stafford, who had known Pavier since their days in the Drapers' Company, printed another quarto in 1611. How the play first left Blount's control isn't certain, but when he turned his hand to the First Folio, *Pericles*'s attribution, like *The Yorkshire Tragedy*'s, would be denied by Heminges and Condell.[68]

The original publishers of *The Merchant of Venice* and *A Midsummer Night's Dream* were dead, and the rights unclear. Lawrence Heyes claimed his father's lapsed rights to *The Merchant of Venice* in July 1619, officially registering the claim on July 8, which has been construed as a response to the 1619 quartos.[69] Jaggard's quarto does not name the senior Heyes but rather James Roberts, who had first registered the work and whose business Jaggard had bought around 1608, and from whose stock the "Heb Ddieu, Heb Ddim" ornament had come.[70] Jaggard may have believed that the rights had reverted from Heyes to Roberts and thereafter transferred to him; he may have discovered Roberts's old right in the play without discovering its later transfer; in any case Lawrence Heyes's entry underscores *Merchant*'s insecure title in early 1619. The apparent extinction of the legitimate rights made these plays especially vulnerable to appropriation; but the King's Men, intent on voiding the extant print rights to their plays, were the most likely to appropriate it, and a new impression was the best defense against their revisions of copyright history.[71]

Mr. William Shakespeare his True Chronicle History of King Lear may have been printed with Nathaniel Butter's permission, as Greg speculates, especially if he felt the King's Men might try to supersede his text, as he had superseded *King Leir*.[72] But his title to the "authorial" *Lear* did not necessarily inspire universal respect, and the 1619 quarto may be a kind of retaliatory trespass, reappropriating the literary property Butter had appropriated from the owners of *Leir* (John Wright and Simon Stafford, the most recent publisher of *Pericles*).[73]

Neither would Arthur Johnson's rights to *Sir John Falstaff* inevitably command recognition from the owner of *Sir John Oldcastle*. Radical differences of genre and tone notwithstanding, the ongoing identification between the title characters would undermine any certain boundary between the two plays as literary properties. One of the titles might even be used to gain possession of the other. The best available protection for a stationer was to assert control of both texts, and as many other texts featuring the lead character as possible, so that his claim on Oldcastle/Falstaff was beyond dispute. *Sir John Oldcastle* was a Shakespeare play in this sense, a play that Shakespeare's partners might appropriate through a textual double. After all, the King's Men had appropriated other plays, which had once belonged to other companies, by providing a new text and naming an author. Shakespeare's name on Jaggard's title page asserts the identity of the publisher's and author's property, so that the differentiating power of the authorial name cannot create a second property from the first.

The King's Men's response to the 1619 quartos, and the property claims they embodied, is inscribed in the First Folio. Of Jaggard's ten quartos, only the two dead men's texts, *Midsummer Night's Dream* and *Merchant of Venice*, enter the Folio largely unchanged. Heminges and Condell discarded three of the other plays and provided new texts for the remaining five. Even the quartos of *Lear* and *Henry V*, which had supplanted earlier texts, were exchanged for revised versions. The Folio also provided a new text for one of the texts Smethwick had printed without a date, *Hamlet*, although the Folio *Romeo and Juliet* shares some emendations with Smethwick's undated quarto of that play. *Romeo and Juliet* is the one play from the standard list of "bad" quartos that did not gain a new substantive text in the Folio. But taken together, Smethwick's undated quartos and the Jaggard quartos (excluding the two plays without a living stationer to claim them) constitute nearly the entire list of "bad" quartos; the sole exception is *The Taming of a Shrew*, also owned by Smethwick.

Sir John Falstaff and the Merry Wives of Windsor not only gained a new text but lost the first half of its title, becoming *The Merry Wives of Windsor* thereafter. Although *Falstaff* might seem the more logical name, the Folio's truncated title bears no dangerous resemblances to the title of *Sir John Oldcastle*. At the same time Shakespeare's name, no longer necessary, is dropped from the title of *Lear*. Shakespeare's authorizing name was now attached to the whole volume and could be removed from individual plays.

At first glance it seems paradoxical that booksellers, who dealt in the permanent medium of the printed text, championed a fluid, inclusive concept of literary property, in which a single work might have many versions, while actors like Heminges and Condell, adapting their scripts to suit opportunity and need, would promote the notion of a fixed and singular literary object, of "the perfect and full originals" that would later be advertised in the first Beaumont and Fletcher Folio.[74] The actors' and stationers' positions were dictated by practical economics more than deep philosophical principle; some individuals, like Butter, might embrace the actors' model for intellectual property (differentiating *Lear* from *Leir*) rather than the Stationers', if it happened to give him a commercial advantage. As a group, the printers and booksellers needed to preserve their expensive, slow-selling wares from any rapid change and to discourage radical revisions (although small-scale additions and corrections, which enhanced the value of a second edition without affecting title, were naturally welcome). The actors, whose art was confined to the moment of performance and whose business demanded swift adaptation, naturally valued their newest texts and sought recompense for the cost and labor of revision. The King's Men's story of "stolen and surreptitious copies" and their related account of Shakespeare's compositional process dehistoricize the texts in the hope of current gain, disowning all previous incarnations and disinheriting previous owners.[75] Heminges and Condell were revisionists committed to denying revision.

In the Folio's address "To the great Variety of Readers," Heminges and Condell offer the elusive ideal of a definitive Shakespeare text, with copies "perfect of their limbs, and . . . absolute in their numbers, as he conceived them," and a yearning for that promised Grail has haunted textual scholars ever since. But Heminges's and Condell's promise is not about the text at all. One of their motives is frankly commercial, and they make no attempt to hide it. The first paragraph of their preface to the general reader exhorts customers to read the work "but buy it first," since payment "commends a Book best, says the Stationer." Heminges and Condell may ascribe their economic motives to a proverbial, straw-man "Stationer," but the message is their own: "whatever you do, buy." Naturally, the charge of "stolen and surreptitious copies" suits their business agenda, by discrediting any rival editions of the plays. But Heminges and Condell's idealized notion of the text is also an expression of their trade.

Margreta de Grazia has explored how the Folio's prefatory materials use the imagery of the natural body and familial succession to construct authorship.[76] But Heminges's and Condell's account of Shakespeare the author also depicts writing in largely theatrical terms. Shakespeare,

> as he was a happy imitator of Nature, was a most gentle expresser of it. His mind and hand went together: And what he thought, he uttered with that easiness, that we have scarce received from him a blot in his papers.

Shakespeare's talent as a poet or "expresser" of nature is linked to his gift as a "happy imitator" on the stage. His effortless "easiness," the synchronized purpose of his mind and hand, suggest not the labors of composition but rather a *performance of composition*, a present-tense speech act with the theatrical illusion of spontaneity. Most interestingly, Heminges and Condell imagine Shakespeare's words not as what he penned but as what he *uttered*, as words spoken aloud at the moment of conception and also, in the prevalent seventeenth-century meaning of "uttered," as things offered for sale upon the market.

Heminges's and Condell's account should not be taken for literal truth; the extent of Shakespeare's borrowings from other sources, and the divergent versions of his texts, disprove it. But the actor's trade demands that he conceal the work preparatory to performance, that his actions in front of the spectators seem unpremeditated and effortless. The idealized Shakespeare text which Heminges and Condell imagine is a copy without compositional history, eclipsing past indecisions and labors in an eternal, superbly consummated present. It is the text on stage: not the legendary playhouse copy, or a faithful record of any performance, but a performance of its own, a self-representation that denies its own prior history. Those who have taken Heminges and Condell at their word, hoping for some unmediated record of the authorial intent, have made a serious miscalculation. The writer, William Shakespeare, is not to be found in the Folio pages. The figure critics have embraced is an actor.

A Local Habitation

Heminges's and Condell's appeal to a heroic author is also a tactical move in the actors' struggle for authority over their audience, an assertion of their right to govern the interpretation of the text. In Heminges's and Condell's formulation, neither performers nor customers are entitled to ultimate control of the play, and both must defer to the original intentions of the author, which the players will take it upon themselves to enact. Of course, the actors also figure themselves as the best available representatives of the playwright. A dead author is more rhetorically useful than a dead actor; when Burbage goes he is gone, but Shakespeare's ghost can be retained as a controlling principle, allowing the players to assert their power over the texts while disowning their private motives and appealing to the (infinitely demanding, infinitely flexible) claims of their departed colleague, the author.

The prefatory material of the Folio Heminges and Condell authorized does many different kinds of cultural work and has been the object of enormously fruitful study over the last few decades. It promotes the plays' economic value on a number of fronts, it consolidates and officially legitimates the discourse of Shakespeare's authorship, it places the author within a dense nexus of literary and patronage relationships, and it delegitimizes the quarto texts of the plays. It furthermore monumentalizes Shakespeare, as Laurie E. Maguire has demonstrated, serving as a kind of bibliographical funeral monument.[77] But it also, tellingly, locates Shakespeare, both within a canon of English dramatists and within a very specific theatrical structure. The Folio begins Shakespeare's special metonymic association with the Globe.

The contributors to 1623's official commemorative volume do not merely celebrate the deceased but also refute rival, and now explicitly "unofficial," attempts at elegy. Some of these hidden polemics are as subtle as the decision to list one poet rather than another among Shakespeare's peers, and other are palpably direct, such as Jonson's response to William Basse's elegy "On Mr. Wm. Shakespeare" and to a Leonard Digges poem ("Poets are born, not made") which was not published until John Benson's 1640 edition of Shakespeare's *Poems* but whose language Jonson specifically engages and refutes. It is clear that Jonson has seen both Basse's and Digges's elegies in manuscript. (Digges provided another, more subdued, poem for the 1623 volume; it is printed between the table of contents and the beginning of *The Tempest*.) Webster, who had once lumped Shakespeare with Dekker and Heywood and damned them all with faint praise about "happy and copious industry,"[78] is not among the contributors to the Folio. Neither is the "Water Poet" John Taylor, who had listed Shakespeare on a roll of poetic honor which included Chaucer, Spenser, Beaumont, and Sidney but also had room in his canon for Robert Greene, Thomas Nashe, Samuel Daniel, Sir John Harington, Sir Edward Dyer, and Joshua Sylvester.[79] This, as seems painfully apparent in retrospect, would never do.

The Folio entrusts the care of Shakespeare's legacy to a circle of designated guardians, who assign Shakespeare a more privileged rank in a more carefully reasoned canon. Ben Jonson does not consign Shakespeare to Sylvester's foothill of Parnassus or rank him alongside Thomas Heywood but places him above his English "peers"—"how far thou didst our *Lilly* out-shine, /Or sporting *Kyd*, or *Marlowe's* mighty line"—and even places him above the classical dramatists: "thund'ring *Aeschylus*, / *Euripides* and *Sophocles*," Marcus Pacuvius, Lucius Annius, Seneca, "tart *Aristophanes*, / Neat *Terence* [and] witty *Plautus*."[80] This is far more exalted company than Sir Edward Dyer, and rather better than Shakespeare enjoys even in such works as Meres's *Palladis Tamia*. But Jonson observes strict limits on his praise. Except for Chaucer and Spenser (who are mentioned because of the William Basse elegy), Shakespeare is compared only to fellow dramatists. (Digges's Folio contribution does manage a glancing allusion to Ovid, to whom Shakespeare was often compared in allusions to his narrative poems.)[81] Neither is there any reference to Shakespeare's nondramatic works, although other tributes routinely praise his *Venus and Adonis* and especially *The Rape of Lucrece*. Shakespeare is figured within the Folio strictly as a dramatic poet, suited to a strictly dramatic collection, even if this means stripping away central elements of his prior reputation.

Moreover, Jonson is careful not to compare Shakespeare to any living playwright. Some of this is politic, of course, in that no working writers are slighted or insulted. But it also places a tacit qualification on all of Jonson's praises: Shakespeare is imagined as the greatest playwright among the dead, a stage poet who triumphed over all of his predecessors and yet not necessarily the better (nor even necessarily the peer) of his best successors. The Folio material is carefully agnostic about the question of John Fletcher, the King's Men's chief playwright in 1623 (and it equivocates about Francis Beaumont, who is also mentioned primarily because of the Basse poem). The King's Men want their old friend and fellow praised, but not at the expense of their new material; the Folio does not even mention Fletcher's existence.

Jonson does not commit John Webster's rudeness by openly rating Shakespeare behind more fashionable or learned Jacobean playwrights (Fletcher, Chapman, Jonson himself), but neither does he present any obstacle to that conclusion. At times, it seems, he praises with the faintest condemnation. Jonson's Shakespeare is "for all time," certainly, as are most or all of the dramatists he has surpassed; just as Aeschylus and Sophocles have remained immortal after being outdone by Shakespeare, Shakespeare will remain immortal after being outdone. And while Shakespeare is the "Soul of the Age," in Jonson's famous phrase,[82] precisely which age is left tantalizingly open. Those still enthusiastic for Shakespeare's plays might take him for the reigning genius of the English stage, while sophisticates might opt to view him as the tutelary spirit of an era that had recently passed away.

But the prefatory matter does not merely place Shakespeare among his literary peers. It also locates him in perfectly literal ways, associating him with particular sites and implicitly excluding him from others. The Folio apparatus makes the first published reference to Shakespeare's Stratford breeding, and it makes the second as well. First Jonson apostrophizes the poet as the "Sweet Swan of Avon,"[83] and then Digges drops a mention of his "Stratford Monument." For the first time in the written discourse about Shakespeare's authorship he is marked as a provincial, native to other ground and now buried beneath it. He is more absent even than the rest of the dead, without so much as a London resting place. Shakespeare is deceased, and Shakespeare is displaced, belonging not to the precincts of the capital city but to the provinces and to the suburbs.

Here is the root of Jonson's famous "monument without a tomb" trope, his forcible revision of William Basse's Poet's Corner fantasy. Basse's verse, circulated widely in manuscript, begins:

> Renowned Spencer, lye a thought more nye
> To learned Chaucer, and rare Beaumont lye
> A little nearer Spenser to make roome
> For Shakespeare in your threefold fowerfold Tombe.[84]

Jonson's riposte, while apparently inviting Shakespeare's apotheosis, spares the poets buried in Westminster this indignity, and indeed any other concession to Shakespeare:

> I will not lodge thee by
> *Chaucer*, or *Spenser*, or bid *Beaumont* lie
> A little further to make thee a room:
> Thou art a Monument without a Tomb,
> And art alive still, while thy Book doth live.

The passage's ambivalence is exquisite. Shakespeare transcends his death but also, taking the words literally, fails to make Westminster Abbey's cut; a figure of Beaumont's magnitude is not to be inconvenienced for a mere Shakespeare. Jonson displaces Basse's manuscript poem with his own "official" printed one, and at the same time he displaces Shakespeare's body, rejecting the imaginary resting place Basse proposes but also, bizarrely, seeming to deny that Shakespeare possesses any burial place at all. It is Digges's contribution to the Folio, not Jonson's, that acknowledges the Stratford monument. Jonson prefers to imagine Shakespeare ascending the heavens as a star, exerting astrological influence on the stage. Jonson describes a restless, groundless spirit, "alive still," whose presence is reconstituted through the appreciation of art.

Where is the proper place for the recuperation of this poet? Not at Westminster Abbey. Not in Stratford (where none of the contributors proposes to go). Jonson's answer is more suggestive than concrete, as he imagines the "Sweet Swan of *Avon*" returning:

> what a sight it were
> To see thee in our waters yet appear,

And make those flights upon the banks of Thames
That so did take our *Eliza*, and our *James*!

The swan alights upon the boundary between London and its southern suburbs. The juxtaposition of James's and Elizabeth's names with the river perhaps evokes Whitehall Palace, just up the Thames from London, although the mention of both monarchs emphasizes Shakespeare's membership in an older generation (Shakespeare not only entertained the king of the last two decades, but the monarch before that as well). But court performances aside, "the banks of Thames" tends to evoke the King's Men's Bankside theater, the playhouse which most Londoners could only reach by crossing the river. Anyone seeking the "flights" of Shakespeare's dramatic poetry should seek the Thames, and the stage that Shakespeare, as "star of poets" will "chide" and "cheer" from the heavens.[85]

Hugh Holland's elegy to "the Famous Scenic Poet, Master William Shakespeare" (still defined exclusively as a dramatist) locates Shakespeare far more concretely, lauding "the dainty Playes,/ Which made the Globe of heav'n and earth to ring."[86] The pun on the theater's name could hardly be more pointed. Shakespeare is specifically the poet of the Globe; no such association is made between the playwright and the Blackfriars. Indeed, the Folio's sole reference to the indoor playhouse gives no sign that the King's Men own it. That information must be supplied by the reader. Heminges and Condell, themselves preeminent among the Blackfriars' owners, allude to their private theater in the same terms and in the same breath as a rival house. "Though you be a Magistrate of wit," they caution the reader, "and sit on the Stage at *Black-friars*, or the *Cock-pit*, to arraign Playes daily," Shakespeare's plays should nonetheless be considered immune from censure.[87] Heminges and Condell are sketching a sophisticated and somewhat prodigal customer, apparently just the kind of *cognoscento* from whom Shakespeare must be protected, but they make no distinction between another company's playhouse and their own. A reader at any great distance from Jacobean London, whether in a distant shire or in the provinces of another century, is given no reason to suppose that the Blackfriars has become the King's Men's principal theater, or that Fletcher has become their principal dramatist. But such a reader will learn about the Globe before reaching the table of contents.

Heminges and Condell have little obvious reason to promote the Globe at the expense of the Blackfriars. The indoor theater was a more profitable venture for them; receipts from the early Caroline period show that the Blackfriars brought in more than twice the average sum for each performance,[88] and the two men themselves owned a significantly larger proportion of the Blackfriars than of the Globe.[89] Quarto editions of individual King's Men's plays in the period mention the Blackfriars as frequently as the Globe, or a bit more often.[90] The Blackfriars was the company's primary theater, but Shakespeare is being connected primarily with the Globe.

Whatever that connection, it was neither natural nor strictly biographical, since the Globe they were promoting was a reconstruction where Shakespeare had never performed, and for which he had written none of his plays. (Shakespeare's dramatic career and the original Globe had ended together, with the fiery debut of *Henry VIII*.) While the King's Men seem to have performed all of their plays at both of their venues, Heminges and Condell evidently perceive some homology between Shakespeare's audience and the customers at the Globe, which leads them to promote each in terms of the other. The leading playwright of the last generation is bound up with the (reconstructed) leading playhouse of that generation, the place where spectators who want him seem most likely to seek him. Shakespeare becomes the poet of the backup venue, the muse of the off-season; his colleagues have left him to the second-best house. The Folio's efforts to link Shakespeare's plays with this particular theater extends beyond the prefatory apparatus into the texts of some of plays, where the original provenance of the script is presented as a crucial interpretive key.

Introducing *Henry V*

Virtually all of the references to the Globe playhouse within Shakespeare's plays come within the Folio versions. Rosencrantz's allusion to the Globe's emblem, "Hercules and his load," comes only in the Folio's *Hamlet* (2.2.345–346), where it is embedded in a topical passage about theatrical events, the infamous "eyrie of little eyases" from twenty years before the Folio's publication. The Chorus's famous plaint about the confines of the "wooden O" appears, as do the rest of the Chorus's lines, only in the Folio *Henry V*. And if the Globe's motto was indeed *Totus mundus agit histrionem*, a premise upon which Tiffany Stern has cast serious doubt, then Shakespeare's winking paraphrase of that motto occurs in *As You Like It*, a play never published in quarto at all.[91]

The *Henry V* and *Hamlet* passages are precisely those that would have needed to be cut to suit varying performance spaces and circumstances. To allude to the wooden O during a performance at Whitehall would be, at best, mysterious. To continue telling Hamlet about the little eyases during the 1620s would be decidedly odd, since the child companies had long been out of business and some of the little eyases themselves were full-grown partners in the King's Men. (It would have been oddest of all in the Blackfriars, the original "eyrie of children" that Rosencrantz describes.) Yet these very passages, crying out for edification from the margin, are included in a monumental collection of plays, as exemplars of the "true original copies." The Folio suggests, repeatedly, that these plays are best understood not in the prestige publishing format in which the reader encounters them but in a specific London playhouse, which the actors involved with the volume happen to own.

Most considerations of *Henry V*'s Chorus have been directed toward original performance conditions, which is precisely where the Chorus directs our attention, but it is worth considering how the play's choral metatheatricality functions in the context of print. The Chorus's apologies for the insufficiency of theatrical illusion, for the discrepancy between the represented action and what the playgoer actually sees, work very differently on the page, where the reader is not a playgoer and has nothing to see. On stage, the Chorus compares a wished-for and an actual spectacle, what the actors would like to show and what they will realize on the stage. In print, the Chorus is actually comparing two spectacles that the reader cannot see, offering both the original historical events and their theatrical representation as objects for the reader's frustrated desire.

The opening lines of the prologue bemoan the impossibility of staging history itself and famously yearn to have "A kingdom for a stage, princes to act,/ And monarchs to behold the swelling scene," and for "warlike Harry, like himself" to portray Henry V (Prologue 3–5).[92] But if *Henry V*'s Chorus draws attention in performance to the inadequacies of theatrical representation, the Chorus on the page calls attention to the lack of even this theatrical substitute. There is not only no kingdom but no stage, no one at all to act, no swelling scene to behold, and very little audience to behold it. If the Chorus's "wooden O" (14) is an imperfect substitute for the battlefield of Agincourt, the reader lacks even that wooden O; the playhouse can only manage "four or five most vile and ragged foils" (4.0.50) for the battle scene, but the printed book cannot manage even that. The playgoer "from a few" must "make a million," but the reader isn't even given the few. If the spectators' imagination must work hard to supplement the staged spectacle, the readers' imagination must work harder.

The Folio text of *Henry V* gives the reader words that make no sense, that have no referent, outside the context of the Southwark playhouse. The complaints about "this cockpit" and "this wooden O" (Prologue 11, 13), like the later reference to "the playhouse" (2.0.36) cannot possibly be explained in terms of the play's nominal action. The reader is not allowed to forget that this play was meant to be staged, so that the text is only a poor substitute for a poor substitute. The Folio provides its reader deliberate aporia, moments when the text points to itself as inherently insufficient and prompts the reader to seek satisfaction or resolution elsewhere.

Moreover, the play is meant to be staged in a specific place, in a specific way, in one of the circular public playhouses which existed only in the London suburbs, and the Chorus offers the reader a literal site for frustrated desire. One may read *Henry V*, but not without being reminded that it would be better to see it staged, and better to see it staged by the King's Men at the Globe in Southwark; no amateur or provincial venue suits the texts. Even the fashionable Blackfriars, or the exalted precincts of Court, are merely substitutes. The text can be read anywhere but always suggests to readers that they should be somewhere else. It works to create a sense of lack: the lack of the right place, the lack of the right people to speak the words.

The 1623 collection is a monument not simply to Shakespeare himself but to the King's Men's own history. Shakespeare's plays are a testament to the company's sustained success over a generation, just as the volume's honor roll of "Principall Actors in all these plays" is, and the book locates a great deal of the plays' value in their longevity. The fashionable theatergoer, it is implied, the playgoer who might censure at the Blackfriars, should understand these long-established plays as part of the King's Men's historic and institutional glory. But to the extent that the Folio tries to lure customers to the playhouse, the fashionable spectator is not its primary audience. The Blackfriars did not want for patrons, and fashionable playgoers were lured there by current fashion. The Folio aims, however subtly, at attracting a rather less chic group who might be attracted to older plays at the more accessible and less expensive playhouse. The Globe, with space for perhaps three times as many spectators as the Blackfriars held, and opened largely during the court vacations, was harder to fill.

The Folio's rhetoric also strives to create dissatisfaction with any unofficial or unsanctioned performance. The company's control over performance rights had always been weak outside London. It is not clear that the notion of exclusive performance rights was well understood outside the capital, where it was enforced by the presence of both the Master of Revels and of the legitimate theatrical owners. And while we know very few of the plays performed by provincial companies in the Jacobean period, the tiny sample of evidence shows trespasses against the King's Men, such as the Yorkshire professionals playing

Pericles and *Lear*,⁹³ and possibly the cast of *Titus Andronicus* in Rutland in 1595. The King's Men might well suspect that their plays were being acted without them in the country.

We also know that nonprofessionals would perform commercial London plays until at least the early seventeenth century. In 1607 a ship's captain anchored on the coast of Sierra Leone allowed his crew to perform *Hamlet* and *Richard II*, to keep them "from idleness and unlawful games or sleepe."⁹⁴ Within London itself, there was a burgeoning (or resurgent) tradition of amateur theatricals by members of various guilds. The number and frequency of such performances are impossible to measure precisely, but the 1615 quarto of one play, *The Hector of Germany*, claims to have been performed by "a company of young men of this city," meaning apprentices, at not one but two public theaters. If apprentices could mount such high-profile performances, then the culture of guild theatricals must have been thriving. There is also literary evidence for amateur citizen performances. In the Induction to Beaumont's *The Knight of the Burning Pestle*, Rafe the apprentice is said to have "played Mucedorus before the wardens of our company" and to have been ready to play Hieronimo on a bet, and he demonstrates his acting ability by reeling off a stretch of Hotspur from *1 Henry IV*. This is parodic and Beaumont is commenting upon these popular plays as much as he comments upon audience behavior, but Rafe's personal repertory involves three widely available printed plays, two of which belonged to the King's Men.⁹⁵ If Rafe's real-life counterparts actually wanted to act these roles, the quartos were for sale.

The very durability and popularity of plays suggest a problem for acting companies trying to control their own repertory over a long period. Hieronimo, Mucedorus, and Hotspur were all still on stage when *The Knight of the Burning Pestle* was published in 1613, but the actors who had made those parts famous were no longer playing them. Whatever public authority derived from those original actors was lost. An apprentice playing Prince Hal in a guildhall during a holiday might be no Richard Burbage, but the actor playing Prince Hal for the King's Men wasn't Richard Burbage either. If someone new could play the great man's role, then why shouldn't Rafe, or a thousand Rafes, give it a try? What the text of the Folio suggests, quite tactically, is that the poet is the presiding genius of the stage, and that his texts are best realized by his own theatrical heirs, the custodians of his legacy, and in the original venue. Any other performance, in any other place, is by implication second-best. Those who wish to enjoy Shakespeare properly can only be gratified on the Bankside.

How this subtle rhetoric operated on seventeenth-century readers is difficult to gauge, but it has worked superbly on literary critics. The Chorus's insistent specificity is a spur to a whole critical enterprise, simultaneously an invitation and a command to reconstruct the lost theatrical context for the plays. It prompts Shakespeare lovers to rebuild the Globe playhouse, as close to the original site as can be managed, and even to reproduce the now-iconic thatched roof, the very fire hazard that burned the original to the ground. The identification of Shakespeare and the Globe has become almost complete in the public imagination. It is now "Shakespeare's theater" in a way that the Theater, the Curtain, and even the Blackfriars are not. The current edifice in Southwark is only the culmination of a series of reconstruction projects: the latest, best, and most prestigiously located in a long series of simulations.[96] If our yearning for one early modern playhouse eclipses our interest in the others, then it is so in large part because Shakespeare's acting partners, John Heminges and Henry Condell, wished it. We still believe that we are not acting or watching Shakespeare in the right place, because the Folio text tells us so.

The Chorus's plea worked astonishingly well on Laurence Olivier, whose 1944 film of *Henry V* spends the entire first act in a painstaking reconstruction of a performance at the Globe. Olivier, with enormous resources at his disposal, with cameras and Technicolor and a veritable army to play his army, a director finally capable of satisfying the Chorus's stated longings, directs those resources to a reconstruction of the very theatrical limits against which the Chorus purports to chafe. Olivier has bought the Chorus's logic of origin and authority completely and seeks to ground his own authority in a performance of a vanished, unattainable original.

Heminges and Condell were already appealing to that lost original in 1623. The authority of the absent playwright is paradoxically more durable for early modern actors, more congenial and easier to use, than their own. A leading man's departure is a loss, but a poet's absence is an opportunity. When the writer is gone, the actor can represent him, can supply his absence, because supplying personal absence is precisely the actor's trade. Actors are professionally second best, the consummate second best. (In fact, the only person an actor cannot easily represent in his absence is another actor. Pretending to be Henry V is easy. Pretending to be Richard Burbage is much, much harder.) The actor presents himself as the substitute for a person who cannot appear: Talbot, Julius Caesar, Prince Hal, and the audience's imagination colludes to make the substitution work. Heminges and Condell, who had made their living for decades by substituting themselves for imaginary and historical characters, merely substituted themselves for William Shakespeare as well. Actors of various stripes have been giving us Shakespeare ever since.

CHAPTER 5

Restorations and Glorious Revolutions

> You kiss by th' book.
> —*Romeo and Juliet*, 1.5

The King's Men's ownership of Shakespeare's plays, and the model of ownership they had proposed for those plays, did not survive the company's demise after the Civil War. The Stationers' registration system, while frequently undermined and adjusted by successive acts of Parliament, nonetheless managed to reassert itself for another fifty years after the Restoration. The booksellers' model of intellectual property, while contested in its details, would not be fundamentally changed until 1710's Statute of Queen Anne. As I observed in the opening of my introduction, Nicholas Rowe's edition of Shakespeare's *Works* closely anticipated this development. Also in 1710, Thomas Betterton, the leading Shakespearean actor in Restoration London and the chief source for Rowe's Shakespearean biography, passed away. The three events together can be taken as the end of a distinct era governed by a set of rules different from those of any time before or since: half a century when Shakespeare's plays had passed out of the King's Men's custody but not yet become public property.

Twice in his career, first at the beginning and then near the end, Betterton appears among a group of unruly actors, defying the authority of patent-wielding courtiers. As a young novice, acting in the unlicensed playing companies which were suppressed by Thomas Killigrew and William D'Avenant in 1660, Betterton was defeated. As an aging but acknowledged master, leading his colleagues in successful rebellion against the United Company in 1695, he triumphed. Together these incidents mark the collapse, first sudden and then gradual, of exclusive performance rights vested in specific companies. In fact, the concept of intellectual property underlying the King's Men's practices had not survived the Civil War and the Commonwealth any more than the King's Men had. An entire way of owning had perished with the owners. The Restoration instituted a system of performance rights which superficially resembled the old practices but was founded upon entirely different principles. The new practices were not devised by the actors and indeed seem to have been imposed despite them; it was the actors' pursuit of professional liberty that ultimately abolished the notion of Shakespeare's plays as private property.

Shakespeare's dramatic ownership, such as it had been, had been corporate and did not survive the corporation of which he had been a member. The Civil War destroyed the instrument of Shakespeare's possession when it destroyed his company. The opening years of the Restoration undermined his identification with that playing company, prying his personal authorial identity loose from the corporate identity of the King's Men, for which it had been a metonymy. Shakespeare ceased to be even a minimal possessor and became instead others' possession: the privatized playwright. Only with Betterton's happy secession did Shakespeare's plays, and those of his contemporaries, begin to enter what could be called the stage's public domain.

Unlicensed to Act

At the outset of the Restoration, Charles II licensed Thomas Killigrew and William D'Avenant to establish new playing companies in London. But Killigrew and D'Avenant were already behind events. The professional actors had returned to the London playhouses without prompting or permission, even before the courtiers had received their royal authorizations. Killigrew received his license on July 9, 1660, and D'Avenant's was granted on August 21; one of the nascent companies had demonstrably performed at the Red Bull on June 24,[1] and the others were active as well. The Red Bull performers were primarily younger Caroline actors from several of the prewar companies, the so-called old actors led by Michael Mohun, Nicholas Burt, and Charles Hart under the management of John Rhodes. William Beeston, who led a troupe at Salisbury Court, had been an impresario before the Civil War but did not thrive during the Restoration.[2] On the other hand, Thomas Betterton and his fellows at the Cockpit were a group of younger men (not the "old actors" but the new ones) with no connection to the prewar players.

However different the actors' professional experiences, the companies shared the same stock of old plays. Drawing on the published corpus of Tudor and Stuart drama, each of the companies developed its own repertory of pre-revolutionary plays without regard for any prior claim, and perhaps inevitably there was a certain overlap. Both the "old" actors at the Red Bull and the young ones at the Cockpit played D'Avenant's *The Unfortunate Lovers*, and both performed *The Tamer Tamed*.[3] *The Taming of the Shrew*, apparently, was less popular with Restoration audiences than Fletcher's sequel. No one asked D'Avenant's permission to play *The Unfortunate Lovers*, as he was merely the poet, and the King's Men, who had owned both *The Unfortunate Lovers* and *The Tamer Tamed*, were extinct. Plays were no longer exclusive possessions, and playing companies could not maintain unrivaled control over them.

Exclusive performance rights had lapsed for several reasons, all of them fundamental. First of all, the most essential component of pre–Civil War performance rights, the license bestowed by the theatrical censor, was no longer in effect. The 1660 companies did not request government licenses for the plays they acted, any more than they sought government license to act. When the Commonwealth regime ended, the actors seem to have presumed that plays were permitted again simply because they were no longer forbidden, and they did not wait for permission. Many of these actors had mounted risky illegal productions during the Commonwealth, often suffering arrest; it was enough to know that troops of soldiers would no longer converge on the playhouses. Only when confronted by officially appointed authorities such as D'Avenant and Killigrew do the players seem to have realized that the new regime would require formal authorization for their art. Without a Master of Revels to assign exclusive performance rights, the old system of theatrical property ceased to function (although the dispossessed Master of Revels himself, Sir Henry Herbert, would return and energetically reassert himself). Since none of the actors felt the need for a government license, there was no licenser to enforce the principle of exclusive performance rights.

Neither could any appeal to prior possession be made. All previous claims had lapsed with the dissolution of the old playing companies who had owned the plays, and no senior member from the years before 1642 lived to perform in the Restoration. Even Mohun, Hart, and Burt's company, most of whose members had acted before the Civil War, seem not to have pressed any special claim upon the old plays. These "old actors" had been distinctly junior members of their original companies, and most were best known before 1642 for acting women's roles. Colley Cibber's précis of their early careers, although based on secondhand recollection, suggests that the Red Bull actors had primarily been apprentices:

> Hart and [Walter] Clun were bred up boys at the Blackfriars and acted women's parts. Hart was Robinson's boy . . . he acted the

Duchess in the tragedy of *The Cardinal*... [William] Cartwright and [William] Wintershall belonged to the private house at Salisbury Court. Burt was a boy first under Shank at the Blackfriars, then under Beeston at the Cockpit; Mohun and [Robert] Shatterall were in the same condition with him at the last place. There Burt used to play the principal women's parts.[4]

Only Mohun is specifically described as having played a man's role before the Civil War. These actors had, at best, recently completed their apprenticeships when the theaters were closed. They had certainly not advanced past the intermediary condition of "hired men" to become sharers themselves, which would have given them partial title to the company's shared properties. None of these former apprentices ever pressed a claim to the theatrical possessions of their old masters or represented themselves as continuing the corporate existence of the old companies. The collection of players at the Red Bull apparently understood itself as a new group, distinct from the prewar companies and with no pretense to their rights. Certainly, they made no claim to be the latter-day King's Men; that title would have to be forced upon them and would carry no sense of a Jacobean or Caroline heritage.

It is also worth noting that no claim to performance rights was ever pressed on the basis of a surviving "allowed book." The prime symbols of theatrical ownership in the old dispensation, the numinous manuscripts signed by the Master of Revels, were no longer discussed. Nor is there any positive sign that any such playhouse manuscripts were passed down to the Restoration actors. What became of most theatrical manuscripts is not clear. Certainly pre-Commonwealth plays were still finding their way into print throughout the 1640s, 1650s, and 1660s, sometimes with the obvious participation of actors as in the case of the 1647 Beaumont and Fletcher Folio. In 1657 Francis Kirkman even published *Lusts Dominion* as "Written by *Christofer Marloe*, Gent."[5] But while theatrical texts were finding their way to the printing houses, the crucial manuscripts were not necessarily being passed down to other players.

No one actor or company could base any special claim to a play on possession of the theatrical manuscript if those manuscripts did not survive; all companies were rendered equal. Perhaps more importantly, the apparent loss of original playhouse texts changed the London theater's relationship with the book trade. Restoration actors largely relied on printed texts for their performance scripts. All of the old plays the early Restoration actors performed—and at the very outset they did nothing but old plays—were published works. The theater no longer provided Shakespeare's copy to the press, but the other way

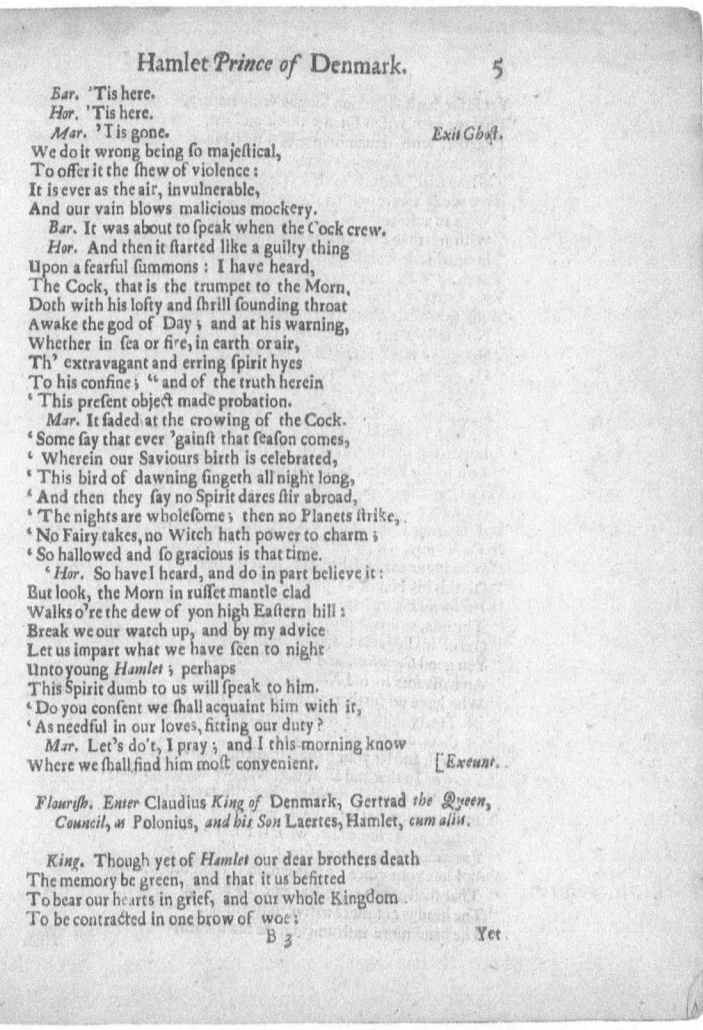

Figure 10. Page from *Hamlet* as played by the Duke of York's Men, with performer's cuts indicated by inverted commas (') at the beginnings of lines, 1676. By permission of the Folger Shakespeare Library.

around. Whatever authority the text possessed was now imagined in the printed word, to which performers might be variably faithful. English actors after 1660 were no longer the owners or inheritors of their scripts but common purchasers who got their scripts from the booksellers like anyone else. Drama was imagined originating in the printing house before making its way to the playhouse.

This would eventually transform the ways in which companies revised their performance texts; starting from a printed copy made the task very different. Consider the 1676 edition of *Hamlet*, based upon the acting edition of the Duke's Men.[6] (The publishers were still interested in texts from the playhouse; the play as acted was apparently a draw for customers.) What the company has provided is an "uncut" *Hamlet*, a text based on earlier published editions, with their own theatrical deletions marked by inverted commas at the beginnings of lines. A note "To the Reader" explains:

> This Play being too long to be conveniently Acted, such places as might be least prejudicial to the Plot or the Sense, are left out upon the Stage: But that we may no way wrong the incomparable Author, are here inserted according to the Original Copy, with this Mark '.[7]

The wrong done to the "incomparable Author" here is not revising his play on the stage (which for the actors was not merely a right but a requirement); it is altering "his" printed text. The "Original Copy" is not the author's personal draft, or the players' manuscript copy, as Heminges and Condell had purported it to be. Rather it is earlier printings of the play; the 1676 edition is set from John Smethwick's 1637 quarto, a direct descendant of the 1604/5 Second Quarto.[8] Shakespeare was now imagined primarily as a creature of the printed word.

Moreover, he was a creature of the master text. The theatrical cuts which the 1676 *Hamlet* makes visible were made from an integral text, rather than from manuscript parts and plots. Restoration actors still relied upon written parts, but it is quite evident that the Duke's Men began editing *Hamlet* from the complete printed text and then had the parts made up from their revised master copy. Their text often cuts away the last line or lines from an actor's speeches, doing away with the words which had originally been the next actor's cue. This would have entailed enormous inconveniences in the Jacobean playhouses but was perfectly efficient and straightforward when beginning with a published quarto. The Civil War had destroyed the old relationship between the playhouse text and the printed word, and the Restoration had restored a status quo that had never quite existed. Before the playhouses closed, the life of a play had resided in its messy, mutable, and evolving performance texts, captured imperfectly by the more static medium of print. Since the Restoration, the printed text has provided a relatively immutable foundation from which essentially disposable performance texts are derived, and to which theater professionals continually return. Since 1660, the basic theatrical text for pre–Civil War plays has been set by publishers.

The Book's the Thing

The Stationers' Company's hold on print rights had not, of course, lapsed with the Restoration. It was, if anything, firmer than it had been during the Commonwealth and far stronger than it had been in the last years before the Civil War, when loosened censorship rules had undermined its monopoly on print. In a political climate defined by the restoration of old properties and prerogatives, the Stationers were positioned to do quite well. While the playing companies had died off, the booksellers' corporation had persisted uninterrupted and the Stationers had their guild's written records to trace the ownership of particular texts over the years. There were occasional errors and misinterpretations, so that the title to Shakespeare's *Hamlet* was confused with the title to a prose *Historie of Hamblett* and the Restoration inheritor of the pamphlet laid claim to the play instead.[9] The successors of Thomas Pavier, rather than those of Nicholas Ling and John Smethwicke, became the publishers of *Hamlet* in the Restoration, but this was not a problem as long no one recalled and prosecuted a separate right to the play. The general principle of printers' rights over a text was largely secure. Indeed, control over theatrical texts was now less troubled without any contentious owners of performance rights. The influence of the players' intellectual property system becomes indirectly visible at the moment of its disappearance, silhouetted by the book trade's response to its absence. Before 1642 the players' claims had sometimes interfered with the Stationers', as in 1619. Plays had been different from other books, with a second category of owner sometimes casting a shadow over the printers' claims. Now the lapse of the players' rights had made plays normal books again, conforming unproblematically to the book dealers' categories of ownership. And consequently, plays could be handled differently. The 1660s saw subtle but quite distinct shift in the way old plays were published and attributed; the Stationers had become the chief authorities.

The security of print rights and the collapse of any claim to exclusive performance rights actually led Michael Mohun, the emerging leader of the Red Bull actors, to ask a publisher for a performance license. A letter from the stationer Humphrey Mosely in August of 1660 indicates that he had made an arrangement with Mohun granting the Red Bull company exclusive rights to perform the plays that Mosely published and barring the other two companies from performing them.[10] Mosely's right to print and sell these plays of course conferred no such authority upon him, and the pact did not keep Mohun and his fellows free of either Thomas Killigrew's or Henry Herbert's control. Mohun's attempt to found a claim to performance rights upon print rights speaks in part of his desperation in the wrangle with Thomas Killigrew and Henry Herbert but also implies his utter lack of conviction in the traditional system of theatrical ownership and the comparative vigor of the Stationers' copyright arrangements. The printers' model of intellectual property was for the moment unassailably dominant.

Some book sellers demonstrated particular confidence in the way they circulated Shakespeare's texts. In 1661, Francis Kirkman and Henry Marsh Jr. published *The merry conceited humors of Bottom the weaver. As it hath been often publikely acted by some of his majesties comedians, and lately, privately, presented, by several apprentices for their harmless recreation, with great applause.*[11] Their text is a short farce or "droll" composed of the mechanicals' scenes from *A Midsummer Night's Dream*. The pre–Civil War tradition of amateur dramatics by apprentices had apparently survived the Commonwealth period at least as well as professional acting had. But something is new here: the publication of a drastically altered version of a commercial play. In 1662, Marsh would go even further, publishing *The Wits*, a collection of twenty-seven drolls from a wide range of pre-Commonwealth plays.[12]

The publishers' dedication to *Bottom the Weaver* makes their motives clear:

> the entreaty of several Persons . . . hath enduced us to the publishing of this Piece, which (when the life of action was added to it) pleased generally well. It hath been the desire of several (who know we have many pieces of this nature in our hands) that we should publish them, and we considering the general mirth that is likely, very suddainly to happen about the Kings Coronation; and supposing that things of this Nature, will be acceptable, have therefore begun with this which we know may be easily acted, and may now be as fit for a private recreation as formerly it hath been for a publike. If you please to encourage us . . . you will enduce us to bring forth our store, and we will assure we are plentifully furnished with things of this Nature.[13]

Kirkman and Marsh expected the new official tolerance for stage plays to lead to a boom in amateur performances, and they set out to supply texts for these imminent "private recreation[s]" out of their allegedly vast theatrical inventory. Perhaps they intended to multiply their inventory by dividing the longer plays of the old professional stage into numbers of brief drolls, or perhaps they felt no need. In an "Advertisement" at the end of the last page, they promise that "if you please to repair to our Shops aforementioned, you may be furnished with all the Plays that were ever yet Printed."[14] Certainly they intended their piece to be performed by their readers and include helpful hints on doubling to that purpose.[15] Just as certainly, the publishers did not imagine *A Midsummer Night's Dream* as subject to any proprietary claims beyond their own. Nothing about the publication of *Bottom the Weaver* suggests that anyone might object to any performance or adaptation of Shakespeare's text. The publication denies any idea of a theatrical authority governing the performance text and presumes no need for any authority but the printer's. Kirkman and Marsh acted as if *A Midsummer Night's Dream* had no theatrical owners. At the beginning of the 1660s they were right. Marsh justifies his publication of the drolls in *The Wits* like this:

> He that knows a Play, knows that Humours [i.e., clowning scenes] have no such *fixedness* and indissoluble *connexion* to the Design, but that without *injury* or *forcible revulsion* they may be *removed* to an *advantage*; which is so demonstrable, that I am sure nothing but a *morose propriety* would offer to deny it.[16]

However "demonstrable" Marsh's claim might be, he can make it without fear of contradiction, and here a publisher rather than an actor gets to define what it means to "know a Play." The only possibility of contradiction Marsh admits comes from "*morose propriety.*" But of course, Marsh knows the plays no longer have proprietors, except in the bookstalls.

Freed from any need to consider the actors' perspective, the Stationers also changed the shape of Shakespeare's dramatic canon. Kirkman and Marsh might confidently cite *The Birth of Merlin* as by Shakespeare and Rowley in 1662, not because they necessarily had any theatrical testimony but because they are no longer concerned with actors' testimony about old plays at all.[17] The contents of the 1623 Shakespeare Folio reflect the involvement of his acting partners, Heminges and Condell, and their sense of his work, so that some plays published in quarto under Shakespeare's name are excluded from the collection. When the Second Folio was printed in 1632, the King's Men were still a thriving concern and the active guardians of their late partner's reputation and his plays. But when Philip Chetwind published the Third Folio in 1663 and 1664 there was no longer any company of actors to testify which "Shakespeare" plays were authentic and which spurious. Instead, Chetwind relied on the testimony of quarto playbooks and their title pages as transparent indicators of authorship. Thus the second issue of Chetwind's folio, in 1664, includes "seven Playes, never before Printed in Folio" but which had been published in quarto with Shakespeare's name or the initials "W.S." Chetwind's new seven plays were *Sir John Oldcastle, Pericles, The Yorkshire Tragedy, The London Prodigal, Thomas Lord Cromwell, The Puritan Widow,* and *Locrine.* Chetwind limited himself to plays "published in [Shakespeare's] life time," or apparently so. This guideline kept him from including such belatedly ascribed plays as *The Birth of Merlin* or *The Two Noble Kinsmen* but demanded the inclusion of *Sir John Oldcastle* on the basis of its falsely dated title page. But within his chosen historical limits, Chetwind essentially chose to believe the attestations of his fellow stationers rather than the (admittedly silent) dissent of the players. That *Oldcastle* had entered the Shakespeare canon again, on the muted testimony of William Jaggard, shows how thoroughly the Stationers' model held sway, and how much implicit credence Chetwind afforded it. There was, frankly, no one to gainsay him.[18]

Meet the New Boss

The happily unlicensed, unpropertied state of affairs that the grassroots acting companies enjoyed in the early summer of 1660 would not last long; Killigrew and D'Avenant, wielding their royal patents, quickly moved to suppress the existing companies of actors. Their grants gave them exclusive rights to playing in the city, with one authorized company each, an arrangement which echoed the old duopoly of the late 1590s, and other companies were by definition unauthorized. In practice, things were more complicated; Killigrew's and D'Avenant's arrangement left out Henry Herbert, who insisted on his old prerogatives to license plays and playing companies, and although Charles II had agreed to the principle of only two playing companies, he then issued a third patent to George Jolly. Killigrew and D'Avenant struggled to accommodate Herbert and marginalize Jolly. Meanwhile, the actors resisted Killigrew's and D'Avenant's authority for several months, quite naturally preferring to be their own masters.

Killigrew and D'Avenant did not recruit new actors for their official companies but simply pressed the unlicensed actors into their service. Indeed, the official companies at the end of 1660 look much like the unofficial companies from the middle of 1660, with minor shuffling of personnel and of course new and well-connected company owners. Killigrew, who was Charles's personal favorite and thus had first choice of players,[19] took Mohun and the rest of the Caroline veterans from the Red Bull, John Lacey from Salisbury Court, and

Edward Kynaston from the upstarts at the Cockpit to form his new King's Men. D'Avenant and his Duke of York's Men had to settle for Thomas Betterton, who would eventually far outshine the rivals. To a large extent, the new King's Men were the old Red Bull players and the Duke's Men the company of youngsters from the Cockpit.

D'Avenant and Killigrew were not launching new enterprises. Rather, they were using their favor with the monarch to take over existing enterprises for their own benefit. D'Avenant had briefly managed something like this before the Civil War; in June of 1640 D'Avenant had been given the disgraced William Beeston's company of actors at the Phoenix, and D'Avenant presumably controlled that company by "power of privilege" from the Lord Chamberlain until being implicated in a royalist plot against Parliament and fleeing London in 1641.[20] Getting the Crown to hand him someone else's business was a familiar procedure for D'Avenant. The grants to D'Avenant and Killigrew were quite typical royal monopolies; although monopolies existed in theory to protect and encourage innovation, the monarch could in practice bestow them where he liked. In essence, the acting companies were notified that two members of the Court now owned their businesses.

Although there was a superficial similarity between the new arrangements and the old system of playing companies, D'Avenant and Killigrew occupied an entirely new role. The patent holder was not the company's patron; the King's and Duke's Men had royal patrons as the old companies had once done. Nor were they necessarily "managers" or impresarios, although they might perform this role if they chose. D'Avenant was particularly energetic in the management of his company and helped build it into the more eminent of the two, but this was a sign of intelligent self-interest. Killigrew was less active but was under no requirement to be more so, and some of the two patent holders' successors would do little more than collect their shares of the profits. The company's manager was quite often a distinct position, with its own remuneration. Charles II's royal fiat had added a new layer of profit-taking middlemen, the patentees, to the old arrangement of patrons and sharing actors. Killigrew and D'Avenant didn't actually have to do anything for their money, although D'Avenant worked hard to maximize the profits he collected.

Killigrew and D'Avenant would also use their royal patents to ensure that every old play, like every professional actor, had a master once again. Creating a theatrical economy that superficially resembled the old dispensation, the two courtiers reestablished the principle of exclusive performance rights confined to a single company. Sir Henry Herbert, who had to be placated, was allowed to charge a commission for the licensing of each play once more. However,

Herbert's license was no longer the core of theatrical ownership; he merely gave his blessing to revivals of plays the companies already controlled. Nor was there even the faintest remaining appeal to natural or inherent property rights; the companies who owned the plays had not commissioned them or paid for them. Companies owned plays for the same reason that patentees owned companies: because it was the royal pleasure.

Various scholars have tried to rationalize the control Killigrew's patent gave him over almost the entire body of pre-Restoration English drama, always by trying to link Killigrew's enormous dramatic holdings to some continuing property claim. Accustomed to thinking of intellectual property as a natural and even a moral right, such scholars look for a natural or moral justification. A typical argument claims that Killigrew somehow "inherited" the performance rights, or that because Killigrew's new company was officially the King's Men, they were considered the owners of the prewar King's Men's plays.[21] However, their repertory contained several plays, such as Jonson's *Epicoene* and *Bartholomew Fair*, which had never belonged to the original King's Men. Some critics have even been misled into believing that Mohun and the other prewar actors, whom Killigrew had taken for his company, were the keys to theatrical possession, that "the old actors still owned the old plays."[22] But if that were so, then Mohun would never have had to negotiate with Humphrey Mosely. Moreover, the Duke's Men would be given a number of old King's Men's plays; previous ownership seems not to have influenced the assignment of plays to companies. Individual property rights were beside the point. Indeed, Killigrew's company was initially assigned *The Unfortunate Lovers*, although D'Avenant had written it.[23] Authorship was not ownership.

Killigrew was granted virtually every play known to English theatergoers simply because the King chose to grant them to him and because the King considered them his to grant. The monopoly model of property was in unchallenged ascendance. Killigrew was given first choice of plays just as he had been given first pick of the actors.[24] Killigrew's patent is far more concerned, in fact, with controlling the actors' labor than with controlling plays. The patent forbids either Killigrew or D'Avenant to employ actors from the other's company except by mutual agreement of the two patent holders (there was, in fact, some movement back and forth in late 1660) but specifies nothing of Killigrew's repertory beyond authorizing "tragedies, comedies, plays, operas, music, scenes, and all other entertainments of the stage whatsoever."[25] Which plays is not a concern.

Twentieth-century critics, conditioned to think of intellectual property in the same terms as real property, as something alienable and heritable, naturally grope to identify some enduring title, whether corporate or individual, at the base of Killigrew's repertory, some connection to previous owners. But Killigrew and his King did not consider any previous owners and did not consider plays things to be owned. Performance rights were not a kind of property but a kind of privilege: Charles was simply granting a monopoly. The arbitrary nature of the grant is underscored by the subsequent assignment of several plays, including *Hamlet*, *Lear*, and *Macbeth*, to D'Avenant on the condition that he "reforme" them.[26] The specificity of this grant indicates how general Killigrew's was; any play not specifically assigned to D'Avenant was Killigrew's. But even Killigrew's plays were not really Killigrew's, because the King could be persuaded to give them to someone else.

The grant also gave D'Avenant six plays (including *The Mad Wife*, *The Maid in the Mill*, *The Spanish Curate*, and *Pericles*) temporarily, for a period of two months after the grant was issued on December 12, 1660, after which they would revert to Killigrew. In fact, the Duke's Men did not relinquish all of these plays so easily, although the King's Men began performing them almost as soon as D'Avenant's two months were up.[27] The temporarily granted plays remained an ongoing irregularity in the system of exclusive performance rights. Once the Duke's Company had learned the plays, they intended to keep performing them. But the fact of the two-month grant itself demonstrates that the plays belonged to neither company, and neither patentee, in any fundamental sense. They were all imagined as the King's, who could take them from one group and lend them to another. The same grant allowed D'Avenant control of his own Caroline-era plays, again as a privilege rather than as possession. This is no formality by which Charles confirmed D'Avenant's "natural" rights to his own labor but rather a royal favor which required D'Avenant to implicitly recognize the King's power to assign the playwright's works.

Why the King should own the acting rights to old plays was neither explained nor asked. They were assets without owners, and the Crown assumed control of them, in every sense of that verb. The restored Royalists, intent on restoring pre-Commonwealth rights and prerogatives as fully as they could imagine them, did not think of property as an individual right, but as a royal grant. The titles to Shakespeare's plays were treated like the title to a lapsed fiefdom. Charles II had in effect nationalized English dramatic literature. As Sandra Clark points out, D'Avenant was "obliged, by the terms of [his] patent, to 'improve'" the old plays he had been assigned.[28] The adaptations that have sometimes been castigated by later critics were in fact necessary to maintain D'Avenant's claim. Charles granted D'Avenant some of Shakespeare's plays much as he might grant a mining concession, and for much the same reasons, so that the petitioner could improve a resource which would otherwise lie dormant. The metal under the ground is the King's, by this logic, but he will allow his faithful subject to mine it, for a price; no-longer-fashionable plays by long-dead poets are the King's, and he will allow his faithful subject to refashion them into something presentable. D'Avenant's control of the plays was both conditional and revocable. Shakespeare, Jonson, Beaumont and Fletcher had become national treasures in the literal sense, assets from which the Crown expected returns.

The Restoration patents had restored the principle that each play was the unique province of a single acting company, but plays had ceased to be private property in any real sense. Nor were they public property, in the sense that they were free for anyone who wished to perform them. They still did not belong to the author, but they no longer belonged to the actors either. Nor did they belong even to the patentees to whom they were assigned. Everyone who performed them professionally was, in essence, a tenant of the Crown. Least of all did they belong to the authors. William Shakespeare was now figured primarily as an individual rather than as a member of a professional company, but this did not emphasize his rights of individual possession. Quite the reverse; the plays were figured as uniquely his precisely because he no longer had partners, assigns, or heirs. Any strictly economic ownership had lapsed. Shakespeare was no longer imagined as a private citizen with private interests but as a public treasure whose works belong to others. Like orphans or heirless estates, the dead man's plays had reverted to Charles.

The most important abstract properties in the Restoration theater were Killigrew's and D'Avenant's royal patents, which approached the condition of property much more nearly than did plays or shares in acting companies. Unlike player's shares or the rights to plays, the two royal patents were heritable, and alienable. This, in fact, was the weakness of the system, and the downfall of exclusive performance rights.

In 1682, for a number of reasons including the poor management of Killigrew's and D'Avenant's successors, the King's and Duke's Companies were merged into a single United Company. The new joint company controlled both of the original patents and, by definition, every play in the original companies' combined repertory. The United Company had an absolute monopoly on the London stage, and upon the entire body of English dramatic literature.

In practice, the amalgamation of the troupes represented a takeover of the King's Men by the Duke's, and the sidelining of such old stars as Michael Mohun and Charles Hart. Although officially the junior company, the Duke's had long been the more powerful, due in part to D'Avenant's assiduous management in the early years and to Betterton's talents. The merger also gave Betterton and his colleagues access to all of the old plays which had belonged to the King's Company. They immediately set about a thorough exploration and refurbishment of the King's Men inventory.[29] The playwright George Powell complains in his general preface to *The Treacherous Brothers* in 1696: "The time was, upon the uniting of the two *Theatres*, that the reviveing of the old stock of Plays, so ingrost the study of the House, that the Poets lay dorment; and a new Play cou'd hardly get admittance."[30] Old plays were potentially valuable commodities, and Betterton was intent on maximizing their value now that they were available to him again. (He had felt free to play anything he liked in 1660, but a large portion of the existing English repertory was denied him for the intervening twenty-two years.)

The United Company's monopoly ended in 1695, when Betterton, aggrieved by the behavior of Christopher Rich, who held both of the original patents, led a walkout of the company's major stars. Rich, as an unchallenged monopolist, had shown none of the competitive motivation that had marked D'Avenant and was considered neither competent nor just by his chief actors. (Rich was more apt to increase his profits by cutting salaries than by improving business.) Rich and his associates lobbied for the breakaway company's suppression, but Betterton, Elizabeth Barry, Anne Bracegirdle, and their confederates were simply too popular among the courtly classes to be denied a hearing of their grievances. Aristocratic admirers interceded for the actors, various negotiations ran aground, and eventually William III issued a new, separate patent to Betterton's rebels.[31] If the basis of company ownership was royal favor, the star actors had built up a fundamental advantage throughout their careers.

However fiercely and futilely Rich argued, he never seems to have argued that his patents gave him control over the United Company's entire stock of plays. Forbidding Betterton and his followers from performing *Hamlet*, or *Lear* or any of the other scripts which Killigrew or D'Avenant had once controlled seems a perfectly straightforward expedient: good at the very least for extracting concessions and delays. But Rich and his Patent Company never attempted anything of the kind. Instead the rebels were allowed to take their signature roles to Lincoln's Inn Fields while, as Judith Milhous notes, the remaining actors at the old company were forced to learn the defectors' parts.[32]

Perhaps a decade and more of universal monopoly had led Rich to forget that plays were once assigned to one specific company to the exclusion of the other, or that his company patents implied control of particular titles.

Perhaps the very encompassing vagueness of Killigrew's patent, which specified no special plays because Killigrew was granted nearly all of them, did not provide sufficient argumentative force in 1695; a more restricted patent, listing allowed titles, might have served Rich's turn far better. Or perhaps the very nature of the royal grants involved made such a line of argument seem dangerous. Rich was grounding his claim upon his rights as the holder of heritable, transferable patents, while the performance rights to plays had been granted at royal pleasure. The royal pleasure was the last principle Rich needed to invoke in a contest with a group of professional entertainers and ingratiators.

Still less would he be served by pressing the a "property" claim based upon a royal grant in the aftermath of the Glorious Revolution and Locke's *Second Treatise of Civil Government*, with its new definition of private property as an inherent personal right derived from personal labor. With Locke's ideas newly fashionable and influential, it would be awkward to press a claim on century-old plays which one had neither written nor acted but possessed at the royal prerogative. After all, even possession of the English throne was no longer solely grounded upon the royal pleasure; one could not expect William III to imagine property as Charles II had. But even a counter-Lockean appeal to the arbitrary powers of the Crown would only raise the inconvenient question of why the Crown could not arbitrarily reassign to new favorites the plays that it had once arbitrarily assigned to old favorites. Whatever the case, Rich failed to press any claim upon performance rights. The effect was that both of the permitted acting companies, the established group with the upstart actors and the upstart group with the established actors, would have unfettered rights to the entire repertory that the United Company had once shared. In seeking to control the actors' labors, he neglected to press any claim upon the plays.

An incident reported by Cibber makes clear the extent to which the actors' schism placed stock plays into a mutually shared domain. The leftover Patent Company decided to sabotage the graying renegades by offering *Hamlet* on the night before the rival company planned to act it. Betterton's group called the younger actors' bluff by moving *Hamlet* up a day, so that both theaters would be offering it on the same night. The official company dared not risk such head-to-head competition, especially since Betterton *was* Hamlet to much of the contemporary audience. They had to content themselves with acting the play the rebels had originally planned for that night, William Congreve's *The Old Bachelor*, and letting their lead actor burlesque Betterton on stage.[33]

The story reflects the enormous difference in prestige between the two sets of actors, but it also reveals how much each company took the other's right to perform stock plays, whether their authors were living or dead, for granted. Their game of musical productions involves both the hundred-year-old *Hamlet* and a comedy that had premiered in 1693; both were equally free for either company's taking, although new plays would subsequently belong to the house that commissioned them. Congreve, for example, had given his new play *Love for Love* to Betterton's company for their premiere.[34] The idea of one company's rights to a particular play, or of rights bestowed on a company by royal grant, was dead.

Betterton's performance of *Hamlet* was a first step into the theatrical public domain for Shakespeare and his coevals, an echo perhaps of the brief freedoms from the summer of 1660, but it was hardly the last step. Although sixteenth- and seventeenth-century plays would never again be the exclusive property of any one company, they would legally be restricted to England's "legitimate" theaters, those legitimated and authorized by government patents, until 1843.[35] Other modes of ownership, not least of print and editorial ownership, would soon be developed, and even with Betterton's success, Shakespeare, Fletcher, Jonson, and Beaumont would only be liberated from the confines of a single theater to the slightly broader bounds of two or four theaters. Even so, when Betterton defied the Patent Company and regained a fraction of his own lost liberty, he also did away with the narrowest restrictions on performing Elizabethan and Jacobean drama. In proving how thoroughly he himself owned Hamlet, a part he had enriched, in the Lockean sense, with decades of his labor, and how deeply his audiences believed in his possession of the role, he made it impossible for any single performer entirely to own Hamlet, or *Hamlet*, again. On that night in Lincoln's Inn Fields, William Shakespeare moved one step closer to being free.

NOTES

INTRODUCTION

1. Andrew Murphy, "Birth of the Editor," in *A Concise Companion to Shakespeare and the Text*, ed. Andrew Murphy (Malden, Mass.: Blackwell, 2007), 93–108, 94–95.

2. Peter Seary, *Lewis Theobald and the Editing of Shakespeare* (Oxford: Clarendon, 1990), 133–35; Margreta de Grazia, *Shakespeare Verbatim: The Reproduction of Authenticity and the 1790 Apparatus* (Oxford: Clarendon, 1991), 192–95.

3. Mark Rose, *Authors and Owners* (Cambridge, Mass.: Harvard University Press, 1993), 4–5, 92–112.

4. The 1923 cutoff date for copyright protection has remained in effect since 1978, when copyright laws were revised and the term of protection greatly extended; subsequent laws have repeatedly extended the term of copyright protection further, with the practical effect that virtually nothing has entered the public domain in the past three decades.

5. Murphy, "The Birth of the Editor," 94.

6. Andrew Murphy, *Shakespeare in Print: A History and Chronology of Shakespeare Publishing* (Cambridge: Cambridge University Press, 2003), 60.

7. *The Works of Mr. William Shakespeare*, ed. Nicholas Rowe, 6 vols. (London, 1709), 1:xxxiv.

8. *The Works of Mr. William Shakespear*, ed. Alexander Pope, 6 vols. (London, 1723), 1:i, ii.

9. Murphy, *Shakespeare in Print*, 70–71.

10. Warburton, Theobald's immediate successor and Pope's personal friend, did attempt a return to primarily aesthetic editing practice but gained little traction and never saw his edition reprinted.

11. Marcus Walsh, *Shakespeare, Milton, and Eighteenth-Century Literary Editing: The Beginnings of Interpretative Scholarship* (Cambridge: Cambridge University Press, 1997), 131.

12. Murphy, "Birth of the Editor," 97.

13. George C. D. Odell, *Shakespeare from Betterton to Irving*, 2 vols. (New York: Scribners, 1920; reprint, New York: Dover, 1966), 1:385–89. Garrick omitted the Gravediggers, Ophelia's funeral, the reported deaths of Rosencranz and Guildenstern, and the Queen's death by poison. Garrick's Hamlet never leaves for England, and stabs the King for reiterating the order to leave.

14. Lewis Theobald, *Shakespeare Restored: or, a Specimen of the Many Errors, As Well*

Committed, and Unamended, by Mr. Pope in his Late Edition of this Poet (London, 1726), iii.

15. Pope 1:xvii.
16. Ibid.
17. Murphy, *Shakespeare in Print*, 65.
18. Pope 1:viii.
19. Steven Urkowitz, *Shakespeare's Revision of "King Lear"* (Princeton, N. J.: Princeton University Press, 1980), 143–44.
20. Pope 1:xvi.
21. London: J. Wenman, 1778; English Short Title Catalog (ESTC) T39351.
22. Q1 1600; ESTC 22302.
23. The revisers who added material to *Doctor Faustus*'s B-text returned to the English Faust Book, *The History of the Damnable Life and Deserved Death of Doctor John Faustus*, for additional material. See David Bevington and Eric Rasmussen, eds., *Doctor Faustus: A- and B- Texts (1604, 1616)* (New York: Manchester University Press, 1993), 6, 79n (note 17).
24. Paul Werstine, "The Science of Editing," in *A Concise Companion to Shakespeare and the Text*, ed. Andrew Murphy (Malden, Mass.: Blackwell, 2007), 109–27. See also E.A.J. Honigmann, "The New Bibliography and Its Critics." in *Textual Performances: The Modern Reproduction of Shakespeare's Drama*, ed. Lukas Erne and Margaret Jane Kidne (Cambridge: Cambridge University Press, 2004), 77–93.
25. Ibid., 113.
26. Werstine provides excellent overviews in "Science of Editing" and also "Narratives about Printed Shakespeare Texts: 'Foul Papers' and 'Bad' Quartos," *Shakespeare Quarterly* 41, no. 1 (Spring 1990): 65–86, and "A Century of 'Bad' Shakespeare Quartos," *Shakespeare Quarterly* 50, no. 3 (Autumn 1999): 310–33.
27. Stanley W. Wells and Gary Taylor, *William Shakespeare: A Textual Companion* (New York: Oxford University Press, 1987), 60. Hereafter *Textual Companion*.

CHAPTER 1

1. *Greenes Groatsworth of Wit*, ed. D. Allen Carroll (Binghamton, N.Y.: Center for Medieval and Early Renaissance Studies, State University of New York at Binghamton, 1994), 84–85.
2. Reproduced in E. K. Chambers, *The Elizabethan Stage*, 4 vols. (Oxford: Clarendon, 1923), 4:164.
3. *Gesta Grayorum,1688*, The Malone Society Reprints, ed. W. W. Greg (London: Malone Society, 1914), 22.
4. Chambers's *Elizabethan Stage* gives an alternate date of "December 27" with an explanatory footnote, although his reason for choosing December 27 rather than December 29 are unclear, and Chambers reproduces the original document. Andrew Gurr's *Shakespearean Playing Companies* (Oxford: Clarendon, 1996) and his *The Shakespeare Company* (Cambridge: Cambridge University Press, 2004) simply print the December 27 date as fact.
5. Roslyn Knutson has recently opened the discussion over who performed *The Com-*

edy of Errors in a provocative essay, "What's So Special about 1594?" delivered at the Shakespeare Association of America, 2009.

6. Chambers, *Elizabethan Stage*, 4:310–11.

7. Scott McMillin and Sally-Beth MacLean, *The Queen's Men and Their Plays* (Cambridge: Cambridge University Press, 1998), passim, especially 37–46.

8. Ibid., 108.

9. Chambers, *Elizabethan Stage*, 4:311–12.

10. McMillin and MacLean, *Queen's Men*.

11. Gurr, *Playing Companies*, 61.

12. Chambers, *Elizabethan Stage*, 4:325.

13. Gurr, *Playing Companies*; Gurr, *The Shakespeare Company*.

14. McMillin and Maclean, *The Queen's Men*, 51–53.

15. The Stationers' charter restricted printing to members of the London company. The only exceptions were the Royal Printer, who was inevitably one of the Londoners, and the two University printers. See Edward Arber, ed., *A Transcript of the Registers of the Company of Stationers of London: 1554–1640*, 5 vols., 1875–94 (New York: Peter Smith, 1950), 1:xxviii–xxxii.

16. The Privy Council granted the license on May 6, 1593, specifying Alleyn as the Admiral's Servant and the other five as Strange's. PRO, PC2/20, p. 351, cited in Wickham 191–92, and Chambers 2:123. Andrew Gurr, oddly, cites Heminges as member of Lord Strange's in 1996 but does not in 2004.

17. W. W, Greg, *A Bibliography of the English Printed Drama to the Restoration*, 4 vols. (London: Printed for the Bibliographical Society at the University Press, Oxford, 1939–59), 1:194–95.

18. Henslowe simply records the combined group as "my lord stranges mene" during their run at his playhouse in 1592, the very run during which *A Knack* debuted, and they appear as Strange's Men in Court performance records and in their petition for the reopening of the Rose. *Henslowe's Diary*, ed. R. A. Foakes, 2nd ed. (Cambridge: Cambridge University Press, 2002), 16, 19.

19. Henslowe 16–21, 207.

20. Henslowe 103; Glynne Wickham, William Gladstone, Herbert Berry, and William Ingram, *English Professional Theatre, 1530–1660*, Theatre in Europe (Cambridge: Cambridge University Press, 2000), 218–20.

21. Mary Edmond has attempted to identify some of Pembroke's Men through the will of Simon Jewell, which mentions the Countess of Pembroke. (Mary Edmond. "Pembroke's Men," *Review of English Studies*, n.s., 25 [1974]: 129–36.) See also Karl P. Wentersdorf, "The Origin and Personnel of the Pembroke Company," *Theatre Research International* (1979): 5:45–68. Scott McMillin ("Simon Jewell and the Queen's Men," *Review of English Studies*, n.s., 27, no. 106 [May 1976], 174-77) interrogates Edmond's claims and persuasively refutes them. Other critics have tried to identify minor players from the Pembroke's company using actors' names from Chamberlain's Men's texts; these claims will be dealt with more fully in the next chapter.

22. Scholars also rely heavily on the manuscript "plot" for the play *The Second Part of the Deadly Sins*, which will be discussed at length in Chapter 2 and which has traditionally been assigned a very early date that has recently been refuted by archival evidence. But even

if the traditional (and itself highly speculative) date were accepted, it would not suffice to support any claims about the Sussex or Pembroke company's personnel.

23. Gurr, *Playing Companies*, 74–75; John Dover Wilson, ed., *The Second Part of King Henry VI* (Cambridge: Cambridge University Press, 1952), xii; Wentersdorf, "The Origin and Personnel of the Pembroke Company," 45–68.

24. Andrew Gurr, for example, argues that "the presence of Queen's Men's plays in the subsequent repertory of the Chamberlain's suggests that some of its players" were also present in the company (*Playing Companies*, 279), but this line of argument risks tautology; Queen's Men's plays found their way into the Chamberlain's Men's repertory, although the precise mechanism is unclear.

25. Gurr, *Shakespeare Company*, 19.

26. Terence G. Schoone-Jongen, *Shakespeare's Companies: William Shakespeare's Early Career and the Acting Companies, 1577–1594*, Studies in Performance and Early Modern Drama (Burlington, Vt.: Ashgate, 2008).

27. Andrew Gurr, "Did Shakespeare Own His Own Playbooks?" *Review of English Studies*, n.s., 60, no. 244 (2008): 206–29. Gurr argues, curiously, that the King's Men's model of joint possession, as exemplified by the 1623 Shakespeare Folio, should not be taken to imply the ownership practices governing Shakespeare's plays.

28. Roslyn L. Knutson, "Evidence for the Assignment of Plays to the Repertory of Shakespeare's Company," *Medieval and Renaissance Drama in England* 4 (1989): 63–89; Roslyn L. Knutson, "Marlowe, Company Ownership, and the Role of Edward II," *Medieval and Renaissance Drama in England* 18 (2005).

29. Henslowe 203, 201; Roslyn L. Knutson, "The Repertory," in *A New History of Early English Drama*, ed. John D. Cox and David Scott Kastan (New York: Columbia University Press, 1997), 461–80, at 470; David Riggs, *Ben Jonson: A Life* (Cambridge, Mass.: Harvard University Press, 1989), 87–91.

30. Henslowe 33–38, 47–48, 323.

31. Henslowe 33–34, 36–37, 47–48.

32. Guy Hamel, "*King John* and *The Troublesome Raigne*: A Reexamination," in *King John: New Perspectives*, ed. Deborah T. Curren-Aquino (Cranbury, N.J.: Associated University Presses, 1989), 41–61. Also see E. A. J. Honigmann's *Arden* 2nd ed. of *King John* (The Arden Edition of the Works of William Shakespeare, 2nd ser. [London: Methuen, 1954]) and Lester A. Beaurline's New Cambridge Shakespeare edition (Cambridge: Cambridge University Press, 1990), which argue for *The Troublesome Reign* as derivative.

33. Henslowe 21.

34. The shift from *The True Tragedy*'s "A horse! A horse! A fresh horse!" to the more familiar "A horse! A Horse! My kingdom for a horse!" shows a bit of Shakespeare at work. (I, like Dominique Goy-Blanquet, find it hard to imagine actors or revisers casting aside the superior line.) The author of *The True Tragedy* has created an ironic coup de theatre: the defeated king will call out for something which, as a character on a stage, he can never receive. Every audience member knows that there will be no horses on the stage; the man crying for a horse is declaring himself lost. Shakespeare improves this sharp irony by expanding it into a full and resonant pentameter line but also adds to it another layer of irony: the man calling for the horse that cannot appear offers in exchange the kingdom he has already lost.

35. The passage can be found B2v of *The True Tragedy* Q1. Reproduced in *Shakespeare's Plays in Quarto: A Facsimile Edition*, ed. Michael J. B. Allen and Kenneth Muir (Berkeley: University of California Press, 1981).

36. *Greenes Groatsworth of Wit*, 85.

37. Nashe, *Works of Thomas Nashe*, ed. R. B. McKerrow, 5 vols. (London: Sidgwick & Jackson, 1910), 1:213.

38. For an examination of how Henslowe used the "ne" annotation, and of the inconsistencies in his usage, see Roslyn L. Knutson, "*Henslowe's Diary* and the Economics of Play Revision for Revival, 1592–1603," *Theatre Research International* 10 (1985):1–18.

39. Henslowe 16–19.

40. Ibid., 19–20.

41. Ibid., 21–22.

42. Nashe 3:315.

43. Henslowe 21. Henslowe often begins the new year on the traditional date of March 25; I have emended Henslowe's dates, here and elsewhere, to fit the modern system.

44. Greg, *Bibliography*, 1:196–98.

45. Ibid.

46. Gustav Ungerer, "Shakespeare in Rutland," *Rutland Record* 7 (1987): 242–48.

47. Gurr, *Shakespeare Company*, 56.

48. Keenan, *Travelling Player's in Shakespeare's England* (New York: Palgrave Macmillan, 2002), 81. Keenan does not accept absolutely that the players in question were the Lord Chamberlain's Men.

49. London, Lambeth Palace MS 6454, no. 167.

50. Douglas A. Brooks, *From Playhouse to Printing House: Drama and Authorship in Early Modern England* (Cambridge: Cambridge University Press, 2000), 71.

51. Greg, *Bibliography*, 1:245–46, 226–29, 230–34.

52. See E. K. Chambers, *William Shakespeare: A Study of Facts and Problems*, 2 vols. (Oxford: Clarendon, 1930), 2:193–201.

53. Urkowitz, *Shakespeare's Revision*.

54. Steven Urkowitz, "'If I mistake in those foundations which I build upon': Peter Alexander's Textual Analysis of *Henry VI Parts 2* and *3*," *English Literary Renaissance* 18, no. 2 (Spring 1988): 230-56, and "Texts with Two Faces: Noticing Theatrical Revision in *Henry VI, Parts 2* and *3*," in *"Henry VI": Critical Essays*, ed. Thomas A. Pendleton (New York: Routledge, 2001), 27–37.

55. *Richard III*, TLN 346–57, in *The Norton Facsimile, the First Folio of Shakespeare*, 2nd ed., ed. Charlton Hinman, intro. Peter W. M. Blayney (New York: Norton, 1996). All further direct quotations of the Folio text will be taken from this edition and will use its through line numbering (TLN) to indicate the cited text's place in the volume.

CHAPTER 2

1. *The Taming of a Shrew: The 1594 Quarto*, ed. Stephen Roy Miller (Cambridge: Cambridge University Press, 1998); *Shakespeare's Plays in Quarto: A Facsimile Edition*, ed. Michael J. B. Allen and Kenneth Muir (Berkeley: University of California Press, 1981).

2. Leah S. Marcus, *Unediting the Renaissance: Shakespeare, Marlowe, Milton* (New York: Routledge, 1996), 101–31.

3. *The Taming of the Shrew*, updated ed., ed. Ann Thompson, New Cambridge Shakespeare (Cambridge: Cambridge University Press, 2003), 2–3.

4. *The Norton Facsimile, the First Folio of Shakespeare*, 2nd ed., ed. Charlton Hinman, intro. Peter W. M. Blayney (New York: Norton, 1996), TLN 93–97.

5. TLN 98.

6. Some scholars give preference to the spelling "Sincler," but I prefer to use "Sincklo," as this spelling or some phonetic variant appears consistently in the contemporary printed texts.

7. See *Norton Facsimile, 3 Henry VI*, TLN 1396–1499; *The Second Part of Henrie the Fourth* . . . (London: 1600), sig. K3v; and John Marston, *The Malcontent*, in *English Renaissance Drama*, ed. David Bevington et al. (New York: W. W. Norton, 2002), 545–613, Ind.17 s.d.-135. The "plat" or plot of *The Second Part of the Seven Deadly Sins* is Dulwich College MS 19.

8. Mark Eccles, "Elizabethan Actors IV: S to End," *Notes and Queries* 238 (1993): 165–76, 168.

9. Ibid., 168–69.

10. *The Taming of the Shrew*, ed. Sir Arthur Quiller-Couch and John Dover Wilson, New Shakespeare (Cambridge: Cambridge University Press, 1928), 114–15. Hereafter cited by the traditional scholarly abbreviation for the original New [Cambridge] Shakespeare editions, NCS.

11. Ibid., 131.

12. Ibid., 131–32.

13. Ibid., 132.

14. Ibid,, 144.

15. Ibid., xiii.

16. Wells and Taylor, *Textual Companion*, 170.

17. Ibid., 169. Wells does suggest that if the Soto speech is indeed a reference to *Women Pleased*, then "the allusion might be a late interpolation, authorial or not" (*Textual Companion*, 170). The idea of an "authorial" interpolation in a Shakespeare play circa 1620 surely cannot be what Wells intends to suggest.

18. Ibid., 170.

19. Eric Sams, "The Timing of the *Shrews*," *Notes and Queries* 32, no. 1 (March 1985): 33–45.

20. *Textual Companion*, 170.

21. Ibid.

22. Thompson 2, 3.

23. *The Taming of the Shrew*, ed. Brian Morris, Arden Edition of the Works of William Shakespeare (London: Methuen, 1981), 50.

24. Wells and Taylor, *Textual Companion*, 169.

25. For a sense of the typical orthodoxy, see Ann Thompson's "Feminist Theory and the Editing of Shakespeare: *The Taming of the Shrew* Revisited," in *The Margins of the Text*,

ed. D. C. Greetham (Ann Arbor: University of Michigan Press, 1997), 98, or Stephen Roy Miller's critical edition of the 1594 Quarto.

26. *The Norton Shakespeare,* ed. Stephen Greenblatt et al. (New York: Norton, 1997), 170. Wells is more cautious in the *Textual Companion,* noting "a combination of the characteristics of a [theatrical] transcript and foul papers" (170); meticulous and detailed editorial theory is simplified into far less cautious practice.

27. Paul Werstine, "McKerrow's 'Suggestion' and Twentieth-century Textual Criticism," *Renaissance Drama* 19 (1988): 149–73, 150.

28. R. B. McKerrow, "The Elizabethan Printer and Dramatic Manuscripts," *The Library* 12, no. 3 (December 1931): 253–75, reprinted in *Ronald Brunlees McKerrow: A Selection of His Essays,* ed. John Phillip Immroth (Metuchen, N.J.: Scarecrow Press, 1974), 149–58.

29. Ibid., 156.

30. Ibid., 153–54.

31. Ibid., 155–56.

32. R. B. McKerrow, "A Suggestion Regarding Shakespeare's Manuscripts," *Review of English Studies* 11, no. 44 (October 1935): 459–65, esp. 464.

33. Werstine, "McKerrow's 'Suggestion.'"

34. Thompson 164–68. Compare G. Blakemore Evans's assertion, in the updated New Cambridge edition of *Romeo and Juliet,* that "there is universal agreement that the printer's copy for Q2 was derived in some way from Shakespeare's rough draft ('foul papers')" (224). Granting that Evans, like Thompson, is updating an edition rather than creating an entirely new one, the work of "updating" might include acknowledging that old agreements are no longer universal. Clearly Evans, like Thompson, feels no need to defend or justify the traditional "foul papers" model.

35. Greg, *Dramatic Documents from the Elizabethan Playhouses* (Oxford: Clarendon, 1931), 215–16.

36. Greg, *The Editorial Problem in Shakespeare: A Survey of the Foundations of the Text,* 2nd ed. (Oxford: Clarendon, 1951), 102–3.

37. Ibid., 73–74.

38. Greg, *The Shakespeare First Folio* (Oxford: Clarendon, 1955), 142.

39. Ibid., 116–17.

40. Ibid., 212–14.

41. Ibid., 183, 266.

42. *The Taming of the Shrew,* ed. H. J. Oliver (Oxford: Clarendon, 1982), 5.

43. Morris 6.

44. TLN 137–78.

45. G. E. Bentley, *The Jacobean and Caroline Stage,* 7 vols. (Oxford: Clarendon, 1941–68), 3:432, 2:551–51.

46. Chambers, *Elizabethan Stage,* 2, 339.

47. Gurr, *Shakespeare Company,* 241.

48. Thompson 58.

49. Fredson Bowers et al., *The Dramatic Works in the Beaumont and Fletcher Canon,* 10 vols. (Cambridge: Cambridge University Press, 1966–96), 5:444.

50. *Playing Companies*, 71–73.

51. Thompson 9.

52. David Kathman, "Reconsidering *The Seven Deadly Sins*," *Early Theatre* 7, no. 1 (2004): 13–44, 14–18.

53. Kathman 28, 30–31.

54. Marston, *Malcontent*, ll. 75–76.

55. Mary Edmond, "Pembroke's Men," *Review of English Studies* n.s. 25 (1974): 129–36; Morris 51–52; Thompson 3; *Norton Shakespeare*, 140.

56. Bowers et al. 5:444.

57. Soto does not by any means win over "the Gentlewoman" in *Women Pleased*, which has led some critics to view the claim that he "woo'd . . . so well" as an inconsistency. But it may also be read as simple irony, and it is by no means clear that the class-conscious Lord of *The Taming* would enjoy the spectacle of a farmer's son winning a gentlewoman.

58. *King Leir*, ed. Tiffany Stern (New York: Routledge, 2002), 1.1.63–64.

59. Stephen Greenblatt, *Will in the World: How Shakespeare Became Shakespeare* (New York: W. W. Norton, 2004), 327–28.

60. *Taming of the Shrew*, 3.169–71.

61. Greenblatt, *Will*, 323–24.

62. *The Tamer Tamed*, 1.1.16.

63. *Norton Shakespeare*, 140.

64. Marcus, *Unediting the Renaissance*, 123–24, 128.

CHAPTER 3

1. Nashe 3:315.

2. *Hamlet*, ed. G. R. Hibbard (Oxford: Oxford University Press, 1987), 13.

3. See Paul Werstine, "The Textual Mystery of *Hamlet*," *Shakespeare Quarterly* 39, no. 1 (Spring 1988): 1–26

4. Ann Thompson and Neil Taylor, eds., *Hamlet*, Arden Shakespeare, 3rd ser. (London: Thomson Learning, 2006), 53, 56.

5. Ibid., 46–47.

6. Wells and Taylor, *A Textual Companion*, 137–38.

7. Ibid., 398.

8. Harold Jenkins, ed., *Hamlet*, Arden Shakespeare, 2nd ser. (London: Methuen, 1982), 1.

9. John Shakespeare was buried on September 8, 1601, in Stratford-on-Avon. E. K. Chambers, *William Shakespeare: A Study of Facts and Problems*, 2 vols. (Oxford: Clarendon, 1930), 2:4.

10. James Burbage, builder and owner of the Theater, was buried on February 2, 1597. Chambers, *Elizabethan Stage*, 2:306.

11. Emma Smith, "Ghost Writing: *Hamlet* and the *Ur-Hamlet*," in *The Renaissance*

Text: Theory, Editing, Textuality, ed. Andrew Murphy (Manchester: Manchester University Press, 2000), 177–90, 178.

12. Ibid., 179.

13. The classic example, in every sense, is E. A. J. Honigmann, "The Date of *Hamlet*," *Shakespeare Survey* 9 (1956): 24–34. More recent attempts at dating can be seen in Philip Edwards's *New Cambridge* edition (Cambridge: Cambridge University Press, 2003) 1–8; Thompson and Taylor 43–53; and Wells and Taylor.

14. Honigmann, "Date."

15. The 1604/5 Quarto and the 1623 Folio have an allusion to *Julius Caesar*; the 1623 Folio makes quite explicit reference to the London boy players and the so-called War of the Theatres.

16. Horace Howard Furness, ed., *Hamlet,* New Variorum Edition of Shakespeare, 2 vols. (Philadelphia: J. B. Lippincott, 1877), 2:114–20.

17. Geoffrey Bullough, *Narrative and Dramatic Sources of Shakespeare,* 7 vols. (London: Routledge, 1957–73), 7:128–58.

18. Greetham, *Textual Scholarship,* 142; Bullough 7:21–22.

19. Greg, *Bibliography,* 1:309–11.

20. The idea of "pirated" texts preceding legitimate editions onto the market misses the point of such piracy completely. Surreptitious books, such as those printed in defiance of monopolies, came after a work had become an established success, and after the risky investment in procuring and setting the text had been made by someone else. The profit lay not in the first edition, but in the fifth.

21. Fredson Bowers, *On Editing Shakespeare and the Elizabethan Dramatists* (Philadelphia: University of Pennsylvania Press, 1955), 41.

22. David Scott Kastan, *Shakespeare and the Book* (Cambridge: Cambridge University Press, 2001), 29; Johnson, "Nicholas Ling, Publisher, 1580–1607." *Studies in Bibliography* 38 (1985): 203–14.

23. Johnson, "Nicholas Ling."

24. Kastan, *Shakespeare and the Book,* 29–30.

25. Ibid., 29.

26. Scott McMillin, "Casting the *Hamlet* Quartos: The Limit of Eleven," in *The Hamlet First Published (Q1, 1603): Origins, Forms, Intertextualities,* ed. Thomas Clayton (Newark: University of Delaware Press, 1992), 179–94, 184.

27. McMillin, "Casting," 179, 183.

28. Random Cloud [Randall McLeod], "What's the Bastard's Name?," in *Shakespeare's Speech-Headings: Speaking the Speech in Shakespeare's Plays,* ed. George Walton Williams (Newark: University of Delaware Press, 1997), demonstrates how much of the regularity of characters' names even in the apparatus is a function of later editing, rather than of the early texts themselves.

29. All citations from Q1 are taken from *The First Quarto of Hamlet,* ed. Kathleen O. Irace (Cambridge: Cambridge University Press, 1998). Since Q1 is not divided into acts, I have cited passages by scene and line number.

30. All citations from the Folio and Second Quarto texts of *Hamlet* are taken from

The Norton Shakespeare, based on the Oxford Edition, ed. Stephen Greenblatt et al., 2nd ed, (New York: Norton, 2008), which marks passages unique to the Second Quarto.

31. Interestingly, Hamlet's ability to name Rosencrantz and Guildenstern degenerates as the Q2 and F1 texts progress. Initially, he greets them by name. By Q2's closet scene, they are merely "my two schoolfellows, whom I will trust/As I will adders fanged" (3.4.185.1–2). (Here as elsewhere the *Norton* edition lineates passages found only in the Second Quarto separately from the rest of its *Hamlet* text; the relevant passage comes between the beginning and end of line 185 in the *Norton's* Folio-based text, and is lineated as lines 185.1–9.) Both Hamlet's relationship with them and his capacity to name them onstage have decayed. Once he has engineered their deaths, he has problems even making his references to them grammatically clear. "In the dark / Groped I to find out them, had my desire, / Fingered their packet," he says (5.2.14–16), providing his pronouns no antecedent and leaving the reader or listener groping in the dark a bit. One must supply Rosencrantz's and Guildenstern's identities to these clauses. Hamlet no longer supplies them. It's left to Horatio to return Rosencrantz's and Guildenstern's names to the language of the play and retroactively put names to Hamlet's tale of doomed messengers (5.2.57). Horatio takes over the task of speaking Rosencrantz's and Guildenstern's names for Hamlet, including reading them aloud from Hamlet's letter (4.6.23–24).

32. Furness, New Variorum, 2:138.

33. The hypothesis is well summarized in Hibbard 74–75.

34. The change of Montano/Reynaldo's name is perfectly straightforward in this respect. Only the old man ever speaks to his servant, and so only one actor's lines need to be revised.

35. A 1558 account entry from Bungay in Suffolk records expenses for preparing such parts, authorizing fourpence "for the interlude and game book" and two shillings "for writing of the parts" (E, K. Chambers, *The Medieval Stage*, 2 vols. (Oxford: Clarendon, 1903), 2:192, 343). E. K. Chambers argues that the difference between the cost of the master text and the cost of making the parts indicates that the Wardens of Bungay had purchased a printed interlude; the printed book was far less expensive than the scribal copies made from it. Although the cost of copying a manuscript play would be greater than the price of a printed copy, it is also clear that the preparation of parts was not a small expense. A typical "interlude" from 1558 would require parts for four men and a boy, while professional Elizabethan plays required minimum casts of eleven or more and were significantly longer than Tudor interludes, requiring more costly labor to copy out.

36. Peter Quince distributes just such partial scripts to the mechanicals ("Masters, here are your parts," *MND* 2.1.80–81) and Snug hopes to receive "the lion's part written" (2.1.55). Flute, famously, has trouble understanding the format of these acting texts, rushing past his colleagues' lines because they aren't written on his page. Quince has to rebuke him: "You speak all your part at once, cues and all" (3.1.86–87).

37. Dulwich MS 1, Item 138.

38. Laurie E. Maguire, *Shakespearean Suspect Texts: The "Bad" Quartos and Their Contexts* (Cambridge: Cambridge University Press, 1996), 78.

39. W. W. Greg, *Two Elizabethan Stage Abridgements: The Battle of Alcazar & Orlando*

Furioso (London: Printed for the Malone Society by F. Hall at the Oxford University Press, 1923), 139.

40. Tiffany Stern, *Making Shakespeare: From Stage to Page* (London: Routledge, 2004), 135–36, and *Rehearsal from Shakespeare to Sheridan* (Oxford: Oxford University Press, 2000), 106–10.

41. Stern, *Making Shakespeare*, 136.

42. Corambis's versions of these lines are closer to F than to Q2. Corambis's catalog of genres ends "pastoral-historical, historical-comical, comical-historical-pastoral, tragedy historical" (7.267–68). His theater criticism reads, "'Mobled queen' is good, faith, very good" (7.325).

43. Irace, *First Quarto of Hamlet*, 7. Irace set out to challenge the Marcellus hypothesis with a computer comparison of the "good" and "bad" texts, and found that the results of her quantitative analysis bore out the old claim ("Origins"; *Quarto* 6–7). However, Irace's test accepts a fundamental premise of the "orthodoxy" she wanted to examine. Her computer analysis asks whether the verbal correspondences Duthie et al. describe really exist (they do) but presumes that if the correspondences exist, then the traditional explanation for them is valid.

44. Peter Stallybrass, "Naming, Renaming and Unnaming in the Shakespearean Quartos and Folio," in *The Renaissance Text: Theory, Editing, Textuality*, ed. Andrew Murphy (Manchester: Manchester University Press, 2000), 108–34, 108–9.

45. Wickham et al. 494.

46. I am grateful to my colleague Richard M. Preiss for the financial context of Kempe's Norwich venture.

47. Gurr, *Playing Companies*, 281–84, 291–94.

48. Henslowe's and Alleyn's contract with the builder of the Fortune specifies various features of their new house which are to be "Contryved and fashioned Like unto . . . the saide Plaiehowse Called the Globe," but unlike the Globe, built from the old timbers of the dismantled Theater playhouse, the Fortune was to be built with "good stronge and substancyall newe Tymber" and the roof would be tile instead of thatch (qtd. in *Riverside*, 1849–50).

49. *Hamlet*, 2.2.325–45; TLN 1385–1408.

50. See James P. Bednarz, *Shakespeare and the Poets' War* (New York: Columbia University Press, 2001).

51. *Hamlet*, *Q1*, 7.247–49.

52. Henslowe 56, 216, 217.

53. Henslowe 219.

54. *Hamlet*, *Q1*, 7.270–76; *Hamlet*, 2.2.392.

55. Henslowe 200–203.

56. Chambers, *Elizabethan Stage*, 2:297.

57. *Hamlet*, 3.2.258; Henslowe 131–34.

58. *Hamlet*, *Q1* 9.55–60; *Hamlet*, 3.2.89–96; Henslowe 201.

59. Ben Jonson, *Poetaster*, ed. Tom Cain, (Manchester: University of Manchester Press, 1995), 1.2.45, 3.4.167, 4.3.24, 4.5.107, 5.3.416.

60. Thomas Dekker, *Satiro-Mastix, Or the Untrussing of a Humorous Poet* (London: William White, 1602), signatures C4v–D2v, F1v–F3v, I3r, L3r.

61. Ibid., C4v, L4r, F3r.
62. Ibid., G3v.
63. Ibid., H2v, C4v.
64. Ibid., F3v.
65. Jenkins, 475–77.
66. Ben Jonson, George Chapman, and John Marston, *Eastward Ho!*, ed. C. G. Petter (New York: W. W. Norton, 1994), 3.2.6.
67. Richard Horwich, "Hamlet and Eastward Ho," *SEL: Studies in English Literature, 1500–1900* 11, no. 2 (1971): 223–33, 233.
68. Ibid., 233.
69. Ibid., 227.
70. Jenkins 9–13.
71. Henslowe 203.

CHAPTER 4

1. The most comprehensive account of *Oldcastle*'s publication can be found in Douglas A. Brooks, *From Playhouse to Printing House: Drama and Authorship in Early Modern England*, Cambridge Studies in Renaissance Literature and Culture (Cambridge: Cambridge University Press, 2000), which illuminates the parallel developments of Oldcastle's and Shakespeare's iconographies. Brooks is deeply engaged with questions of material culture and of the dialectical relationships between rival texts, but less concerned with the exact nature and consequences of the 1619 attribution, or with the inconsistencies in traditional accounts of that attribution, which have been my chief interests here. Brooks's argument allows for, but by no means depends upon, the narrative that I contest, and my conclusions would tend to strengthen his basic claims about authorship while recognizing the complications and significance that previous explanations for Jaggard's quartos deny.

2. Sonia Massai, *Shakespeare and the Rise of the Editor* (Cambridge: Cambridge University Press, 2007), 114, has recently argued that the players would not be deceived by Jaggard's false dating, objecting that they "would probably have realized that at least some" of the quartos were falsely dated , but Massai does not detail how or why the players would have come to such a realization.

3. De Grazia and Stallybrass, "The Materiality of Shakespeare's Text," *Shakespeare Quarterly*, 44, no. 3 (Fall 1993): 255–83. 255.

4. McKerrow, *Devices*, 110.

5. W. W. Greg, "On Certain False Dates in Shakespeare Quartos," *The Library*, 2nd ser., no. 9 (1908): 113–31.

6. Greg made the first case for the 1619 quartos' fraudulent dates, converting Pollard to his cause, and Neidig provided the conclusive proof. Pollard recounts these events in *Shakespeare's Fight with the Pirates*, 2nd ed. (Cambridge: Cambridge University Press, 1920), viii–xiii. See also Greg's "On Certain False Dates in Shakespeare Quartos"; and Neidig's essay "The Shakespeare Quartos of 1619," *Modern Philology* 8, no. 2 (October 1910): 145–64.

7. Pollard, *Fight with the Pirates*, viii–ix; Greg, *Bibliography*, 3:1107–9.

8. Sonia Massai argues that Pavier was talked into the deception partway through the printing process by William Jaggard's son, Isaac (*Shakespeare and the Rise of the Editor*, 107). How Massai has divined these parties' particular intentions, or why she believes the idea stemmed from Isaac Jaggard rather than from William or from Thomas Pavier, is not clear.

9. Johnson, "Thomas Pavier, Publisher, 1600–1625," *The Library*, 6th ser., 14, no. 1 (March 1992): 12.

10. For example, the play's 1908 Malone Society facsimile still identifies the 1619 *Oldcastle* as the first publication and the genuine 1600 printing, without Shakespeare's name, as the second.

11. A. W. Pollard and J. Dover Wilson, "The 'Stolne and Surreptitious' Shakespearian Texts I: Why Some of Shakespeare's Plays Were Pirated," *Times Literary Supplement*, January 9, 1919: 18.

12. Maguire, *Shakespearean Suspect Texts*, 66–67.

13. Greg, "Dates," 58.

14. Ibid., 37–38.

15. Early English Books Online (EEBO); ESTC.

16. De Grazia, *Shakespeare Verbatim: The Reproduction of Authenticity and the 1790 Apparatus* (Oxford: Clarendon, 1991), 30; Kastan, *Shakespeare after Theory* (New York: Routledge, 1999), 84–85; Leo Kirschbaum, *Shakespeare and the Stationers* (Columbus: Ohio State University Press, 1955), 198–99, 298–300; Wells and Taylor, *Textual Companion*, 35–36.

17. Transcribed in W. A. Jackson, *Records of the Court of the Stationers' Company, 1602 to 1640* (London: Bibliographic Society, 1957), 110.

18. Joseph Loewenstein, *The Author's Due: Printing and the Prehistory of Copyright* (Chicago: University of Chicago Press, 2002), 98–100, 106–7, 141.

19. Ibid., 142. The book in question was William Fulke's *Confutation of the Rhemish Testament*, already a vexed case because the royal printer also claimed a privilege in it.

20. Gurr, *Playing Companies*, 186.

21. Chambers, *Elizabethan Stage*, 2:308.

22. Loewenstein, *Author's Due*, 122.

23. Ibid., 142.

24. Ibid., 27.

25. The 1619 title page is reproduced on p. xxi of the Malone Society edition: *The Life of Sir John Oldcastle, 1600*, ed. Percy Simpson (London: Printed for the Malone Society by Charles Whittingham & Co. at the Chiswick Press, 1908).

26. Johnson, "Pavier," 21–22, 35, 36.

27. De Grazia, *Shakespeare Verbatim*, 30–31, 44.

28. De Grazia and Stallybrass 261–62.

29. The constitution of the Folio has been examined recently by Jeffrey Masten, who also considers the Jonson and Beaumont and Fletcher folios, in his *Textual Intercourse Collaboration, Authorship, and Sexualities in Renaissance Drama* (Cambridge: Cambridge University Press, 1997); Peter Blayney in his *First Folio of Shakespeare* (Washington, D.C.:

Folger Library, 1991); and Kastan, *Shakespeare after Theory*. Arthur Marotti explores the parallel topic of Shakespeare's lyric canon, including Jaggard's *Passionate Pilgrim* anthology and his successor John Benson's *Poems Written by William Shakespeare*, in "Shakespeare's Sonnets as Literary Property," in *Soliciting Interpretation: Literary Theory and Seventeenth-Century English Poetry*, ed. Elizabeth D. Harvey and Katharine Eisaman Maus (Chicago: University of Chicago Press, 1990), 143–73.

30. *Sir John Oldcastle*, lines 6–7, printed in *The Oldcastle Controversy: Sir John Oldcastle, Part 1 and The famous Victories of Henry V*, ed. Peter Corbin and Douglas Sedge (Manchester: Manchester University Press, 1991).

31. *2 Henry IV*, TLN 3348.

32. Kawachi, *Calendar of English Renaissance Drama, 1558–1642* (New York: Garland, 1986), 111, 113, 122, 207, 232.

33. Roslyn L. Knutson, *The Repertory of Shakespeare's Company, 1594–1613* (Fayetteville: University of Arkansas Press, 1991), 95–96.

34. Henslowe 125–26; Gurr, *Companies*, 245.

35. Kawachi 111, 113; Gurr, *Companies*,116, 294; Knutson, *Repertory*, 79.

36. Gurr, *Companies*, 76, 245, 287.

37. Ibid., 245, 320.

38. Kawachi 122; Gurr, *Companies*, 245, 320.

39. Henslowe 213–16.

40. Kawachi 113; Knutson, *Repertory*, 95.

41. Kinney, *Titled Elizabethans: A Directory of Elizabethan State and Church Officers and Knights, with Peers of England, Scotland, and Ireland, 1558–1603* (Hamden, Conn.: Archon Books, 1973), 4, 31.

42. The King's Men are also recorded giving a play called "Sir John Falstaff" at court twice, in 1612–13 and in 1625, and performing a piece John Greene referred to as "Falstaff" at the Blackfriars in 1635. Gurr, *Companies*, 389; Bentley, *Jacobean*, 1:28; Sir Henry Herbert, *The Dramatic Records of Sir Henry Herbert, Master of the Revels 1623–1673*, ed. Joseph Quincy Adams (New Haven, Conn.: Yale University Press, 1917), 52.

43. Kastan, *Shakespeare after Theory*, 93–96.

44. Herbert, *Dramatic Records*, 76; Bentley, *Jacobean*, 1:28.

45. *Shakespeare after Theory*, 105.

46. Oldcastle and Falstaff had parallel careers in print as well as on stage. *Oldcastle* was registered and published hot on the heels of the Chamberlain's Men's *Henry V*, which had connections to the Oldcastle and Falstaff material; *2 Henry IV* followed immediately after that (Greg, *Bibliography*, 1:268–72). This seems to be a case where, as Blayney argues, the players used publication as advertising ("The Publication of Playbooks," in *A New History of Early English Drama*, ed. John D. Cox and David Scott Kastan [New York: Columbia University Press, 1997], 386). Here, the publicity for each company's property spurred the other troupe to advertise its counteroffering.

47. Greg, *Bibliography*, 1:243–44.

48. Blayney, "Publication of Playbooks," 399.

49. Greg, *Bibliography*, 1:243–44, 268–70.

50. Ibid., 1:16.

51. Blayney presents a somewhat different explanation of these events, including the "staying" of the later *Henry V* ("Publication of Playbooks," 399). My main difference from Blayney lies in our views of Millington and Busby's role; that they published the 1600 quarto, with Creed as printer-for-hire, might indicate that they gained control over a separate property, but there were other instances where the printers, rather than the "publishers," were the registered owners of a copy.

52. Greg, *Bibliography*, 1:16; Greg, *Folio*, 64.

53. Greg, *Bibliography*, 1:243–44.

54. Ibid., 1:203–5

55. Ibid., 1:178–80. For the chronology of the Folio's production, see Peter Blayney's *First Folio* and his introduction to the second edition of Charlton Hinman's *Norton Facsimile* (New York: W. W. Norton, 1996), xxvii–xl.

56. R. Carter Hailey, "The Dating Game: New Evidence for the Dates of Q4 *Romeo and Juliet* and Q4 *Hamlet*," *Shakespeare Quarterly* 58, no. 3 (Fall 2007): 367-87, 372.

57. Greg, *Bibliography*, 1:197; Hailey 372.

58. Hailey, "Dating Game," 379–81.

59. Greg, *Bibliography*, 1: 33.

60. Blayney, *First Folio* 2; Kastan, *Shakespeare after Theory*, 82.

61. Blayney, "Publication of Playbooks," 399.

62. De Grazia and Stallybrass 275–76.

63. Greg, *Bibliography*, 1:11, 20, 337–38.

64. Ibid., 1:24, 398–401.

65. Stallybrass, "Individual," 597; Kastan, *Shakespeare after Theory*, 37, 81.

66. De Grazia, *Shakespeare Verbatim*, 39.

67. Greg, *Bibliography*, 1:34–35.

68. Ibid., 1:419–22, 3:1107–9; Johnson, "Pavier," 14, 24.

69. Greg, *Bibliography*, 1:31, 278–81.

70. Ibid., 3:1107–9; McKerrow et al., *A Dictionary of Printers and Booksellers in England, Scotland and Ireland, and of Foreign Printers of English Books, 1557–1640* (London: Bibliographical Society, 1968), 227.

71. Technically, the rights to such "derelict" titles, in Greg's phrase, would revert to the Stationers' Company at large, but without an interested party to press his claims, such titles would likely be left undefended (Greg, *Folio*, 67).

72. Greg, *Bibliography*, 3:1107–9.

73. Ibid., 1:337, 420.

74. G. E. Bentley, *The Profession of Dramatist in Shakespeare's Time* (Princeton, N.J.: Princeton University Press, 1971), 241.

75. Heminges and Condell's note "To the great Variety of Readers" occupies signature A3r of the First Folio, and subsequent citations are taken from that page. The text is widely reproduced including in Chambers, *William Shakespeare*, 2:229–230 and in *The Riverside Shakespeare*, ed. G. Blakemore Evans et al. (Boston: Houghton Mifflin, 1974), 63.

76. *Shakespeare Verbatim*, 40–42.

77. See, for example, David M. Bergeron, "The King's Men's King's Men: Shakespeare and Folio Patronage," in *Textual Patronage in English Drama, 1570–1640* (Hants, UK: Ash-

gate, 2006), 141–60; de Grazia, *Shakespeare Verbatim*; Laurie E. Maguire, "Composition/Decomposition: Singular Shakespeare and the Death of the Author," in *The Renaissance Text: Theory, Editing, and Textuality*, ed. Andrew Murphy (Manchester: Manchester University Press, 2000), 135–53; and Leah Marcus, *Puzzling Shakespeare: Local Reading and Its Discontents* (Berkeley: University of California Press, 1988).

78. John Webster, *The White Devil*, ed. Elizabeth M. Brennan (New York: W. W. Norton, 1989), 6.

79. Chambers, *Shakespeare*, 2:226–27.

80. *Norton Facsimile*, 9–10.

81. Ibid., 15.

82. Ibid., 9.

83. Swans, of course, were royal birds, the property of the monarch.

84. Chambers, *Shakespeare*, 2:226.

85. *Norton Facsimile*, 10.

86. Ibid., 15.

87. Folio, signature A3r.

88. Irwin Smith, *Shakespeare's Blackfriars Playhouse: Its History and Design* (New York: New York University Press, 1964), 263–64.

89. The Burbage family owned half the lease on the Globe themselves, leaving the other half to be divided between all of the other partners, while the Blackfriars was originally divided into equal portions for each investor; each of Heminge's and Condell's Globe shares was in fact only half of a share.

90. Between 1617 and 1623, three King's Men quartos cited the Blackfriars, two the Globe, and two cited both theaters. In 1623 itself, one cited the Blackfriars and one both theaters (Greg, *Bibliography*, 2:493–537).

91. Tiffany Stern, "Was Totus Mundas Agit Histriunem Ever the Motto of the Globe Theatre?" *Theatre Notebook* 51, no. 3 (1997): 122–27.

92. All citations from *Henry V* are taken from *The Norton Shakespeare*, 2nd ed.

93. C. J. Sisson, "Shakespeare Quartos as Prompt-Copies, with Some Account of Cholmley's Players and a New Shakespeare Allusion," *Review of English Studies* 70 (1942): 129–43.

94. For discussion of this record's authenticity, see Thompson and Taylor's edition of *Hamlet*, 54–55.

95. *Mucedorus*, *1 Henry IV*, and *The Spanish Tragedy* are three of the four most frequently printed plays in the era, with *Mucedorus* the most frequently printed of all.

96. Gurr, "Shakespeare's Globe," 27–30.

CHAPTER 5

1. Arthur Colby Sprague, *Beaumont and Fletcher on the Restoration Stage* (Cambridge, Mass.: Harvard University Press, 1926), 8.

2. DNB. It may be that Beeston's inability to thrive came from a lack of courtly connections; he was eclipsed by D'Avenant both before and after the Civil War.

3. Allardyce Nicoll, *A History of English Drama, 1660–1900*, 7 vols. (Cambridge: Cambridge University Press, 1952), 1:289–90.

4. Qtd. in David Thomas and Arnold Hare, *Restoration and Georgian England, 1660–1788* (Cambridge: Cambridge University Press, 1989), 129.

5. *Lusts dominion; or, The Lascivious Queen: A Tragedie. Written by Christofer Marloe, Gent.* (London: Printed by Jane Bell for F. Kirkman, 1657), Wing L3504A.

6. William D'Avenant and William Shakespeare, *The Tragedy of Hamlet, Prince of Denmark as It Is Now Acted at His Highness the Duke of York's Theatre* (London: Printed for J. Martyn and H. Herringman, 1676), Wing S2950. ESTC R561.

7. D'Avenant and Shakespeare, A4r.

8. Greg, *Bibliography*, 1:313.

9. Ibid., 1:312–13.

10. John Freehafer, "The Formation of the London Patent Companies in 1660," *Theatre Notebook* 20, no. 1 (1965): 6–29.

11. ESTC R208092.

12. ESTC R38726.

13. A2r.

14. D4v.

15. A2v.

16. A3v.

17. Wing R2096; ESTC R7261; Greg, *Bibliography*, 2:882.

18. Chetwind did segregate his seven new plays into a separate section at the rear of the volume, with its own pagination, and some eighteenth-century editors would extend this practice. But this derives from the exigencies of printing itself. Adding each of the new plays in its proper place among the comedies, histories, or tragedies would have required Chetwind to typeset the entire volume from scratch. One of the chief economic attractions of reprinting an early modern book was that the compositor's most complicated work, casting off forms, had already been done.

19. Alfred Harbage, *Thomas Killigrew, Cavalier Dramatist, 1612–83* (Philadelphia: University of Pennsylvania Press, 1930), 117.

20. Wickham et al. 635–36.

21. Richard W. Bevis, *English Drama: Restoration and Eighteenth Century, 1660–1789* (London: Longman, 1988), 36; Allardyce Nicoll, *A History of English Drama, 1660–1900*, 7 vols. (Cambridge: Cambridge University Press, 1952), 1:303.

22. Gary Taylor, *Reinventing Shakespeare: A Cultural History, from the Restoration to the Present* (New York: Weidenfeld & Nicolson, 1989), 14.

23. Nicoll, *History*, 1:296.

24. Harbage, *Killigrew*, 117.

25. Thomas and Hare 16–17.

26. Nicoll, *History*, 1:352–53.

27. Sprague 13–17, 23–24.

28. Sandra Clark, "Shakespeare and Other Adaptations," in *A Companion to Restoration Drama*, ed. Susan J. Owen (Oxford: Blackwell, 2001), 274–90, 274.

29. Sprague 54.

30. George Powell, *The Treacherous Brothers, a tragedy, as it is acted at the Theatre-royal by His Majesty's servants* (London: W. Freeman, 1696), Wing P3057, signature A3r.

31. Odell 1:13.

32. Judith Milhous, *Thomas Betterton and the Management of Lincoln's Inn Fields, 1695–1708* (Carbondale, Ill.: Southern Illinois University Press, 1979), 97.

33. Ibid., 88–89.

34. William Congreve, *Love for Love, a Comedy: Acted at the Theatre in Little Lincolns-Inn Fields by His Majesty's servants* (London: Jacob Tonson, 1695), Wing C5851, signature A1r.

35. Odell 2:237.

WORKS CITED

Alexander, Peter. "The Taming of a Shrew." *Times Literary Supplement*. September 16, 1926. 614.
Arber, Edward, ed. *A Transcript of the Registers of the Company of Stationers of London: 1554–1640*. 5 vols. 1875–1894. New York: Peter Smith, 1950.
Aubrey, John. *Brief Lives*. Ed. Oliver Lawson Dick. Ann Arbor: University of Michigan Press, 1957.
Bakhtin, M. M. (Mikhail Mikhailovich). *The Dialogic Imagination: Four Essays*. Trans. Caryl Emerson and Michael Holquist. Ed. Michael Holquist. Austin: University of Texas Press, 1981.
Bale, John. *Brefe chronycle concernynge the examinacyon and death of the martyr Syr J. Oldecastell*. [Antwerp: A. Goinus,] 1544. STC 1276.
Barthes, Roland. "The Death of the Author." Barthes, *Image, Music, Text*. Trans. Stephen Heath. New York: Hill and Wang, 1977
Bednarz, James P. *Shakespeare and the Poets' War*. New York: Columbia University Press, 2001.
Beaumont, Francis, and John Fletcher. *The Dramatic Works in the Beaumont and Fletcher Canon*. Ed. Fredson Bowers et al. 10 vols. Cambridge: Cambridge University Press, 1966–96.
Bentley, Gerald Eades. *The Jacobean and Caroline Stage*. 7 vols. Oxford: Clarendon, 1941–68.
———. *The Profession of Dramatist in Shakespeare's Time*. Princeton, N.J.: Princeton University Press, 1971.
Bergeron, David M. "The King's Men's King's Men: Shakespeare and Folio Patronage." In *Shakespeare and Theatrical Patronage in Early Modern England*, ed. Paul Whitfield White and Suzanne R. Westfall. Cambridge: Cambridge University Press, 2002. 45–63.
Bevington, David. "Determining the Indeterminate: The Oxford Shakespeare." *Shakespeare Quarterly* 38, no. 4 (Winter 1987): 501–19.
Bevington, David, and Eric Rasmussen, eds., *Doctor Faustus: A- and B- Texts (1604, 1616)*. New York: Manchester University Press, 1993.
Bevis, Richard W. *English Drama: Restoration and Eighteenth Century, 1660–1789*. London: Longman, 1988.
Blagden, Cyprian. *The Stationers' Company; a History, 1403–1959*. London: Allen & Unwin, 1960.

Blayney, Peter W. M. *The First Folio of Shakespeare*. Washington, D.C.: Folger Library, 1991.
———. "The Publication of Playbooks." In *A New History of Early English Drama*, ed. John D. Cox and David Scott Kastan. New York: Columbia University Press, 1997. 383–422.
Bowers, Fredson. *On Editing Shakespeare and the Elizabethan Dramatists*. Philadelphia: University of Pennsylvania Press, 1955.
Brooks, Douglas A. "Sir John Oldcastle and the Construction of Shakespeare's Authorship." *SEL: Studies in English Literature, 1500–1900* 38, no. 2 (Spring 1998): 333–61.
———. *From Playhouse to Printing House: Drama and Authorship in Early Modern England*. Cambridge: Cambridge University Press, 2000.
Brown, Cedric C., and Arthur F. Marotti. *Texts and Cultural Change in Early Modern England*. Early Modern Literature in History. New York: St. Martin's Press, 1997.
Bullough, Geoffrey. *Narrative and Dramatic Sources of Shakespeare*. 7 vols. London: Routledge, 1957–73.
Burnett, Mark Thornton, and John Manning. *New Essays on Hamlet*. New York: AMS Press, 1994.
Carson, Neil. *Companion to Henslowe's Diary*. Cambridge: Cambridge University Press, 1988.
Chambers, E. K. *The Elizabethan Stage*. 4 vols. Oxford: Clarendon, 1923.
———. *The Medieval Stage*. 2 vols. Oxford: Clarendon, 1903.
———. *William Shakespeare: A Study of Facts and Problems*. 2 vols. Oxford: Clarendon, 1930.
The Charter of the Company of the Stationers of London. Rpt. Arber 1:xxviii–xxxii.
Chartier, Roger. *The Cultural Uses of Print in Early Modern France*. Princeton, N.J.: Princeton University Press, 1987.
———. *The Order of Books: Readers, Authors, and Libraries in Europe between the Fourteenth and Eighteenth Centuries*. Stanford: Stanford University Press, 1994.
———. *Publishing Drama in Early Modern Europe*. London: British Library, 1999.
Chettle, Henry. *The Tragedy of Hoffman, 1631*. London: Malone Society, 1951.
Cibber, Colley. *An Apology for the Life of Mr. Colley Cibber: Comedian, and Late Patentee of the Theatre-Royal. With an Historical View of the Stage During His Own Time*. London: Printed by John Watts for the author, 1740.
Clare, Janet. *"Art Made Tongue-Tied by Authority": Elizabethan and Jacobean Dramatic Censorship*. Manchester: Manchester University Press, 1990.
Clark, Sandra. "Shakespeare and Other Adaptations." In *A Companion to Restoration Drama*, ed. Susan J. Owen. Oxford: Blackwell, 2001. 274–90.
Clayton, Thomas. *The Hamlet First Published (Q1, 1603): Origins, Form, Intertextualities*. Newark: University of Delaware Press, 1992.
Cloud, Random [McLeod, Randall]. "What's the Bastard's Name?" In *Shakespeare's Speech-Headings*, ed. George Walton Williams. Newark: University of Delaware Press, 1997. 133–209.
Congreve, William. *Love for Love, a Comedy: Acted at the Theatre in Little Lincolns-Inn Fields by His Majesty's servants*. London: Jacob Tonson, 1695. Wing C5851.

Cox, John D., and David Scott Kastan. *A New History of Early English Drama*. New York: Columbia University Press, 1997.
Curren-Aquino, Deborah T. *King John: New Perspectives*. Cranbury, N.J.: Associated University Presses, 1989.
D'Avenant, William, and William Shakespeare. *The Tragedy of Hamlet, Prince of Denmark as It Is Now Acted at His Highness the Duke of York's Theatre*. London: Printed for J. Martyn and H. Herringman, 1676. Wing S2950.
De Grazia, Margreta. *Shakespeare Verbatim: The Reproduction of Authenticity and the 1790 Apparatus*. Oxford: Clarendon, 1991.
De Grazia, Margreta, Maureen Quilligan, and Peter Stallybrass. *Subject and Object in Renaissance Culture*. Cambridge: Cambridge University Press, 1996.
De Grazia, Margreta, and Stallybrass, Peter. "The Materiality of Shakespeare's Text." *Shakespeare Quarterly* 44, no. 3 (Fall 1993): 255–83.
De Grazia, Margreta, and Stanley W. Wells. *The Cambridge Companion to Shakespeare*. Cambridge Companions to Literature. Cambridge: Cambridge University Press, 2001.
Dekker, Thomas. *Satiro-Mastix. Or the Untrussing of a Humorous Poet. . . .* London: William White, 1602. STC 6521.
———. *Satiromastix*. In *The Dramatic Works of Thomas Dekker*, ed. Fredson Bowers. 4 vols. Cambridge: Cambridge University Press, 1953. 1:299–395.
Dictionary of National Biography (DNB). Ed. Leslie Stephen and Sidney Lee. 22 vols. New York: Macmillan, 1908–9.
Downes, John, and John Clyde Loftis. *Roscius Anglicanus (1708)*. Los Angeles: William Andrews Clark Memorial Library University of California, 1969.
Duncan-Jones, Katherine. *Ungentle Shakespeare: Scenes from His Life*. London: Arden, 2001.
During, Simon. *The Cultural Studies Reader*. New York: Routledge, 1993.
Dutton, Richard. *Licensing, Censorship, and Authorship in Early Modern England*. New York: Palgrave, 2000.
———. *Mastering the Revels: The Regulation and Censorship of English Renaissance Drama*. Iowa City: University of Iowa Press, 1991.
———, and Jean E. Howard. *A Companion to Shakespeare's Works*. Malden, Mass.: Blackwell, 2003.
Early English Books Online (EEBO). ProQuest Information and Learning Company, 2003–10. http://eebo.chadwyck.com/.
Eccles, Mark. "Elizabethan Actors IV: S to End." *Notes & Queries* 238 (1993): 165–76.
Edmond, Mary. "Pembroke's Men." *Review of English Studies* n.s. 25 (1974): 129–36.
English Renaissance Drama. Ed. David Bevington et al. New York: W. W. Norton, 2002.
English Short-Title Catalog. The British Library and ESTC/North America, 1981–2010. http://eureka.rlg.org/Eureka/zgate2.prod.
Erne, Lukas. *Shakespeare as Literary Dramatist*. Cambridge: Cambridge University Press, 2003.
Fletcher, Alan J. *Drama, Performance and Polity in Pre-Cromwellian Ireland*. Cork: Cork University Press 2000.

Foster, Maxwell E., Anne Shiras, and William Shakespeare. *The Play behind the Play: Hamlet and Quarto One*. Portsmouth, N.H.: Heinemann, 1998.
Foucault, Michel. "What Is an Author?" In *The Foucault Reader*, ed. Paul Rabinow. New York: Pantheon Books, 1984. 101–20.
Freehafer, John. "The Formation of the London Patent Companies in 1660." *Theatre Notebook* 20, no. 1 (1965): 6–29.
Furness, Horace Howard. *A Concordance to Shakespeare's Poems: An Index to Every Word Therein Contained*. Philadelphia: Lippincott, 1875.
Gesta Grayorum. 1688. The Malone Society Reprints. Ed. W. W. Greg. London: Malone Society, 1914.
Goy-Blanquet, Dominique. *Shakespeare's Early History Plays: From Chronicle to Stage*. Oxford: Oxford University Press, 2003.
Greco, Albert N. *The Book Publishing Industry*. Boston: Allyn and Bacon, 1997.
Greenblatt, Stephen. *Shakespearean Negotiations*. Berkeley: University of California Press, 1988.
———. *Will in the World*. New York: Norton, 2004.
Greene, Robert. *Greenes Arcadia. Or Menaphon: Camillaes Alarum to Slumber Euphues in His Melancholy Cell at Silexedra*. . . . London: Printed for Iohn Smethwicke, 1599. STC 12275
———. *The Historie of Orlando Furioso, One of the Twelue Pieres of France. as It Was Plaid before the Queenes Maiestie*. London: Printed by Iohn Danter for Cuthbert Burbie and are to be sold at his shop nere the Royall Exchange, 1594. STC 12265.
———. *Menaphon. Camillas Alarum to Slumbering Euphues, in His Melancholie Cell at Silexedra*. . . . London: Printed for Sampson Clarke, 1589.
Greenes Groats-Vvorth of Witte, Bought with a Million of Repentance. . . . London: Imprinted for William Wright, 1592. STC 12245.
Greenes Groatsworth of Wit. Ed. D. Allen Carroll. Binghamton, N.Y.: Center for Medieval and Early Renaissance Studies, State University of New York at Binghamton, 1994.
Greenfield, Jon. "Design as Reconstruction: Reconstruction as Design." In *Shakespeare's Globe Rebuilt*, ed. J. R. Mulryne and Margaret Shrewring. Cambridge: Cambridge University Press, 1997. 81–96.
Greetham, D. C. *Textual Scholarship: An Introduction*. New York: Garland, 1994.
Greg, W. W. *A Bibliography of the English Printed Drama to the Restoration*. 4 vols. London: Printed for the Bibliographical Society at the University Press, Oxford, 1939–59.
———. *A Companion to Arber: Being a Calendar of Documents in Edward Arber's "Transcript of the Registers of the Company of Stationers of London, 1554–1640" with Text and Calendar of Supplementary Documents*. Oxford: Clarendon, 1967.
———. *Dramatic Documents from the Elizabethan Playhouses*. Oxford: Clarendon, 1931.
———. *The Editorial Problem in Shakespeare: A Survey of the Foundations of the Text*. 2nd ed. Oxford: Clarendon Press, 1951.
———. *The Evidence of Theatrical Plots for the History of the Elizabethan Stage*. London: Sidwick & Jackson Ltd., 1925.
———. "On Certain False Dates in Shakespeare Quartos." *The Library*, 2nd ser., 9 (1908): 113–31.

———. *Principles of Emendation in Shakespeare*. London: H. Milford, 1928.
———. *The Shakespeare First Folio*. Oxford: Clarendon, 1955.
———. *Sir Walter Wilson Greg: A Collection of His Writings*. Ed. Joseph Rosenblum. Lanham, Md.: Scarecrow Press, 1998.
———. *Two Elizabethan Stage Abridgements: The Battle of Alcazar & Orlando Furioso*. London: Printed for the Malone Society by F. Hall at the Oxford University Press, 1923.
Gurr, Andrew. "Did Shakespeare Own His Own Playbooks?" *Review of English Studies*, n.s., 60, no. 244 (2008): 206–29
———. "The First Plays at the New Globe." *Theatre Notebook* 51, no. 1 (1997): 4–7.
———. *Playgoing in Shakespeare's London*. Cambridge: Cambridge University Press, 1987.
———. *The Shakespeare Company, 1594–1642*. Cambridge: Cambridge University Press, 2004.
———. *The Shakespearean Stage, 1574–1642*. 3rd ed. Cambridge: Cambridge University Press, 1992.
———. "Shakespeare's Globe: A History of Reconstructions and Some Reasons for Trying." In *Shakespeare's Globe Rebuilt*, ed. J. R. Mulryne and Margaret Shewring. Cambridge: Cambridge University Press, 1997. 27–47.
———. *The Shakespearian Playing Companies*. Oxford: Clarendon, 1996.
———. "Staging at the Globe." In *Shakespeare's Globe Rebuilt*, ed. J. R. Mulryne and Margaret Shewring. Cambridge: Cambridge University Press, 1997. 159–68.
Hailey, R. Carter. "The Dating Game: New Evidence for the Dates of Q4 *Romeo and Juliet* and Q4 *Hamlet*." *Shakespeare Quarterly* 58, no. 3 (2007 Fall): 367–87.
Hamel, Guy. "King John and The Troublesome Raigne: A Reexamination." In *King John: New Perspectives*, ed. Deborah T. Curren-Aquino. Cranbury, N.J.: Associated University Presses, 1989. 41–61.
Harbage, Alfred. *Shakespeare and the Rival Traditions*. New York: Macmillan, 1952.
———. *Sir William Davenant, Poet Venturer, 1606–1668*. Philadelphia: University of Pennsylvania Press, 1935.
———. *Thomas Killigrew, Cavalier Dramatist, 1612–83*. Philadelphia: University of Pennsylvania Press, 1930.
Hayashi, Tetsumaro, and Robert Greene. *A Textual Study of Robert Greene's Orlando Furioso, with an Elizabethan Text*. Muncie, Ind.: Ball State University Press, 1973.
Henry VI: Critical Essays. Ed. Thomas A. Pendleton. New York: Routledge, 2001.
Henslowe, Philip. *Henslowe's Diary*. Ed. R. A. Foakes. 2nd ed. Cambridge: Cambridge University Press, 2002.
Henslowe, Philip, et al. *Henslowe Papers, Being Documents Supplementary to Henslowe's Diary*. London: A. H. Bullen, 1907.
Herbert, Sir Henry. *The Dramatic Records of Sir Henry Herbert, Master of the Revels 1623–1673*. Ed. Joseph Quincy Adams. New Haven, Conn.: Yale University Press, 1917.
Holzknecht, Karl J. *The Backgrounds of Shakespeare's Plays*. New York: American Book Company, 1950.
Honigmann, E. A. J., and Susan Brock, eds. *Playhouse Wills, 1558–1642: An Edition of Wills by Shakespeare and His Contemporaries in the London Theatre*. Manchester: Manchester University Press, 1993.

E. A. J. Honigmann, "The Date of *Hamlet*." *Shakespeare Survey* 9 (1956): 24–34.

———. "The New Bibliography and Its Critics." In *Textual Performances: The Modern Reproducton of Shakespeare's Drama*, ed. Lukas Erne and Margaret Jane Kidnie. Cambridge: Cambridge University Press, 2004. 77–93.

Horwich, Richard. "Hamlet and Eastward Ho." *SEL: Studies in English Literature, 1500–1900* 11, no. 2 (1971): 223–33.

Hume, Robert D., and Arthur Hawley Scouten. *The London Theatre World, 1660–1800*. Carbondale: Southern Illinois University Press, 1980.

Ingram, William. *The Business of Playing: The Beginnings of the Adult Professional Theater in Elizabethan London*. Ithaca, N.Y.: Cornell University Press, 1992.

Irace, Kathleen O. "Origins and Agents of Q1 *Hamlet*." In *The Hamlet First Published (Q1, 1603): Origins, Forms, Intertextualities*, ed. Thomas Clayton. Newark: University of Delaware Press, 1992. 90–122.

———. *Reforming the "Bad" Quartos: Performance and Provenance of Six Shakespearean First Editions*. Newark: University of Delaware Press, 1994.

Jackson, W. A. *Records of the Court of the Stationers' Company, 1602 to 1640*. London: Bibliographic Society, 1957.

Jaggard, William. *A catalogue of such English bookes, as lately haue bene, and now are in printing for publication From the ninth day of October, 1618.* . . . London: Printed by W. Iaggard, 1618. STC 14341.

Johns, Adrian. *The Nature of the Book: Print and Knowledge in the Making*. Chicago: University of Chicago Press, 1998.

Johnson, Gerald D. "Nicholas Ling, Publisher, 1580–1607." *Studies in Bibliography* 38 (1985): 203–14.

———. "Thomas Pavier, Publisher, 1600–1625." *The Library*, 6th ser., 14, no. 1 (March 1992): 12–50.

Jonson, Ben. *Bartholomew Fair*. Ed. Suzanne Gossett. Manchester: Manchester University Press, 2000.

———. *Ben Jonson*. Ed. C. H. Herford, Percy Simpson, and Evelyn Simpson. 11 vols. Oxford: Clarendon, 1925–52.

———. *Poetaster*. Ed. Tom Cain. Manchester: University of Manchester Press, 1995.

———, George Chapman, and John Marston. *Eastward Ho!* Ed. C. G. Petter. New York: Norton, 1994.

Kastan, David Scott. *A Companion to Shakespeare*. Malden: Blackwell, 1999.

———. *Shakespeare after Theory*. New York: Routledge, 1999.

———. *Shakespeare and the Book*. Cambridge: Cambridge University Press, 2001.

Kastan, David Scott, and Peter Stallybrass. *Staging the Renaissance: Essays on Elizabethan and Jacobean Drama*. New York: Routledge, 1991.

Kathman, David. "Reconsidering *The Seven Deadly Sins*." *Early Theatre* 7, no. 1 (2004): 13–44.

Kawachi, Yoshiko. *Calendar of English Renaissance Drama, 1558–1642*. New York: Garland, 1986.

Keenan, Siobhan, *Travelling Players in Shakespeare's England*. New York: Palgrave Macmillan, 2002.

Keenan, Siobhan, and Peter Davidson. "The Iconography of the Bankside Globe." In *Shakespeare's Globe Rebuilt*, ed. J. R. Mulryne and Margaret Shewring. 147–56.

Kemp, William. *Nine Daies Wonder* 1600. Ed. G. B. Harrison. London: Bodley Head, 1923.

Kewes, Paulina. *Authorship and Appropriation: Writing for the Stage in England, 1660–1710*. Oxford: Clarendon, 1998.

King Leir. Ed. Tiffany Stern. New York: Routledge, 2002.

Kinney, Arthur F. *Titled Elizabethans: A Directory of Elizabethan State and Church Officers and Knights, with Peers of England, Scotland, and Ireland, 1558–1603*. Hamden, Conn.: Archon Books, 1973.

Kirschbaum, Leo. *Shakespeare and the Stationers*. Columbus: Ohio State University Press, 1955.

Knutson, Roslyn L. "Evidence for the Assignment of Plays to the Repertory of Shakespeare's Company," *Medieval and Renaissance Drama in England* 4 (1989): 63–89.

———. "Influence of the Repertory System on the Revival and Revision of the Spanish Tragedy and Dr. Faustus." *English Literary Renaissance* 18, no. 2 (Spring 1988): 257–74.

———. "*Henslowe's Diary* and the Economics of Play Revision for Revival, 1592–1603." *Theatre Research International* 10 (1985): 1–18.

———. "Marlowe, Company Ownership, and the Role of Edward II." *Medieval and Renaissance Drama in England* 18 (2005).

———. *Playing Companies and Commerce in Shakespeare's Time*. New York: Cambridge University Press, 2001.

———. "The Repertory." In *A New History of Early English Drama*, ed. John D. Cox and David Scott Kastan. New York: Columbia University Press, 1997. 461–80.

———. *The Repertory of Shakespeare's Company, 1594–1613*. Fayetteville: University of Arkansas Press, 1991.

Kyd, Thomas. *The Spanish Tragedy*. Ed. J. R. Mulryne. 2nd ed. New York: Norton, 1989.

Landro, Philip. "Henslowe's Relocation to the North: Playhouse Management in Renaissance London." *Theatre Survey* 38, no. 2 (November 1997): 31–47.

The Life of Sir John Oldcastle, 1600. Malone Society Reprint. Ed. Percy Simpson. [London]: Printed for the Malone Society by Charles Whittingham & Co. at the Chiswick Press, 1908.

Lodge, Thomas, and Robert Greene. *A Looking Glasse for London and England. Made by Thomas Lodge Gentleman, and Robert Greene. In Artibus Magister*. London: Printed by Thomas Creede, 1594. STC 16679.

Loewenstein, Joseph. *The Author's Due: Printing and the Prehistory of Copyright*. Chicago: University of Chicago Press, 2002.

———. *Ben Jonson and Possessive Authorship*. Cambridge Studies in Renaissance Literature and Culture, [43]. New York: Cambridge University Press, 2002.

———. "The Script in the Marketplace." *Representations* 12 (Fall 1985): 101–14.

———. "Spenser's Retrography: Two Episodes in Post-Petrarchan Bibliography." In *Spenser's Life and the Subject of Biography*, ed. Judith H. Anderson, Donald Cheney, and David A. Richardson. Amherst: University of Massachusetts Press, 1996. 99–130.

Lusts Dominion, or, The Lascivious Queen, a tragedie. London: Printed for F.K. and are to be sold by Robert Pollard, 1657. Wing L3504A.

Maguire, Laurie E. "Composition/Decomposition: Singular Shakespeare and the Death of the Author." In *The Renaissance Text: Theory, Editing, Textuality*, ed. Andrew Murphy. Manchester: Manchester University Press, 2000. 135–53.

———. *Shakespearean Suspect Texts: The "Bad" Quartos and Their Contexts*. New York: Cambridge University Press, 1996.

Maguire, Laurie, and Thomas L. Berger. *Textual Formations and Reformations*. Newark: University of Delaware Press, 1998.

Marcus, Leah. *Puzzling Shakespeare: Local Reading and Its Discontents*. Berkeley: University of California Press, 1988.

———. *Unediting the Renaissance: Shakespeare, Marlowe, Milton*. London: Routledge, 1996.

Marotti, Arthur. "Shakespeare's Sonnets as Literary Property." In *Soliciting Interpretation: Literary Theory and Seventeenth-Century English Poetry*, ed. Elizabeth D. Harvey and Katharine Eisaman Maus. Chicago: University of Chicago Press, 1990. 143–73.

Martone, Michael. *Double-Wide: Collected Fiction of Michael Martone*. Bloomington, Ind.: Quarry Press, 2007.

Marston, John. *Antonio's Revenge*. Ed. G. K. Hunter. Lincoln: University of Nebraska Press, 1965.

Massai, Sonia. *Shakespeare and the Rise of the Editor*. Cambridge: Cambridge University Press, 2007.

Masten, Jeffrey. *Textual Intercourse. Collaboration, Authorship, and Sexualities in Renaissance Drama*. Cambridge: Cambridge University Press, 1997.

McGann, Jerome J. *A Critique of Modern Textual Criticism*. Chicago: University of Chicago Press, 1983.

McKenzie, D. F. *Bibliography and the Sociology of Texts*. New York: Cambridge University Press, 1999.

———. *Stationers' Company Apprentices, 1605–1640*. Charlottesville: Bibliographical Society of the University of Virginia, 1961.

———. *Stationers' Company Apprentices, 1641–1700*. Oxford: Oxford Bibliographical Society, 1974.

McKerrow, Ronald Brunlees. "The Elizabethan Printer and Dramatic Manuscripts." *The Library* 12, no. 3 (December 1931): 253–75. Reprinted in *Ronald Brunlees McKerrow: A Selection of His Essays*, ed. John Phillip Immroth. Metuchen, N.J.: Scarecrow Press, 1974. 139–58.

———. *An Introduction to Bibliography for Literary Students*. 2nd impression. Oxford: Clarendon Press, 1928.

———. *Printers' & Publishers' Devices in England & Scotland, 1485–1640*. London: The Bibliographical Society, 1949.

———. *Ronald Brunlees McKerrow: A Selection of His Essays*. Metuchen, N.J.: Scarecrow Press, 1974.

———. "A Suggestion Regarding Shakespeare's Manuscripts." *Review of English Studies* 11, no. 44 (October 1935): 459–65.

McKerrow, Ronald Brunlees, and F. S. Ferguson. *Title-Page Borders Used in England & Scotland, 1485–1640*. London: Printed for the Bibliographical society at the Oxford University Press, 1932.

McKerrow, Ronald Brunlees et al. *A Dictionary of Printers and Booksellers in England, Scotland and Ireland, and of Foreign Printers of English Books, 1557–1640.* London: Bibliographical Society, 1968.

McMillin, Scott. "Casting the *Hamlet* Quartos: The Limit of Eleven." In *The Hamlet First Published (Q1, 1603): Origins, Forms, Intertextualities,* ed. Thomas Clayton. Newark: University of Delaware Press, 1992. 179–94.

———. "Simon Jewell and the Queen's Men." *Review of English Studies,* n.s., 27, no. 106 (May 1976): 174-77.

McMillin, Scott, and Sally-Beth MacLean. *The Queen's Men and Their Plays.* Cambridge: Cambridge University Press, 1998.

The Merry conceited humors of Bottom the weaver. As it hath often been publikely acted. . . . London: Printed for F. Kirkman and H. Marsh, 1661. Wing S2937.

Milhous, Judith. *Thomas Betterton and the Management of Lincoln's Inn Fields, 1695–1708.* Carbondale: Southern Illinois University Press, 1979.

Milhous, Judith, and Robert D. Hume. *A Register of English Theatrical Documents, 1660–1737.* Carbondale: Southern Illinois University Press, 1991.

Morash, Christopher. *A History of Irish Theatre, 1601–2000.* Cambridge: Cambridge University Press, 2002.

Morrison, Paul G. *Index of Printers, Publishers and Booksellers in A. W. Pollard and G. R. Redgrave a Short-Title Catalogue of Books Printed in England, Scotland & Ireland: And of English Books Printed Abroad, 1475–1640.* Charlottesville, Va.: Bibliographical Society of the University of Virginia, 1950.

A most pleasant and merie nevv comedie, intituled, A knacke to knowe a knaue.... London: Richard Iones, 1594. STC 15027.

Muir, Kenneth. *Shakespeare's Sources. I: Comedies and Tragedies.* London: Methuen, 1961.

Munday, Anthony, Henry Chettle, Michael Drayton, and Robert Wilson. *The first part of the true and honorable historie, of the life of Sir Iohn Old-castle, the good Lord Cobham....* London: Printed for Thomas Pauier, 1600. STC 18795.

———. *The first part of the true & honorable history, of the life of Sir Iohn Old-castle, the good Lord Cobham....* London: Printed for T[homas] P[auier], n.d. [1619]. STC 18796.

Mulryne, J. R., and Margaret Shewring, eds. *Shakespeare's Globe Rebuilt.* Cambridge: Cambridge University Press, 1997.

Murphy, Andrew. "Birth of the Editor." In *A Concise Companion to Shakespeare and the Text,* ed. Andrew Murphy. Malden, Mass.: Blackwell, 2007. 93–108.

———, ed. *A Concise Companion to Shakespeare and the Text.* Malden, Mass.: Blackwell, 2007.

———, ed. *The Renaissance Text: Theory, Editing, Textuality.* New York: Manchester University Press, 2000.

———. *Shakespeare in Print. A History and Chronology of Shakespeare Publishing.* Cambridge: Cambridge University Press, 2003.

Myers, Robin, and Michael Harris. *The Stationers' Company and the Book Trade, 1550–1990.* New Castle, Del.: Oak Knoll Press, 1997.

Nashe, Thomas. *Works of Thomas Nashe.* Ed. R. B. McKerrow. 5 vols. London: Sidgwick & Jackson, 1910.

———. *The Unfortunate Traveller and Other Works*. Ed. J. B. Steane. London: Penguin, 1971.

Neidig, William. "False Dates on Shakespeare Quartos." *Century Magazine* (October 1910): 912–19.

———. "The Shakespeare Quartos of 1619." *Modern Philology* (October 1910): 145–64.

Nicoll, Allardyce. *A History of English Drama, 1660–1900*. 7 vols. Cambridge: Cambridge University Press, 1952.

———. *A Short-Title Alphabetical Catalogue of Plays: Produced or Printed in England from 1660 to 1900*. Cambridge: Cambridge University Press, 1959.

North, Marcy L. *The Anonymous Renaissance: Cultures of Discretion in Tudor-Stuart England*. Chicago: University of Chicago Press, 2003.

The Norton Facsimile, the First Folio of Shakespeare. Ed. Charlton Hinman. 2nd ed. Intro. Peter W. M. Blayney. New York: Norton, 1996.

Norton, Thomas, and Thomas Sackville. *The tragedie of Gorboduc*. . . . London: William Griffith, 1565. STC 18684.

Odell, George C. D. *Shakespeare from Betterton to Irving*. 2 vols. New York: Scribners, 1920. Reprint, New York: Dover, 1966.

The Oldcastle Controversy: Sir John Oldcastle, Part 1, and The Famous Victories of Henry V. Ed. Peter Corbin and Douglas Sedge. Manchester: Manchester University Press, 1991.

Orgel, Stephen. "What's the Globe Good For?" *Shakespeare Quarterly* 49, no. 2 (1998): 191–93.

Orrell, John. "Designing the Globe: Reading the Documents." In *Shakespeare's Globe Rebuilt*, ed. J. R. Mulryne and Margaret Shewring. Cambridge: Cambridge University Press, 1997. 51–65.

Owen, Susan J. *A Companion to Restoration Drama*. Blackwell Companions to Literature and Culture. Oxford: Blackwell, 2001.

The Oxford English Dictionary. 2nd ed. Prepared by J. A. Simpson and E. S. C. Weiner. Oxford: Clarendon, 1989.

Palfrey, Simon, and Tiffany Stern. *Shakespeare in Parts*. Oxford: Oxford University Press, 2007.

Patterson, Annabel. "Censorship and Interpretation." In *Staging the Renaissance: Reinterpretations of Elizabethan and Jacobean Drama*, ed. David Scott Kastan and Peter Stallybrass. New York: Routledge, 1991. 40–48.

Peters, Julie Stone. *Theatre of the Book, 1480–1880: Print, Text, and Performance in Europe*. Oxford: Oxford University Press, 2000.

Plomer, Henry Robert, et al. *A Dictionary of the Printers and Booksellers Who Were at Work in England, Scotland and Ireland from 1726 to 1775*. [Oxford]: Printed for the Bibliographical Society at the Oxford University Press, 1932.

Pollard, Alfred W. *Early Illustrated Books: A History of the Decoration and Illustration of Books in the 15th and 16th Centuries*. 3rd. ed. New York: Empire State Book Company, 1927.

———. *Shakespeare's Fight with the Pirates and the Problems of the Transmission of His Text*. 2nd ed. Cambridge: Cambridge University Press, 1920.

———. *Shakespeare Folios and Quartos: A Study in the Bibliography of Shakespeare's Plays, 1594–1685*. London: Methuen, 1909.
——— et al. *Shakespeare's Hand in the Play of Sir Thomas More*. Cambridge: Cambridge University Press, 1923.
——— and J. Dover Wilson, "The 'Stolne and Surreptitious' Shakespearian Texts I: Why Some of Shakespeare's Plays Were Pirated." *Times Literary Supplement*, January 9, 1919: 18.
Poole, Kristen. "Saints Alive! Falstaff, Martin Marprelate, and the Staging of Puritanism." *Shakespeare Quarterly* 46, no. 1 (Fall 1995): 47–75.
Powell, George. *The Treacherous Brothers, a tragedy, as it is acted at the Theatre-royal by His Majesty's servants*. London: W. Freeman, 1696. Wing P3057.
Rasmussen, Eric. "The Revision of Scripts." In *A New History of Early English Drama*, ed. John D. Cox and David Scott Kastan. New York: Columbia University Press, 1997. 441–60.
Records of the Court of the Stationers Company, 1602 to 1640. Ed. William A. Jackson. London: Bibliographic Society, 1957.
Riggs, David. *Ben Jonson: A Life*. Cambridge, Mass.: Harvard University Press, 1989.
Rose, Mark. *Authors and Owners: The Invention of Copyright*. Cambridge, Mass.: Harvard University Press, 1993.
Rosenthal, Laura J. *Playwrights and Plagiarists in Early Modern England: Gender, Authorship, Literary Property*. Ithaca, N.Y.: Cornell University Press, 1996.
Rowley, William. *The birth of Merlin, or, The childe hath found his father as it hath been several times acted with great applause / written by William Shakespear and William Rowley*. London: Printed by Tho. Johnson for Francis Kirkman and Henry Marsh, 1662. Wing R2096.
Saint-Amour, Paul K. *The Copywrights: Intellectual Property and the Literary Imagination*. Ithaca, N.Y.: Cornell University Press, 2003.
Sams, Eric. "The Timing of the *Shrews*." *Notes and Queries* 32, no. 1 (March 1985): 33-45
Schoenbaum, S. *Renaissance Drama*. Vol. 7. Evanston, Ill.: Northwestern University Press, 1964.
Schoone-Jongen, Terence G. *Shakespeare's Companies: William Shakespeare's Early Career and the Acting Companies, 1577–1594*. Studies in Performance and Early Modern Drama. Burlington, Vt.: Ashgate, 2008.
Seary, Peter. *Lewis Theobald and the Editing of Shakespeare*. Oxford: Clarendon 1990
Sedgwick, Eve Kosofsky. *Between Men: English Literature and Male Homosocial Desire*. Gender and Culture. New York: Columbia University Press, 1985.
Shakespeare, William. *The Complete Oxford Shakespeare*. Ed. Stanley W. Wells and Gary Taylor. Oxford: Oxford University Press, 1987.
———. *The First Part of King Henry VI*. Ed. Michael Hattaway. The New Cambridge Shakespeare. Cambridge: Cambridge University Press, 1990.
———. *The First Quarto of Hamlet*. Ed. Kathleen O. Irace. Cambridge: Cambridge University Press, 1998.
———. *The First Quarto of King Henry V*. Ed. Andrew Gurr. Cambridge: Cambridge University Press, 2000.

---. *The First Quarto of King Richard III*. Ed. Peter Davison. Cambridge: Cambridge University Press, 1996.

---. *Hamlet*. Ed. A. R. Braunmuller. New York: Penguin, 2001.

---. *Hamlet*. Ed. Philip Edwards. The New Cambridge Shakespeare. Cambridge: Cambridge University Press, 2003.

---. *Hamlet*. Ed. Horace Howard Furness. New Variorum Edition of Shakespeare. 2 vols. Philadelphia: J. B. Lippincott, 1877.

---. *Hamlet*. Ed. G. R. Hibbard. Oxford: Oxford University Press, 1987.

---. *Hamlet*. Ed. Harold Jenkins. The Arden Edition of the Works of William Shakespeare. 2nd ser. New York: Methuen, 1982.

---. *Hamlet*. Ed. Ann Thompson and Neil Taylor. The Arden Shakespeare. 3rd ser. London: Thomson Learning, 2006.

---. *Henry VI, Part I*. Ed. J. Dover Wilson. The New Shakespeare. Cambridge: Cambridge University Press, 1952.

---. *Henry VI, Part II*. Ed. J. Dover Wilson. The New Shakespeare. Cambridge: Cambridge University Press, 1952.

---. *Henry VI, Part III*. Ed. J. Dover Wilson. The New Shakespeare. Cambridge: Cambridge University Press, 1952.

---. *King John*. Ed. E. A. J. Honigmann. The Arden Edition of the Works of William Shakespeare. 2nd ser. London: Methuen, 1954.

---. *King John*. Ed. Lester A. Beaurline. The New Cambridge Shakespeare. Cambridge: Cambridge University Press, 1990.

---. *Mr. VVilliam Shakespeares comedies, histories, & tragedies Published according to the true originall copies*. London: Printed by Isaac Iaggard, and Ed. Blount [at the charges of W. Iaggard, Ed. Blount, I. Smithweeke, and W. Aspley], 1623. STC 22273.

---. *Mr. William Shakespear's comedies, histories and tragedies published according to the true original copies: and unto this impression is added seven plays never before printed in folio*. London: Printed for P. C. (Philip Chetwind), 1664. Wing S2914.

---. *The most lamentable Romaine tragedie of Titus Andronicus As it was plaide by the right honourable the Earle of Darbie, Earl of Pembrooke, and Earl of Sussex their seruants*. London: Printed by Iohn Danter, 1594. STC 22328.

---. *The most lamentable Romaine tragedie of Titus Andronicus As it hath sundry times beene playde by the Right Honourable the Earle of Pembrooke, the Earle of Darbie, the Earle of Sussex, and the Lorde Chamberlaine theyr Seruants*. London: Printed for Edward VVhite, 1600. STC 22329.

---. *The Norton Shakespeare*. Ed. Stephen Greenblatt et al. New York: Norton, 1997.

---. *The Norton Shakespeare. Based on the Oxford Edition*. Ed. Stephen Greenblatt et al. 2nd ed. New York: Norton, 2008.

---. *Richard III*. Ed. Anthony Hammond. The Arden Edition of the Works of William Shakespeare. 2nd ser. London: Methuen, 1981.

---. *Richard III*. Ed. J. Dover Wilson. The New Shakespeare. Cambridge: Cambridge University Press, 1954.

---. *The Riverside Shakespeare*. Ed. G. Blakemore Evans et al. Boston: Houghton Mifflin, 1974.

———. *Romeo and Juliet*. Updated ed. Ed. G. Blakemore Evans. The New Cambridge Shakespeare. Cambridge: Cambridge University Press, 2003.

———. *Shakespeare's Hamlet: The First Quarto, 1603*. Cambridge, Mass.: Harvard University Press, 1931.

———. *Shakespeare's Hamlet, the Second Quarto, 1604*. San Marino, Calif.: Huntington, 1938.

———. *Shakespeare's Plays in Quarto: A Facsimile Edition*. Ed. Michael J. B. Allen and Kenneth Muir. Berkeley: University of California Press, 1981.

———. *The Taming of the Shrew: Texts and Contexts*. Ed. Frances E. Dolan. Boston: Bedford/St. Martin's, 1996.

———. *The Taming of the Shrew*. Ed. Brian Morris. The Arden Edition of the Works of William Shakespeare. 2nd ser. London: Methuen, 1981.

———. *The Taming of the Shrew*. Ed. H. J. Oliver. Oxford: Clarendon, 1982.

———. *The Taming of the Shrew*. Ed. Sir Arthur Quiller-Couch and John Dover Wilson. The New Shakespeare. Cambridge: Cambridge University Press, 1928.

———. *The Taming of the Shrew*. Updated ed. Ed. Ann Thompson. The New Cambridge Shakespeare. Cambridge: Cambridge University Press, 2003.

———. *The Third Part of King Henry VI*. Ed. Michael Hattaway. The New Cambridge Shakespeare. Cambridge: Cambridge University Press, 1993.

———. *The Three-Text Hamlet*. Ed. Paul Bertram Kliman and Bernice W. Kliman. New York: AMS Press, 1991.

———. *The tragicall historie of Hamlet Prince of Denmarke by William Shake-speare*.... London: Printed for N[icholas] L[ing] and Iohn Trundell, 1603. STC 22275.

———. *The tragicall historie of Hamlet, Prince of Denmarke By William Shakespeare*. London: Printed for N. L[ing], 1605. STC 22276a.

———. *The Works of Mr. William Shakespear*. Ed. Alexander Pope. 6 vols. London, 1723.

———. *The Works of Mr. William Shakespeare*. Ed. Nicholas Rowe. 6 vols. London, 1709.

Sharpe, Robert Boies. *The Real War of the Theaters: Shakespeare's Fellows in Rivalry with the Admiral's Men, 1594–1603: Repertories, Devices, and Types*. Published by the Modern Language Association of America. Boston: D. C. Heath, 1935.

Sisson, C. J. "Shakespeare Quartos as Prompt-Copies, with Some Account of Cholmley's Players and a New Shakespeare Allusion." *Review of English Studies* 70 (1942): 129–43.

Smith, Emma. "Ghost Writing: *Hamlet* and the *Ur-Hamlet*." In *The Renaissance Text: Theory, Editing, Textuality*, ed. Andrew Murphy. Manchester: Manchester University Press, 2000. 177–90.

Smith, Irwin. *Shakespeare's Blackfriars Playhouse: Its History and Design*. New York: New York University Press, 1964.

Sprague, Arthur Colby. *Beaumont and Fletcher on the Restoration Stage*. Cambridge, Mass.: Harvard University Press, 1926.

Stallybrass, Peter. "Naming, Renaming and Unnaming in the Shakespearean Quartos and Folio." In *The Renaissance Text: Theory, Editing, Textuality*, ed. Andrew Murphy. Manchester: Manchester University Press, 2000. 108–34.

———. "Shakespeare, the Individual, and the Text." In *Cultural Studies*, ed. Lawrence Grossberg, Cary Nelson, and Paula Treichler. New York: Routledge, 1992. 593–610.

Stern, Tiffany. *Making Shakespeare: From Stage to Page*. London: Routledge, 2004.

———. *Rehearsal from Shakespeare to Sheridan*. Oxford: Oxford University Press, 2000

———. "Was Totus Mundus Agit Histrionem Ever the Motto of the Globe Theatre?" *Theatre Notebook* 51, no. 3 (1997): 122–27.

The Taming of a Shrew: The 1594 Quarto. Ed. Stephen Roy Miller. Cambridge: Cambridge University Press, 1998.

Taylor, Gary. "The Fortunes of Oldcastle." *Shakespeare Survey* 38 (1985): 85–100.

———. *Reinventing Shakespeare: A Cultural History, from the Restoration to the Present*. New York: Weidenfeld & Nicolson, 1989.

Taylor, Gary, and Michael Warren. *The Division of the Kingdoms: Shakespeare's Two Versions of King Lear*. New York: Oxford University Press, 1983.

Theobald, Lewis. *Shakespeare Restored: or, a Specimen of the Many Errors, As Well Committed, and Unamended, by Mr. Pope in his Late Edition of this Poet*. London, 1726.

Thomas, David, and Arnold Hare. *Restoration and Georgian England, 1660–1788*. Cambridge: Cambridge University Press, 1989.

Thompson, Ann. "Feminist Theory and the Editing of Shakespeare: *The Taming of the Shrew* Revisited." In *The Margins of the Text*, ed. D. C. Greetham. Ann Arbor: University of Michigan Press, 1997. 83–103.

Ungerer, Gustav. "Shakespeare in Rutland." *Rutland Record* 7 (1987): 242–48.

Urkowitz, Steven. "'If I mistake in those foundations which I build upon': Peter Alexander's Textual Analysis of *Henry VI Parts 2 and 3*." *English Literary Renaissance* 18, no. 2 (Spring 1988): 230-56

———. *Shakespeare's Revision of King Lear*. Princeton, N.J.: Princeton University Press, 1980.

———. "Texts with Two Faces: Noticing Theatrical Revision in *Henry VI, Parts 2 and 3*." In *"Henry VI": Critical Essays*, ed. Thomas A. Pendleton. New York: Routledge, 2001. 27–37.

Veeser, H. Aram. *The New Historicism Reader*. New York: Routledge, 1994.

Walsh, Marcus. *Shakespeare, Milton, and Eighteenth-Century Literary Editing*. Cambridge: Cambridge University Press, 1997.

Webster, John. *The Duchess of Malfi*. Ed. Elizabeth M. Brennan. New York: Norton, 1983.

———. *The White Devil*. Ed. Elizabeth M. Brennan. New York: Norton, 1989.

Weimann, Robert. *Author's Pen and Actor's Voice: Playing and Writing in Shakespeare's Theatre*. Cambridge: Cambridge University Press, 2000.

———. *Shakespeare and the Popular Tradition in the Theater: Studies in the Social Dimension of Dramatic Form and Function*. Baltimore: Johns Hopkins University Press, 1978.

Wells, Stanley W., and Sarah Stanton. *The Cambridge Companion to Shakespeare on Stage*. Cambridge Companions to Literature. New York: Cambridge University Press, 2002.

Wells, Stanley W., and Gary Taylor, with John Jowett and William Montgomery. *William Shakespeare: A Textual Companion*. New York: Oxford University Press, 1987.

Wentersdorf, Karl P. "The Origin and Personnel of the Pembroke Company." *Theatre Research International* 5 (1979): 45–68.
Werstine, Paul. "A Century of 'Bad' Shakespeare Quartos." *Shakespeare Quarterly* 50, no. 3 (Autumn 1999): 310–33.
———. "McKerrow's 'Suggestion' and Twentieth-century Textual Criticism." *Renaissance Drama* 19 (1988): 149–73.
———. "Narratives about Printed Shakespeare Texts: 'Foul Papers' and 'Bad' Quartos." *Shakespeare Quarterly* 41, no. 1 (Spring 1990): 65–86.
———. "The Science of Editing." In *A Concise Companion to Shakespeare and the Text*, ed. Andrew Murphy. Malden, Mass.: Blackwell, 2007. 109–27.
———. "The Textual Mystery of *Hamlet*." *Shakespeare Quarterly* 39, no. 1 (Spring 1988): 1–26.
White, Paul Whitfield. *Marlowe, History, and Sexuality: New Critical Essays on Christopher Marlowe*. New York: AMS Press, 1998.
Wickham, Glynne, William Gladstone, Herbert Berry, and William Ingram. *English Professional Theatre, 1530–1660*. Theatre in Europe. Cambridge: Cambridge University Press, 2000.
Wilson, John Harold. *A Preface to Restoration Drama*. Cambridge, Mass.: Harvard University Press, 1968.
The Wits, or, Sport upon sport. in select pieces of drollery, digested into scenes by way of dialogue: together with variety of humors of several nations, fitted for the pleasure and content of all persons, either in court, city, countrey, or camp: the like never before published. London: Printed for Henry Marsh. 1662. Wing W3218.

INDEX

Acts and Monuments, 123
Act for the Encouragement of Learning, 1, 143
Admiral's Men, Lord, playing company, 24, 36, 119, 121–22; competition with Lord Chamberlain's company, 32–33, 98, 124; favored position of, 23–24, 26; playhouses of 98, 101; repertory of, 24–27, 32–33, 35–36, 43–44, 99–108, 121–25. *See also* Alleyn, Edward; Fortune playhouse; Henslowe, Philip; Rose playhouse
Alexander, Peter, 52, 54, 76
Alexander and Lodowick, 101
Alleyn, Edward, 35, 38, 66, 101, 105, 163n, 171 n.48, 174n; as colleague and rival of Lord Strange's Men, 24–27, 97–99, 163 n.16, 163 n.18; "part" from *Orlando Furioso*, 88–90. *See also* Admiral's Men, Lord
Alsop, Bernard, 126
Antonio's Revenge, 104–5
Arcadia, 44
Arden Shakespeare, The, 2, 76, 102
Ariosto, Ludovico, 68
As You Like It, 138

Bacon, Sir Francis, 11, 117
bad quarto hypothesis, 13, 15–16, 41, 43–44, 131; and *Hamlet*, 80; and *Taming of a Shrew*, 58, 65
bad stationer hypothesis. *See* piracy narratives
Bakhtin, Mikhail Mikhailovich, 123, 134
Bale, John, 123
Barlow, Timothy, 126
Barry, Elizabeth, 157
Bartholomew Fair, 154
Basse, William, 134–36
Battle of Alcazar, The, 27, 100
Beaumont, Francis, 141; burial in Westminster and prestige relative to Shakespeare, 134–36; Folio publication with Fletcher,

131, 146, 173 n.29; plays controlled by Crown privilege, 156, 159
Beeston, William, 144, 146, 153, 176 n.2
Believe as You List, 64
Belin Dun, 36
Belt, Thomas, 66
Bentley, Gerald Eades, 64
bestrafte Brudermord, Der, 76, 79–80, 87, 96–97, 99
Betterton, Thomas, 4, 17, 143–44, 153, 157–59
Bevington, David, 14, 123, 162 n.23
Birth of Merlin, The, 151, 152
Blackfriars, Children of, playing company, 67, 98–99, 101, 108, 139
Blackfriars playhouse, 142, 145–46, 176 n.90; occupied by boy players 98, 103, 108, 139; owned by King's Men, 28, 137–39, 176 n.89; treatment of in Folio, 137–40
Blayney, Peter W. M., 120, 127, 174 n.46, 175 n.51, n.55
Blount, Edward, 126–27, 130
Bottom the Weaver, Merry Conceited Humors of, 150–51
Bowers, Fredson, 80
Bracegirdle, Anne, 157
Brooke, William, Lord Cobham, 122
Brooks, Douglas A., 42, 172 n.1
Bryan, George, 25, 27
Burbage, Cuthbert, 118, 176 n.89
Burbage, James, 27, 28, 108; death, 77, 168 n.10
Burbage, Richard, 20, 133, 141, 142; death, 118; early career, 27–28; as Hamlet, 76–77, 105; as playhouse owner, 98, 176 n.89. *See also* King's Men
Burt, Nicholas, 144–46
Busby, John, 125, 128, 175 n.51
Butter, Nathaniel, 111, 128–29, 130, 132

Caesar's Fall, 32, 100
Cambyses, King of Persia, 101
Cardinal, The, 145–46
Cardinal Wolsey, 32
Carey, George, Lord Chamberlain, 122
Carey, Henry, Lord Chamberlain, 23
Cartwright, William, 66, 146
Catalogue of Such English Books as Lately Have Been and Now Are in Printing for Publication, A, 114–15
Catiline, 32
censorship, 88, 89, 123, 145, 149. See also Master of Revels
Chamberlain's Men, Lord, playing company, 9, 12, 84, 125–26, 174n; authority of, 12; competition with Admiral's Men, 32, 98–101, 106, 124; formation of, 20–29; membership of, 20, 27–29, 50, 61, 65–67, 97, 164 n.24; ownership of plays, 12, 40, 72, 93, 97; playhouses of, 75–76, 98, 122, 124; repertory of, 9–10, 16–17, 19–47, 49, 65–67, 75–76, 100–106, 107–8, 111, 121–25; shaping narratives about Shakespeare, 21–22, 30–32, 41–43. See also King's Men
Chambers, E. K., 64, 80, 162 n.4, 170 n.35
Chapman, George, 102, 135
Charles II, 144, 152, 153, 155–56, 158
Chaucer, Geoffrey, 134, 136
Chettle, Henry, 100, 105
Chetwind, Philip, 151–52, 177 n.18
Children of the Chapel, playing company. See Blackfriars, Children of
Cibber, Colley, 145, 158
Clark, Sandra, 155
"Cloud, Random." See McLeod, Randall
Cobham. See Brooke, William; Oldcastle, Sir John
Cockpit playhouse, 137, 144–46, 153
Comedy of Errors, The, 20–21, 36
competition, theatrical, 9, 24, 43–44, 97–106, 121–22, 158–59; and imitation of repertories, 24, 33, 43–44, 99–100, 104–5, 116, 121–25
Condell, Henry, 27, 176 n.89; role in publication of First Folio, 7, 42, 129–33, 137–38, 142, 148, 151, 175 n.75
Congreve, William, 158–59
copy, Stationers', 1, 48, 80–84, 108–20, 125–32, 143–44, 146–52
copyright law, 1–3, 6–7, 143, 161 n.4
Corbin, Peter, 125

Covent Garden Theater, 10
Cowley, Richard, 65
Creed, Thomas, 125–26, 175 n.51
Curtain playhouse, 142
Cutlack, 36

Damon and Pythias, 100, 101, 102
Daniel, Samuel, 117, 134
Danish Tragedy, The, 105
D'Avenant, William, 143–45, 152–57, 176 n.2
Dearing, Vinson, 80
Declaration of Egregious Popish Imposters, 44
De Grazia, Margreta, 14, 108, 120, 129, 132
Dekker, Thomas, 98, 99, 100–101, 122, 134
Derby's Men. See Strange's Men
Digges, Leonard, 134–36
Doctor Faustus, 12, 92, 101, 107, 162 n.23
Drayton, Michael, 100, 121, 124
Drury Lane Theater, 10
Dudley, Robert, Earl of Leicester, 118
Duke of York's Men, playing company, 147–48, 152–56
Duthie, G. I., 80, 171 n.43
Dyer, Sir Edward, 134
Dyrmonth, Adam, 42–43

Eastward Ho!, 102–3
Edmond, Mary, 163 n.21
Edward II, 31, 114
Elizabeth I, 23–24, 34
Epicoene, 154
Evans, G. Blakemore, 167 n.34
Exton, Rutland, 40, 141

Fair Em, 31
Famous Victories of Henry the Fifth, The, 34, 67, 123, 125–29. See also *Henry V*
First Part of the Contention between Lancaster and York, The, 35, 45, 127; 1619 quarto, 111, 120, 127, 130. See also *Henry VI, Part 2*
First Part of the Life of Sir John Oldcastle, The, 17, 32, 107–32, 151–52, 172 n.1
Fletcher, John, 56, 68, 135; chief dramatist for King's Men, 56, 70, 135, 137; Folio publication with Beaumont, 131, 146, 173 n.29; known collaboration with Shakespeare, 32; plays controlled by Crown privilege, 156, 159; *The Tamer Tamed*, 69–70, 72, 145; *Women Pleased*, 51–53, 67–68
Folio, First (Folio of 1623): actors' names

INDEX

in, 50–51, 62–65, 67; allusions to King's Men's repertory, 51, 70; and canon of Shakespeare's plays, 22, 30, 108, 117, 120, 126–27, 129–31; construction of Shakespeare, 17, 132–38; copy registration for, 126–27; dedication of, 117; imagined priority to quarto texts, 41, 48–49, 54, 65–66, 72–73; promise of ideal text, 42, 132–33; publishers of, 108–11, 126–27; textual differences from quartos, 30–31, 34–40, 43–47, 132–33, 138; textual differences from Quarto of *Henry V*, 30, 34, 138–40; textual differences from quartos of *Hamlet*, 30, 76, 80, 90, 97–98, 138; textual differences from Quarto of *Taming of a Shrew*, 30, 36, 43, 48, 68–70, 125; textual problems of, 71; theatrical provenance, 7, 11, 22, 132–42, 151; topical passages in, 98, 138–39
Fortune playhouse, 98, 100, 103, 171 n.48
foul papers hypothesis, 13, 16–17, 58–64, 71
Foxe, John, 123
Friar Bacon and Friar Bungay, 26, 27

Gabler, Hans Walter, 65, 67
Gammer Gurton's Needle, 101
Garrick, David, 6, 161 n.14
Gascoigne, George, 68, 72
Gesta Grayorum. *See* Gray's Inn
Globe playhouse, 97, 99, 101, 121, 176 n.89; advertised by playbooks, 129, 138, 140, 176 n.90; building of, 97–98, 122, 171 n.48; *Hamlet* performed at, 76, 103, 105; peculiarly associated with Shakespeare, 22, 103, 134, 137–42; proximity to Rose playhouse, 122, 124
Gorboduc, 101
Goy-Blanquet, Dominique, 164 n.34
Gray's Inn, 20, 36
Greenblatt, Stephen, 68–69
Greene, Robert, 26, 66, 134
Greenes Groatsworth of Wit, 19, 35
Greg, W. W. (Walter Wilson), 13–16, 112, 125, 130; foul papers hypothesis, 13, 62–63; memorial reconstruction hypothesis, 13, 88–89; piracy narratives, 15–16, 111–12; quartos of 1619, 111–14, 172 n.6
Gurr, Andrew, 23, 29, 30, 64–65, 122, 162 n.4, 163 n.16, 164 nn. 24, 27

Hailey, R. Carter, 126
Hall, Edward, 46

Hamblett, History of, 149
Hamlet, 75–106; adaptation of, 6, 11, 155–56; allusions to, 36, 38, 75, 78, 102–3; editions after 1623, 2, 126, 131, 147–48; First Quarto of, 30–31, 76, 79–88, 92–94, 96–97, 171 n.43; imagined composition of, 69–70, 76, 78–79, 103–6; ownership of print rights, 80–84, 126, 149; parts and prompt books, 85–97; performance records of, 36, 75, 76, 11, 157–59; revision of, 17, 47, 79, 85–97, 125; textual difficulty of, 12, 30, 75–76, 79–80; theatrical references in, 86, 97–103, 107, 138–39; and *ur-Hamlet* hypothesis, 75, 76–79, 105
Harington, Sir John, 134
Harington, Sir John of Exton, 40
Harsnett, Samuel, 44
Hart, Charles, 144–46, 156
Harvey, Gabriel, 42, 78
Hathway, Richard, 121
Hector of Germany, The, 141
Heminges, John, 27, 29, 66, 97, 176 n.89; member of Lord Strange's players, 25, 27, 29; role in publication of First Folio, 7, 42, 129–33, 137–38, 142, 148, 151, 175 n.75
Henry IV, Part 1, 34, 122–24, 141; as cycle play, 34, 125
Henry IV, Part 2, 3, 121, 124; actors' names in, 50, 51, 62, 67; as cycle play, 34, 125
Henry V, 1, 30, 34, 111, 125–26, 138–42, 175 n.51; 1619 quarto, 120, 125, 130–31; shared subject matter, 32, 33, 127. *See also Famous Victories of Henry the Fifth*
Henry VI, Part 1, 35–36, 127; Folio text's quality, 43, 125; as part of cycle, 45, 46
Henry VI, Part 2, 30, 35; Folio text's quality, 43, 125; as part of cycle, 45, 46, 67. *See also First Part of the Contention between Lancaster and York*
Henry VI, Part 3, 19, 30, 35; actors' names in, 50, 62, 65; Folio text's quality, 43, 125; as part of cycle, 45, 46, 67. *See also True Tragedy of Richard, Duke of York*
Henry VIII, 32, 138
Henslowe, Philip, 23, 26, 38, 98, 165 n.43, 171 n.48; payments for plays, 98–105, 121–22, 124; payments for revisions, 12, 32–33, 122; records performances, 27, 32, 34–36, 163 n.18, 165 n.38
Herbert, Sir Henry, Master of the Revels, 122–23, 145, 149–50, 152–54
Herbert, William, Earl of Pembroke, 116–19

Hester and Ahasuerus, 31, 36
Heywood, Thomas, 33, 99, 114, 134
Hibbard, G. R., 170 n.33
Holinshed, Raphael, 33, 44, 46
Holland, Hugh, 137
Honigmann, E. A. J., 13, 169 n.13
Horwich, Richard, 102–3
Hosley, Richard, 66
Howard, Charles, Lord Admiral, 23, 24–26, 108
Hunsdon's Men, playing company. *See* Chamberlain's Men; King's Men

inherent rights, 155, 158–59. *See also* Locke, John
intellectual property. *See* copy, Stationers'; copyright law; inherent rights; monopoly; performance rights
Irace, Kathleen O., 93, 171 n.43

Jaggard, Isaac, 126–27, 173 n.8
Jaggard, William, 34, 108–26, 130–31, 152, 172 nn. 1, 2, 173 n.8, 174 n.29. *See also* quartos of 1619
James I and VI, 22, 107, 118
Jenkins, Harold, 77, 101–2
Jephthah, 86, 99, 101–4
Jew of Malta, The, 26, 27, 38
Jewell, Simon, 67, 163 n.21
Johnson, Arthur, 130–31
Johnson, Gerald D., 80, 112, 120
Johnson, Samuel, 6
Jolly, George, 152
Jonson, Ben, 30, 32, 42, 100, 102; contributions to First Folio, 134–37; and Poets' Quarrel, 98, 100–101; post-Restoration performance rights, 9, 154, 156, 159
Julius Caesar, 100, 101, 107, 169 n.15

Kastan, David Scott, 80–81, 84, 122–23, 128
Kathman, David, 66
Keenan, Siobhan, 165 n.48
Kemp, William, 65; membership in Chamberlain's Men, 20, 27, 65, 97–98; role in *A Knack to Know a Knave*, 25–26, 97, 99; as Strange's Man, 25, 27
Killigrew, Thomas, 143–44, 149–50, 152–58
King John, 30, 34, 125, 127; attribution to Shakespeare, 34, 128; shared subject matter, 33. *See also The Troublesome Reign of King John*
King Lear, 112, 130, 141; attribution to Shakespeare, 34, 42, 120, 128–29, 131; in Chamberlain's Men's repertory, 30, 31, 33–34, 111; as Duke of York's Men play, 155, 157; relationship to *King Leir*, 34, 44, 128–30, 132; revision of, 12, 44–46, 68, 131
King Leir, 30–31, 42; publication history, 3, 128, 130; relationship to *King Lear*, 34, 44–45, 68, 128–29, 132
King's Men, playing company, 8, 9, 52, 56; and attributions to Shakespeare, 38, 108, 116, 128–29, 131; competition with other companies, 32, 128; demise of, 143–44; and John Fletcher, 70, 135; longevity of, 9, 22, 50, 71, 73, 140, 151; and Lord Chamberlain's edict, 115–20, 130; membership, 64, 67, 141; as owners of plays, 12, 143–44; performance records, 121, 123, 128–29, 174 n.42; playhouses of, 137–40; relationship to patrons, 116–18; and revision, 17, 46–47, 128; repertory, 31, 34, 50–52, 64, 67–73, 111, 116–17, 125–26, 128–29, 131, 135, 140–42, 145, 151–52; shaping narratives about Shakespeare, 22, 108, 116, 128, 132–51; subsequent company in reign of Charles II, 152–57. *See also* Chamberlain's Men
King's Men (Restoration), playing company, 152–57
Kirkman, Francis, 146, 150–51
Knack to Know a Knave, A, 25–27, 37, 38, 97, 99
Knight of the Burning Pestle, The, 141
Knutson, Roslyn Lander, 31, 121, 162 n.5, 165 n.38
Kyd, Thomas, 44, 66, 105, 134. *See also Spanish Tragedy*
Kynaston, Edward, 152–23

Lacey, John, 152–53
Leicester, Earl of. *See* Dudley, Robert
Leicester's Men, Earl of, playing company, 118
Lincoln's Inn's Fields playhouse, 4, 157, 159
Ling, Nicholas, 80–84, 149
Locke, John, 158–59
Locrine, 152
Lodge, Thomas, 75–78, 105
Loewenstein, Joseph, 42, 118–19
London Prodigal, The, 152
Long Meg of Westminster, 101
Love for Love, 159

Loves Labors Lost, 8, 42
Lust's Dominion, 146
Lyly, John, 66, 134

Macbeth, 32, 71, 155
MacLean, Sally-Beth, 23
Mad Wife, The, 155
Maguire, Laurie, 80, 88, 112, 134
Mahomet, 100
Maid in the Mill, The, 155
Malcolm, King of Scots, 32
Malcontent, The, 50, 64, 67
Malone, Edmond, 12
Marcus, Leah S., 8, 14, 49, 58, 72
Marlowe, Christopher, 31, 44, 114; canonical position, 66, 134; plays owned by Admiral's Men, 26, 43
Marston, John, 50, 98, 102, 104
Marsh, Henry, 150–51
Marshal Osric. See Osric
Massacre at Paris, The, 27
Massai, Sonia, 172 n.2, 173 n.8
Masten, Jeffrey A., 14, 173 n.29
Master of the Revels, 9, 122–23, 129, 145; licenser of exclusive performance rights, 26, 38, 89, 140, 145, 146. *See also* censorship; Herbert, Sir Henry; performance rights
McKerrow, R. B. (Ronald Brunlees), 13–16, 83, 109, 112; foul papers hypothesis of, 13, 58–63
McLeod, Randall, 14, 169 n.28
McMillin, Scott, 23, 84, 163 n.21
memorial reconstruction hypothesis, 13, 15–16, 17; and *Hamlet*, 80, 87–88, 93; and *Taming of a Shrew*, 57–58
Merchant of Venice, The, 111–12, 120, 130, 131
Meres, Francis, 34, 38, 42, 78, 134
Merry Conceited Humors of Bottom the Weaver. See *Bottom the Weaver*
Merry Wives of Windsor, The, 31, 48, 93, 123–24, 131; quarto, 111, 119, 120
Midsummer Night's Dream, A, 10, 88, 150–51, 170 n.36; 1619 quarto, 111–12, 120, 130, 131
Milhous, Judith, 157
Miller, Stephen Roy, 166 n.25
Millington, Thomas, 125, 175 n.51
Milton, John, 11
Mohun, Michael, 144–46, 149–50, 152, 154, 156
monopoly, 23–24, 104, 117–20, 149, 152–59

Montaigne, Michel de, 11
Morris, Brian, 57, 63
Mosely, Humphrey, 149, 154
Much Ado About Nothing, 65
Munday, Anthony, 99, 100, 121, 124
Murphy, Andrew, 2

Nashe, Thomas, 35, 100, 134; allusion to *Hamlet*, 36, 75, 77–78, 105
Neidig, William, 111, 172 n.6
New Bibliography movement, 12–17, 41, 43, 54, 80, 88, 112. *See also* bad quarto hypothesis; foul papers hypothesis; memorial reconstruction hypothesis; piracy narratives
New Cambridge Shakespeare, The, 2, 52–55, 57, 167 n.34
Newington Buttes playhouse, 36
Norton Shakespeare, The, 53, 55, 58, 71

Okes, Nicholas, 117
Old Bachelor, The, 158
Oldcastle, Sir John, 121–24
Oliver, H. J., 53, 63
Olivier, Laurence, 142
Orlando Furioso (play), 27, 88–89, 91, 101
Osric, 97, 99, 102, 103–4
Oxford Shakespeare, The, 2, 16, 55–57, 58, 76, 123

Palfrey, Simon, 88
Palladis Tamia. See Meres, Francis
Parnassus plays, 42
Paul's Boys, playing company, 98, 100, 104
Pavier, Thomas, 111–13, 120, 125–26, 130, 149, 173 n.8
"Pavier quartos." *See* quartos of 1619
Peele, George, 66
Pembroke, Earl of. *See* Herbert, William
Pembroke's Men, Earl of, playing company, 9, 23, 24, 40; plays of, 31, 35–38, 45, 46, 49, 65–67, 73; speculations about membership, 27–29, 65, 66, 163 n.21; successor company, 30, 31
performance rights, 30, 117, 126, 153; end of exclusive, 143–45, 149–50, 153–59; licensing basis, 26–27, 38, 89, 145–46, 153–54; potential weakness of, 40, 140–41. *See also* Master of the Revels
Pericles, 141, 152, 155; 1619 quarto, 111, 119, 120–21, 130
Phillips, Augustine, 25, 27, 97

piracy narratives, 13, 15–16, 42, 132, 169 n.20; and *Hamlet*, 80, 87–88, 104; and quartos of 1619, 110–15, 120
Poetaster, The, 100–101
"Poet's Quarrel," 98, 100–101, 169 n.15
Pollard, Alfred W., 13–16, 60; bad quarto theory, 13; and "Pavier quartos," 110–12, 119–20, 172 n.6; piracy narratives of, 15–16, 104, 111–12, 119–20
Poole, Kristen, 123
Pope, Alexander, 1–11, 48
Pope, Thomas, 25, 27, 97
Powell, George, 157
Preiss, Richard, 171 n.46
privilege. *See* monopoly
Privy Council, 22–24, 163 n.16
Pullen, Robert, 88
Puritan Widow, The, 152

quartos of 1619, 34, 35, 107–33, 149, 172 nn. 2, 6, 173 n.10
Queen's Men, playing company, 9, 24, 28, 34; membership, 27, 29, 30; plays of, 26, 29, 33–35, 42, 45–46, 67, 125–26, 164 n.24
Quiller-Couch, Sir Arthur, 52–55, 57, 61, 67

Rape of Lucrece, 19, 33, 43, 135
Rasmussen, Eric, 14, 162 n.23
Red Bull playhouse, 144–46, 149, 152–53
REED (Records of Early English Drama) Project, 24
repertories, theatrical: Admiral's Men's, 24–27, 32–33, 35–36, 43–44, 99–106, 107, 108, 121–25; Chamberlain's Men's, 9–10, 16–17, 19–47, 49, 65–67, 75–76, 100–106, 107–8, 111, 121–25, 164 n.24; competitive imitation of, 24, 33, 43–44, 99–100, 104–5, 116, 121–25; King's Men's, 1, 34, 50–52, 64, 67–73, 111, 116–17, 125–26, 128–29, 131, 135, 140–42, 145, 151–52; post-Restoration, 9, 144–46, 152–57
revision: critical attitudes toward, 13–15, 49, 54–56, 67–68, 70–71, 76–79, 105; as editorial taboo, 4–6; incremental, 17, 79, 84–85, 93, 132; minor, 54–55, 77, 97, 132; non-theatrical, 11, 136; part-based, 84–97; in post-Restoration theater, 7–8, 10, 147–48; plot-based, 92; as property claim, 17, 33, 41, 49, 72–73, 107, 116, 125–28, 131–32; routine, 11, 12, 33,

73–74, 105, 107; by Shakespeare, 8, 42, 44–49, 55–56, 67–70, 76–79, 84, 93, 104–6, 164 n.34; and sources, 44–45, 46, 68, 72; topical, 50–52, 73, 97–106, 107, 124, 138–39; to unify repertory, 45–47, 73, 107, 139
Rhodes, John, 144
Rich, Christopher, 157–58
Richard Crookback, 32
Richard II, 40, 42, 141
Richard III, 34, 42, 43, 164 n.34; as cycle play, 45–46; shared subject matter, 30, 32–33. *See also True Tragedy of Richard III*
Riverside Shakespeare, The, 2, 53
Roberts, James, 80–84, 103–4, 130
Robin Hood, Parts 1 and 2, 101
Robinson, Richard, 145–46
Romeo and Juliet, 31, 65, 126, 131, 143
Rose playhouse, 26–27, 35, 38, 103; possible allusions in *Hamlet*, 98–101; proximity to Globe, 122–24; and *Sir John Oldcastle*, 121–22, 124
Rowe, Nicholas, 1–4, 6, 11, 143
Rowley, Samuel, 32
Rowley, William, 51, 151

Salisbury Court playhouse, 144, 146
Sams, Eric, 56, 58, 64, 73
Satiro-Mastix, 100–101
Schoone-Jongen, Terence G., 29–30
Sedge, Douglas, 125
Seven Deadly Sins, The Second Part of, 50–51, 64, 66–67, 163 n.22
Shakespeare, John, 77, 168 n.9
Shakespeare, William: as actor, 7–8, 19–22, 29–30, 71, 132–33, 140; association with Globe, 22, 103, 134–42; attribution of plays to, 16–17, 19–20, 30–31, 34–35, 38, 42, 67, 108, 111, 116, 119–21, 126–31, 151–52, 177 n.18; authority, 4–7, 13–17, 21–22, 38, 43, 45–46, 49, 67, 120, 129, 131, 134, 142, 146–48; biography, 20–22, 77, 135; canon, 15–17, 21–22, 31, 33–47, 111, 128–33, 151–52; contemporary reputation, 19, 21–22, 38, 42–43, 133–38; critical reverence for, 4–7, 14, 22, 31–32, 45–46, 50, 55, 66, 70–72, 136, 146–48; early career, 19–20, 29–30; editing, 1–7, 13–17, 19, 41, 48–49, 52–63, 71–73, 78–80, 84, 99, 101–2, 143, 148–50, 159; imagined as individual owner of playbooks, 21, 29–30,

164 n.27; imagined composition habits, 13, 16, 45, 47, 49, 56, 58–64, 71, 78–79, 93, 105, 132–33; as non-dramatic poet, 19, 33, 43, 134–35, 173 n.29; as partner in Chamberlain's and King's Men, 7–12, 19–22, 27–36, 41–47, 67–72, 97–106, 108, 116–22, 125–42, 143–44; posthumous revisions to plays of, 7–8, 49–51, 73–74, 133–42, 155–56; post-Restoration performance rights, 155–59; as reviser, 8, 42, 44–49, 55–56, 67–70, 76–79, 84, 93, 104–6, 164 n.34; use of sources, 44–47, 68–69
Shatterall, Robert, 145–46
Sidney, Sir Philip, 44, 68, 112, 118, 134
Sincklo, John, 50–54, 56–58, 61–68, 72–73
Sir John Oldcastle. See *First Part of the Life of Sir John Oldcastle*
Sir John Olden Barnavelt, 64
Sly, William, 27, 50, 67
Smethwick, John, 84, 126, 131, 148, 149
Smith, Emma, 78
Smith, Wentworth, 99
Spanish Curate, The, 155
Spanish Gypsy, The, 51
Spanish Tragedy, The, 12, 27, 66, 101; additions of 1602, 90–92, 104, 105
Spenser, Edmund, 134, 136
Stafford, Simon, 128, 130
Stallybrass, Peter, 14, 96, 108, 128
Stationers, Worshipful Company of, 1, 81, 109, 112, 163 n.15; alleged piracy by, 80, 104, 111; concepts of intellectual property, 1, 15, 82–84, 107–8, 113–19, 125–32, 143, 149–52, 175 n.71; identification of multiple texts as single properties, 48, 114, 121, 125. *See also* copy, Stationers'; Stationers' Register
Stationers' Register, 34–37, 48, 80, 104, 125–30, 143
Statute of Queen Anne, 1, 143. *See also* copyright law
Stern, Tiffany, 88, 90, 138
Strange's Men, Lord, playing company, 9, 23, 27, 29, 163 n.18; combination with Edward Alleyn, 24–27, 29, 35, 66, 97, 163 n.16; plays of, 27, 31, 36–39, 45
Supposes, 68, 72
Suppositi, I, 68
Sussex's Men, Earl of, playing company, 24, 27–29, 34, 40; plays of, 26, 36–38
Sylvester, Joshua, 134

Tamar Cham, 27, 35, 100, 101
Tamburlaine, 35, 100, 101
Tamer Tamed, The, 69–70, 143
Taming of a Shrew, The; Taming of the Shrew, The, 17, 48–74, 131, 145; attributed to Shakespeare, 36, 38, 126; in Chamberlain's Men's repertory, 30, 36, 43, 65, 67, 72–73, 125; chronology of texts, 48–49, 51–58, 61, 65–67, 70–71, 73, 76–78; differences between texts, 30–31, 36, 48, 72, 75–76; features specific to 1594 text, 48, 68–69, 107; features specific to 1623 text, 48, 50–58; imagined composition of, 49, 62–63; perceived as single property, 48, 75, 126–27; performance records, 36, 76
Taylor, Gary, 16, 58, 123. *See also Oxford Shakespeare*
Taylor, John, 134
Taylor, Neil, 76
Theater playhouse, 27, 75, 142, 168 n.10, 171 n.48
Theobald, Lewis, 1–2, 3–6
Thomas, Lord Cromwell, 152
Thompson, Ann, 57, 61–62, 64–66, 76, 166 n.25
Titus Andronicus, 31, 36–40, 140–41
Tonson, Jacob, 1–2, 4, 11
Tonson, publishing family, 4, 6, 11
Treacherous Brothers, The, 157
Tristram de Lyons, 101
Troilus and Cressida, 32–33
Troublesome Reign of King John, The, 33–34, 126–28. *See also King John*
True Tragedy of Richard, Duke of York, The, 19, 35, 45, 65, 127; 1619 quarto, 111, 120, 127, 130. *See also Henry VI, Part 3*
True Tragedy of Richard III, The, 3, 42, 46, 164 n.34. *See also Richard III*
Trundle, John, 80–83
Two Gentlemen of Verona, 58
Two Noble Kinsmen, 152

Unfortunate Lovers, The, 145, 154
ur-Hamlet. See *Hamlet*
Urkowitz, Steven, 8, 14, 45

Venus and Adonis, 19, 43, 135

Walsh, Marcus, 5
Webster, John, 100, 134, 135
Weever, John, 42

Wells, Stanley W., 56–57, 58, 166 n.17, 167 n.26. See also *Oxford Shakespeare*
Werstine, Paul, 13, 14, 58, 61, 162 n.26
White, Rowland, 122
Whole Contention between Lancaster and York, The. See *First Part of the Contention between Lancaster and York*; *True Tragedy of Richard, Duke of York*
William III, 157, 158
Wilson, John Dover, 13–16; as editor of *Taming of the Shrew*, 52–55, 57, 61, 67; piracy narratives, 112

Wilson, Robert, 30, 121
Wintershall, William, 145–46
The Wits, 150–51
Wolfe, John, 118–19
Women Pleased, 51–57, 64, 67–68, 73, 107, 168 n.57
Woman's Prize, The. See *Tamer Tamed*
Worcester's Men, Earl of, playing company, 98, 99, 121, 122
Wright, John, 128, 130

Yorkshire Tragedy, The, 111, 119–21, 13, 152

ACKNOWLEDGMENTS

This book is an argument against an idea of solitary authorship, and I freely admit that I could not have written it alone. My first debts are of course due to Stephen Orgel, who believed in this book before it was a book and in me before I was entirely capable of writing it. I owe him more of a debt than I can repay, or than he would ask of me. I have also profited enormously from the generosity and learning of David Riggs, Jennifer Summit, Seth Lerer, Arthur Kinney, and Pat Parker, to all of whom I am in grateful debt.

I have been helped along the way by the professional advice, exceptional kindness, and attentive reading of more colleagues than I can name, among them James Bednarz, Douglas Brooks, Douglas Bruster, Frances Dolan, Alan Farmer, Jennifer Feather, Bill Germano, Barbara Hodgdon, Peter Holland, Mary Ellen Lamb, Zachary Lesser, Jeffrey Masten, Lori Newcomb, Tiffany Stern, Sarah Wall-Randell, and Paul Werstine. I have been fortunate in my exceptional and supportive colleagues at Cleveland State University, including Jeff Karem, Rachel Carnell, Gary Dyer, Mike Geither, Adam Sonstegard, David Larson, and Glending Olson, and have been blessed in the generous colleagues I made in Stanford's Early Modern Reading Group, including Richard Preiss, Amy Tigner, David Goldstein, Shawn Kairschner, Carolyn Sale, Elizabeth Pentland, Deanne Williams, and Bradin Cormack.

Part of Chapter 2 of this book previously appeared, in a different form, as an article in *Shakespeare Quarterly*. I am grateful to Gail Kern Paster, the editor of *Shakespeare Quarterly*, to Barbara Mowat, the executive editor, and to *SQ*'s superb staff and editorial board. Part of Chapter 4 previously appeared, in a different form, as an article in *Renaissance Drama*, and I am grateful to the editors of *Renaissance Drama*, Jeffrey A. Masten and Wendy Wall, to their staff, and to their editorial board.

I have been given generous support during the writing of this book from the Huntington Library, from Cleveland State's College of Liberal Arts and Social Sciences and its dean, Greg Sadlek, and from the Stanford University English Department. I hope that my efforts repay some of their kindly optimism.

Jerry Singerman doesn't need to be told how much this book, and I, owe him, but I am happy to acknowledge it. Without Jerry, my manuscript and I would be a mess. And most of all, I am grateful to Brooke Conti, who got me down the home stretch and who makes everything worth doing.

www.ingramcontent.com/pod-product-compliance
Lightning Source LLC
Chambersburg PA
CBHW020332240426
43665CB00043B/449